SETTING
NATIONAL
PRIORITIES
The 1975 Budget

SETTING NATIONAL PRIORITIES
The 1975 Budget

Barry M. Blechman
Edward M. Gramlich
Robert W. Hartman

THE BROOKINGS INSTITUTION
Washington, D.C.

Copyright © 1974 by
THE BROOKINGS INSTITUTION
1775 Massachusetts Avenue, N.W., Washington, D.C. 20036

ISBN 0-8157-0994-3 (cloth)
ISBN 0-8157-0993-5 (paper)

Library of Congress Catalog Card Number 74-282

9 8 7 6 5 4 3 2 1

THE BROOKINGS INSTITUTION is an an independent organization devoted to nonpartisan research, education, and publication in economics, government, foreign policy, and the social sciences generally. Its principal purposes are to aid in the development of sound public policies and to promote public understanding of issues of national importance.

The Institution was founded on December 8, 1927, to merge the activities of the Institute for Government Research, founded in 1916, the Institute of Economics, founded in 1922, and the Robert Brookings Graduate School of Economics and Government, founded in 1924.

The Board of Trustees is responsible for the general administration of the Institution, while the immediate direction of the policies, program, and staff is vested in the President, assisted by an advisory committee of the officers and staff. The by-laws of the Institution state, "It is the function of the Trustees to make possible the conduct of scientific research, and publication, under the most favorable conditions, and to safeguard the independence of the research staff in the pursuit of their studies and in the publication of the results of such studies. It is not a part of their function to determine, control, or influence the conduct of particular investigations or the conclusions reached."

The President bears final responsibility for the decision to publish a manuscript as a Brookings book or staff paper. In reaching his judgment on the competence, accuracy, and objectivity of each study, the President is advised by the director of the appropriate research program and weighs the views of a panel of expert outside readers who report to him in confidence on the quality of the work. Publication of a work signifies that it is deemed to be a competent treatment worthy of public consideration; such publication does not imply endorsement of conclusions or recommendations contained in the study.

The Institution maintains its position of neutrality on issues of public policy in order to safeguard the intellectual freedom of the staff. Hence interpretations or conclusions in Brookings publications should be understood to be solely those of the author or authors and should not be attributed to the Institution, to its trustees, officers, or other staff members, or to the organizations that support its research.

Foreword

THE President's annual submission to Congress of the budget proposed for the next fiscal year stimulates national debate on the proper functions of the government in society. Questions about the magnitude of government spending, the allocation of resources between competing domestic and national security programs, and the distribution of the tax burden are all addressed within the context of the federal budget.

The first principle of budgeting is that resources are limited. At any time there will be a long list of projects people feel the government ought to undertake—programs that require various types of expenditures or reductions in taxes—that become feasible only if enough resources are available. Since available resources are never adequate to satisfy the claims of all such proposals, the President and the Congress have to make difficult choices. They must distinguish high priority objectives from those lower on the list and undertake some programs but not others. For this reason, the process through which the federal budget is formulated and revised is, in fact, the way national priority judgments are translated into program proposals and actions.

Setting National Priorities: The 1975 Budget is the fifth in a series of Brookings publications analyzing the President's budget. Like its four predecessor volumes, it discusses the big decisions reflected in the President's budget, examines alternative policies, and compares the budgetary implications of both in the short and long run.

This year's volume describes and analyzes the budget as a whole and deals in depth with several major issues that seem likely to be prominent in the debate over national priorities in the coming year:

economic stabilization policy, changes in the nation's defense posture, the development of national policy on energy resources, federal responsibilities for income support, and national health insurance. By focusing on these major issues, the authors hope to contribute to public understanding of the key decisions that must be made in the near future.

The present volume is written so that Chapters 1 and 9 can be read together as a brief summary of the budget outlook. The other seven chapters supplement this summary in various ways—Chapter 2 gives more detail on the specific decisions underlying the 1975 budget, Chapter 3 on the economic implications of the budget, Chapters 4 and 5 on national security policy, Chapter 6 on energy policy, Chapter 7 on income support programs, and Chapter 8 on national health insurance.

Research for the defense chapters was carried out as part of a continuing program of studies supported by a grant from the Ford Foundation. The project as a whole is supported by grants from the Carnegie Corporation of New York and the Richard King Mellon Foundation.

The combined efforts of many people have made this volume possible. The authors benefited greatly from the advice and comments of Edward R. Fried, Alice M. Rivlin, and Charles L. Schultze, three authors of previous editions of *Setting National Priorities*, and from the guidance of Joseph A. Pechman, director of the Economic Studies program at Brookings, and Henry Owen, director of the Foreign Policy Studies program. The authors are also grateful to Carl R. Gerber of the Federal Energy Office, and Robert P. Berman, Martin Binkin, Jerry A. Kotchka, Wilfred Owen, Alton H. Quanbeck, Jeffrey Record, and William D. White of the Brookings staff for preparing background materials, and to Michael C. Barth and John L. Palmer of the Department of Health, Education, and Welfare, Nancy H. Teeters of the Congressional Research Service, and Robert I. Lerman of the Joint Economic Committee of the U.S. Congress, who were consulted in the preparation of various chapters. For reading and commenting on preliminary drafts, the authors express their appreciation to Henry J. Aaron, Barry Bosworth, John A. Brittain, Philip J. Farley, William E. Gibson, Lawrence B. Krause, Laurence Lynn, Jr., Richard P. Nathan, Benjamin A. Okner, Arthur M. Okun, Robert D. Reischauer, Michael Timpane, Archie L. Wood, and Joseph A. Yager, of the Brookings staff, and to Robert M. Ball of the National Academy of Sciences, Samuel M. Cohn of Robert R. Nathan Associates, Joel Darmstadter of Resources for the Future, William W. Kaufmann of the Massachusetts Institute of Technology, F. Ray Marshall of the University of Texas, Arnold H. Packer of the Committee for Economic Development, Dorothy P. Rice of the Social Security Administration, and Alair A. Townsend of the Joint Economic Committee of the U.S. Congress.

The authors were ably assisted by Arthur M. Hauptman, Stephanie Levinson Rabinowitz, Roger A. Reynolds, and Frederick C. Ribe. Catherine Armington and Peter G. Gould provided computer programming assistance. The risk of factual error was minimized by the work of Evelyn P. Fisher. Kathryn S. Breen, Charlotte Kaiser, Annette M. Solomon, and Margaret H. Su carried the major secretarial burden. Barbara P. Haskins edited the volume.

The views expressed here are those of the authors and should not be attributed to any of the persons whose assistance is acknowledged above; to the trustees, officers, or other staff members of the Brookings Institution; or to the Carnegie Corporation, the Ford Foundation, or the Richard King Mellon Foundation.

KERMIT GORDON
President

May 1974
Washington, D.C.

Contents

Tables

Figures

SETTING
NATIONAL
PRIORITIES
The 1975 Budget

1. Introducing
the Budget

ON FEBRUARY 4, 1974, the administration presented to Congress its proposed federal budget for fiscal year 1975. Besides a detailed plan for federal spending between July 1974 and July 1975, the budget includes revisions of the previous year's expenditure program, projections of future spending plans, and a summary of the taxes and government borrowing needed to finance the proposals. Moreover, the documents supporting the budget presentation explain the administration's foreign and domestic policies and set off a stream of legislation and congressional hearings that eventually culminates in new laws.

Even though the budget influences just about everyone's job or business and determines a large part of the congressional agenda, few citizens or their representatives ever study it carefully. Part of the reason for this is that the budget is a gigantic and very complicated document using specialized jargon to describe the fiscal activities of everything from the Agency for International Development to the National Zoological Park. An additional factor limiting its usefulness is that the budget is necessarily "one-sided," attempting to present the program of the administration in its most favorable light. Finally, despite congressional attempts to reform budgetary procedures and the administration's effort to present projections, the budget is still usually treated in a piecemeal, one-year-at-a-time fashion in Congress.

In this book we attempt to make the budget more accessible by, first, focusing on only the key budgetary and policy issues; second,

1

examining important alternatives to the administration's recommendations; and, third, paying particular attention to the future implications of the administration's decisions and alternative choices.

Specifically, this chapter presents an overview of long-term trends
in federal expenditures and receipts and a summary of the key decisions made in developing the 1975 budget. Chapter 2 is a detailed
examination of the current budget, highlighting recent changes in defense spending and in federal assistance to programs in the education,
manpower, and urban community development fields. In Chapter 3,
the relation of the budget and the outlook for employment and price
stability is analyzed. Chapters 4 and 5 discuss the current defense
budget and the debate over major policy issues that will affect future
defense expenditures.

Alternative policies for meeting energy needs and how these policies
relate to present and future budgets are discussed in Chapter 6. Chapter 7 is a review of federal income support programs and a discussion
of some policy options for reforming welfare programs. Major proposals for national health insurance are contrasted in Chapter 8.
The book concludes with a chapter on the outlook for federal receipts
and expenditures to 1980.

Budget Decision Making

To analyze an administration's budget proposal in any given year
it is necessary to understand the nature of the decisions that must be
made. Generally speaking, these decisions are molded by the balanc-
ing of objectives and constraints.

The objectives of the budgetary plan in their broadest interpreta-
tion reflect the administration's perception of the federal government's role in the economic and social system and in world affairs.
To what extent is the U.S. government to be a guarantor of the security of other nations? To what degree should the federal government
use the public purse to change the distribution of income, to provide
urban transportation, or to aid schools? While this general government mandate typically changes very slowly, it sets the boundaries for
specific budget plans. In the long run, the consensus reached on these
issues is the most important determinant of the level of federal activity.

Once these guidelines are set the federal role is then to allocate funds among the various functional activities in a manner consistent with these principles. Certainly, the most important allocative decision in federal spending is the division of outlays between those that satisfy national security objectives and those that satisfy domestic needs. Within these categories a balance must further be struck between, for example, nuclear forces and conventional forces, and between aid to education and aid to the aged. It is probably at this level of decision making that the greatest opportunity for the general public to make its voice heard exists. Often, lobbies are organized around these broad issues (a strong defense, more money for education, and the like) and much of the political rhetoric is in these general terms.

But in order to produce a budget, important choices must be made at a lower level than that. There are a number of possible strategies for achieving a specific goal in, say, the provision of aid to the aged, and these must be weighed against one another. So, for example, the aged can be aided directly through tax benefits (not a spending program at all), through the provision of in-kind aid—subsidized housing, medical care, food stamps—or through cash assistance programs. Aid in the form of cash payments can be based on need or past earnings. Alternatively, assistance can be provided to older people through service programs sponsored by state and local governments or private groups, financed in part or in full by the federal government. If service programs are the route selected, the federal government must decide whether to control the specific projects or to give a consolidated grant to a state, local, or private agency to cover a variety of services to the aged and let that body decide the details.

Spending choices for the federal government are not simply a matter of drawing up a wish list; there are constraints. Because the federal government is so large, the rates at which it spends money and raises taxes have a major impact on the level of jobs, production, and prices in the country. Moreover, particularly since the Employment Act of 1946, the federal government has tried to gear its spending and taxing to the objective of full employment with stable prices. While in principle either tax rates or expenditure programs could be adjusted each year to meet desired employment goals, the practical constraint is usually on the spending side: federal spending should be related to the capacity of the economy to absorb its demands and yet maintain a reasonably balanced level of employment and price stability.

Just as employment and price stability policies govern the level of aggregate spending, many institutional and historical factors limit the functional and strategic choices within a given total budget. First, many programs commit the government to pay certain people money. It would be a breach of faith to renege on such commitments. Second, every year budgets are fought out in congressional committees dominated by the same representatives, with the same views. Finally, even the most activist and radical administration has neither enough new ideas nor enough political power to alter priorities in wholesale fashion from one year to another. So changes in the allocation of federal spending are usually gradual.

For the annual budget, then, the need to balance the levels of economic activity—through macroeconomic or fiscal policy—generally determines overall spending levels. Functional and strategic choices are limited by past commitments. Thus the grand design of decision making often has little to do with year-to-year budgetary changes. Moreover, since Congress seldom looks ahead more than one year at a time, long-run shifts in budget priorities are likely to be the unintended result of a series of small steps rather than the deliberate result of a long-term plan. Nonetheless, over a period of years the cumulation of gradual changes has produced large shifts in national priorities. Thus we begin our review of the 1975 federal budget with an analysis of these long-term trends.

Trends in Government Spending

An important way to look at the federal budget over time is to examine trends in federal spending, grouped according to the different things the government does. Table 1-1 summarizes outlay levels for major expenditure categories over the last fifteen years arranged in such a way. Aside from defense, space, and foreign affairs, the domestic categories have been determined, for the most part, by *how* the federal government acts to help attain national goals. The objective of attaining income security is reflected in cash income maintenance programs and programs to help people buy essentials. Federal outlays designed to expand specific services or to influence their nature and their beneficiaries are grouped under aid for social programs and investment in the physical environment. Revenue sharing programs encompass those in which federal outlays are used to increase the resources available to state and local governments without concern for how—or for whom—the money is spent. Direct subsidies to producers are intended to stabilize or expand output in specific industries. Net interest is self-explanatory, while the catchall "other" category covers the remaining government expenditures except for some financial devices and contributions by the federal government for civil service retirements, which are grouped under "financial adjustments."[1]

The distribution of federal funds among these categories indicates how much national priorities have changed over the years. For example, defense outlays in fiscal 1975 are estimated at only about 32 percent of the total of $304 billion, a proportion which has been steadily declining. Cash income maintenance programs, on the other hand, are also about 32 percent, a considerably larger proportion of total outlays than in previous years. Other categories showing significant growth are helping people buy essentials (11 percent) and aid for

---

1. *Cash income maintenance* refers to the set of programs that provide cash benefits to people, such as social security benefits to the aged, unemployment compensation to the jobless, and public assistance to the poor and disabled. All of the programs in this category allow the recipients to use their benefits as they wish. The programs in the *helping people buy essentials* category, on the other hand, offer people cash or vouchers to help them buy specific goods and services. About two-thirds of the funds now expended in this category provide aged and poor people with medical care under the Medicare and Medicaid programs. The rest of the money is for programs enabling various classes of people to buy food, higher education, and housing. *Aid for social programs* encompasses programs in which the federal government assists states and localities or, in some cases, private institutions to provide various types of social and economic services to the public. Aid to education (other than student aid counted in the previous category) and aid for manpower programs account for about half of the spending in this category, which also includes some smaller programs to provide health services, to revitalize urban communities, to help provide general social services, and to aid in area and regional development. Programs of *investment in physical environment* are aimed at developing the transportation, recreation, environmental, and water resources of the nation through direct federal investments, or through the provision of assistance to other government agencies or private firms. *Revenue sharing* programs, unlike the above two categories, provide more or less untied aid to state and local governments. The principal program is general revenue sharing initiated in 1972. Others are relatively small grants-in-aid, such as those to the District of Columbia, Puerto Rico, and the Virgin Islands. *Direct subsidies to producers* include federal programs intended to stabilize incomes or expand output in specified industries; the most important of these are in farm income stabilization, the postal service, and the maritime industry. *Net interest* covers interest payments on the federal debt made to the public. The principal components of *other programs* (those not elsewhere classified) are general government (mostly pay for executive, legislative, and judicial branches), research, and veterans' programs not incorporated in other categories. Certain financial adjustments and contributions by the federal government for civil service retirement, and revenues from mineral deposits are grouped under *financial adjustments*. All of the categories are explained in greater detail in Edward R. Fried and others, *Setting National Priorities: The 1974 Budget* (Brookings Institution, 1973).

Table 1-1. Federal Budget Outlays, by Major Category, Fiscal Years 1960, 1970, and 1975

Dollar amounts in billions

Category[a]	1960		1970		1975 estimate	
	Amount	Percent of total	Amount	Percent of total	Amount	Percent of total
Defense, space, foreign affairs	$49.5	53.7	$ 87.7	44.6	$ 96.1	31.6
Cash income maintenance	20.6	22.3	46.6	23.7	98.2	32.2
Helping people buy essentials	1.1	1.2	14.2	7.2	33.2	10.9
Aid for social programs	1.3	1.4	10.3	5.3	18.2	6.0
Investment in physical environment	5.4	5.8	9.4	4.8	17.3	5.7
Revenue sharing[b]	0.1	c	0.5	c	6.8	2.2
Direct subsidies to producers	4.5	4.9	6.7	3.4	3.7	1.2
Net interest	6.9	7.5	14.4	7.3	22.0	7.2
Other programs	3.9	4.2	10.8	5.5	23.0	7.6
Financial adjustments	−1.1	−1.2	−4.1	−2.1	−14.1	−4.6
Total	**92.2**	**100.0**	**196.6**	**100.0**	**304.4**	**100.0**
Total as percent of gross national product	18.6	...	20.6	...	20.9	...

Sources: *The Budget of the United States Government*, together with *Appendix* and *Special Analyses*, for relevant years. Expenditures are reclassified by the authors. Detail may not add to totals because of rounding.
a. For an explanation of the categories see page 5, note 1.
b. Includes small amounts of payments in lieu of taxes on federal lands.
c. Less than 0.05 percent.

social and environmental programs (12 percent). Only about 1 percent of federal outlays in fiscal 1975 are devoted to subsidies to producers in certain industries, which is a smaller share than in earlier years. The remaining expenditure categories have maintained a fairly constant 10 percent level over the 1960–75 period. As a whole, federal outlays grew considerably faster than gross national product between 1960 and 1970, but since then the federal share of GNP has remained constant.

Trends in Government Receipts

The $200 billion growth in federal outlays between 1960 and 1975 was financed by a corresponding growth in federal revenues. Table 1-2 shows that the single most important source of federal revenues is the individual income tax. It has accounted for about 45 percent of federal receipts throughout the 1960–75 period. Corporate income taxes, which in 1960 were the second most important source of federal re-

Table 1-2. Federal Budget Receipts, by Source, Fiscal Years 1960, 1970, and 1975
Dollar amounts in billions

	1960		1970		1975	
Source	Amount	Percent of total	Amount	Percent of total	Amount[a]	Percent of total
Individual income taxes	$40.7	44.0	$ 90.4	46.7	$129.0	43.7
Proposed legislation	...	...	...	...	(−1.9)	...
Corporation income taxes	21.5	23.2	32.8	16.9	43.0	14.6
Proposed legislation	...	...	...	...	(−2.0)[b]	...
Social insurance taxes	14.7	15.9	45.3	23.4	85.6	29.0
Excise taxes	11.7	12.6	15.7	8.1	22.4	7.6
Proposed legislation	...	...	...	...	(5.0)[b]	...
All other	3.9	4.2	9.5	4.9	15.0	5.1
Total	**92.5**	**100.0**	**193.7**	**100.0**	**295.0**	**100.0**

Sources: *The Budget of the United States Government, Fiscal Year 1975*, pp. 46 (n. 2), 297–99, and relevant preceding years; *Special Analyses, Budget of the United States Government*, relevant years. Detail may not add to totals because of rounding.

a. The 1975 figures are estimates. Amounts shown in parentheses for proposed legislation are included in the receipts shown for each tax.

b. The administration has proposed an emergency windfall profits tax that would result in estimated gross receipts of $5 billion. However, the administration estimates that corporate profits tax receipts would be lowered by $2 billion under this tax, so the net revenue effect is $3 billion. In this table, the gross receipts of $5 billion are allocated to excise taxes (see Chapter 6). *The Budget of the United States Government* treats the net revenue as a component of corporation income taxes.

ceipts, have grown comparatively slowly and in 1975 will account for only about 15 percent of the total. Social insurance receipts, most of which are payroll taxes for the social security and unemployment insurance systems, have grown rapidly throughout the period and in 1975 will supply 29 percent of federal revenues. Excise taxes, customs duties, estate and gift taxes, and miscellaneous receipts have all become much less important sources of federal revenue over the years.

It is interesting to compare the trends in outlays and receipts and what they tell about the federal government's impact on redistributing incomes. Although outlays are shifting toward programs designed to aid the aged and low-income populations (see the categories *cash income maintenance* and *helping people buy essentials* in Table 1-1), social insurance taxes that weigh relatively heavily on low-income people are growing the most (see Table 1-2). Similarly, although direct subsidies to producers are a declining fraction of federal outlays, corporate income taxes—which are at least partly borne by producers—have become a less important revenue source. Thus the growing regressivity of the federal tax system may be offsetting the growing expenditures for these programs that benefit low-income people.

Tax Expenditures

The federal government can affect incomes and production not only by spending money but also by offering special tax advantages to persons or corporations. These tax advantages might even be considered a different type of expenditure. "Tax expenditures" therefore represent the cash value of the special tax provisions (that is, the additional amount of tax that would be collected if these special provisions were not on the books). If one were to draw up a tax expenditure budget, it would show a very different set of priorities than the outlay budget shown in Table 1-1. For example, a recent compilation shows that out of a total of $78 billion in tax expenditures at least $14 billion could be considered subsidies to producers.[2] Agriculture will receive over $1 billion in reduced tax liability, about the same as federal outlays for farm income stabilization. Special tax provisions relating to oil and gas production account for another $3 billion, more than the government is now planning to spend on energy research and development. Investment tax credits, accelerated depreciation allowances, and other special aids to manufacturing and service industries make up the remaining portion of the $14 billion, though here the subsidies are available to investors of all types and the case for their being "special tax advantages" is not so clear. Beyond tax subsidies to producers the tax expenditure budget includes such major items as lower tax rates and exclusion from taxation at death of capital gains, various provisions that encourage the consumption of housing and medical services, and exemptions and deductions from federal taxation of interest on state and local government bonds and taxes, respectively.

Although we concentrate on federal spending decisions in this book, when general or special provisions of the tax code offer alternatives to spending programs, they are also discussed.

Changes in the Composition of Expenditures

Without doubt, over the 1960–75 period, the big change in the federal budget is the diminishing share allocated to defense, space, and

2. See Tax Analysts and Advocates, "Fiscal Year 1975 Tax Expenditure Budget," *Tax Notes*, Vol. 2 (January 21, 1974), pp. 4–19.

foreign affairs activities. This is not surprising. Expenditures for programs such as social security or health care are likely to grow at least as fast as the population, while defense spending need not inevitably grow so fast. However, the rate at which the defense share of the budget declined has accelerated since 1970, because domestic programs have been growing at a fast pace.

In the 1960s, the major programs which grew relatively faster were those helping people to buy essentials and those for categorical grants in social areas. Programs such as Medicare and Medicaid, along with other Great Society initiatives in housing and student aid, accounted for most of the growth in the first category; the multitude of federal aid projects in the education, health, and manpower fields created in the 1960s greatly expanded the second. The popular image of the federal government identifying a needy group or functional sector and creating a program for it is not far from the truth. Largely because of the growth of these social aid programs, federal grants became an increasingly important component of state and local expenditures, rising from 13.5 percent in 1960 to 18.3 percent in 1970.

Almost half of the increase in the federal budget in the 1970–75 period went to cash income maintenance programs, which represents a sharp acceleration in the long-term trend. Most of the growth is in social security. Over the 1970–75 period, benefits are expected to rise about 120 percent, whereas the increase in beneficiaries is expected to be under 25 percent. In the future, growth in social security payments are guaranteed under law to rise enough to offset inflation, and if the past pattern persists they will rise even more than that. Public assistance programs have grown, too, both for assistance to adult groups (the aged, blind, and disabled) and for aid to families with dependent children. In the last few years, however, the rate of growth of aid to families with dependent children has slowed, while that of assistance to adults has accelerated. (Social security and public assistance programs are discussed further in Chapter 7.)

The combined total of social grants and general revenue sharing is absorbing more of the domestic budget in the first half of the 1970s than in the previous decade, and an increasing proportion is not subject to detailed federal control. Moreover, in the last two years these grant-in-aid programs have failed to keep pace with state and local expenditures, suggesting a diminished federal influence over activities in the areas of education, manpower, health, and the like.

In perspective, recent trends in federal domestic programs suggest that the federal government is taking on much greater responsibility for providing cash or in-kind assistance to various needy groups. At the same time, it is handing over control and financial responsibility to state and local governments to ensure that social services are provided effectively and to the right people. The latter is a complete turnabout from the sixties when it was regarded as in the federal domain to attempt to affect the delivery of social services through the development of federal priorities and guidelines.

Budget Philosophies in the Seventies

The 1970–75 trends in federal budget activity have been influenced by the Nixon administration's budget priorities as well as congressional preferences. In the national security field, the broad pattern of the administration's policy up to the present has been to keep baseline (peacetime) forces nearly constant. Congress has voted minor reductions in the administration's requests, but generally accepted the administration's defense policy. Changes in defense outlays have been dominated by the Vietnam war: between 1970 and 1974, real outlays for defense including those for Vietnam fell about 25 percent, but real baseline spending fell only 5 percent.

In domestic policy, the major clear-cut departure from previous administrations is in intergovernmental fiscal relations. The Nixon administration's new federalism has two principal components. First, general revenue sharing, a program initiated in 1972, provides about $6 billion a year in virtually untied aid to state and local governments; the funds are distributed on the basis of population, income, urbanization, and tax revenues.[3] This program has received wide bipartisan support. Supporters have given the following rationale: the program strengthens state and local governments, redistributes funds to poorer areas, reduces state and local tax burdens, and decentralizes power. For the most part general revenue sharing was expected to supplement, not to replace, other forms of aid granted to state and local governments; but since its advent, the growth of grant programs in the social area has slowed down.

The second component of the Nixon administration's intergovern-

3. For details of this program, see *Setting National Priorities: The 1974 Budget*, Chapter 7.

mental reform program is special revenue sharing. In four social grant areas (elementary and secondary education, urban community development, law enforcement assistance, and manpower training) and one physical investment field (transportation), the administration proposed the consolidation of a number of existing programs. The consolidated (or block) grant was to be distributed to state or local governments by an appropriate formula and was to be used by the recipient governments for any purpose within fairly broad guidelines set by federal law. While the degree of federal guidance varies in the administration's proposals in the different functional areas, in all cases federal control is much weaker than in predecessor programs. So far, Congress has accepted (in somewhat modified form) the administration's initiatives in the manpower and law enforcement fields; in May 1974, education, urban community development, and transportation proposals were still under consideration.

The special revenue sharing proposals have raised two related issues in Congress. One is the broad issue of whether the federal government ought to set fairly detailed guidelines for the use of federal funds in the social aid fields. The administration consistently argues against federal control and for decentralization; Congress seems willing to reduce federal control, but not to the degree that the administration has in mind. The other issue raised is how much money the federal government should spend for social aid. The Nixon administration has usually coupled its proposals for consolidation with reduced—drastically, in some cases—levels of federal activity. Moreover, President Nixon has vetoed Labor–Health, Education, and Welfare spending bills on several occasions and has blocked spending in several Housing and Urban Development programs. Congress has generally tried to resist these cutbacks, typically with only partial success. (See Chapter 2 for an extended discussion of changes in aid for social programs.)

In the area of income support (encompassing the cash income maintenance programs and programs to help people buy essentials), it is difficult to sort out the Nixon administration's position. In the early years of his administration, "reform" of assistance programs for low-income people was listed as the highest domestic priority. The reforms advocated were to establish a national guaranteed income and to cover poor working families not previously included in any assistance programs; the small in-kind food stamp program was to be converted to cash assistance. These measures passed the House, but did not succeed in the Senate. Although a new reform proposal has been promised for 1974 by the administration, it no longer seems to be of such high priority.

Congress has taken the initiative in expanding programs to help people buy essentials but the administration has for the most part supported the measures. With congressional leadership—and the administration's support—the food stamp program has grown from almost nothing to a $3 billion to $4 billion operation in a few years. Aid for students in postsecondary education has also grown rapidly, with the administration backing direct federal loan and grant assistance, and Congress supporting the distribution of student aid through postsecondary institutions. Medicaid and Medicare, providing federal assistance for the indigent and the aged, have both expanded considerably—with the administration's support after it had made several attempts to reduce some benefits. The administration has recently proposed that these programs be replaced by a national health insurance program covering everyone. (See Chapter 8 for a discussion of health insurance alternatives.)

The large increases in social security came about after an elaborate minuet danced by the administration and Congress. Congress typically suggested very large increases and the administration smaller ones. In the end, Congress voted higher benefits than the administration wanted, but the President signed the bill and took credit for the increase.

There have been a few significant changes in the tax laws during the seventies. The payroll tax rate has risen from 8.4 percent in 1970 to 11.7 percent in 1974, while the maximum earnings taxed have risen from $7,800 to $13,200. These changes were mandatory under the present system in which social security benefits are financed from a trust fund whose main source of income is the payroll tax. Despite rising payroll rates, personal and business taxes were cut in 1971.

In sum, the budget history of the period 1970–75 indicates that Congress has played a more important role in determining domestic spending patterns than before. The administration has shaped spending principally by the way it has reacted to Congress in vetoing some spending bills and withholding spending in the area of aid for social programs, and by proposing major reductions and consolidations of programs. As a result, outlays for cash income maintenance have grown very rapidly compared to aid for social programs. Moreover, the only major administration spending proposals passed by Congress —general revenue sharing and some smaller consolidations of grant-in-aid programs—have shifted the composition of federal aid to state and local governments toward more loosely tied forms. The only other significant form of federal assistance to have expanded rapidly in the last five years is aid for environmental programs. Outlays for direct subsidies to producers have declined though tax expenditures for the same purpose have expanded.

The 1975 Federal Budget

In its budget proposal for fiscal year 1975, the administration is proposing several measures to reallocate federal expenditures. It seeks to end the decline in the defense share of the budget, to continue the rapid growth in cash income maintenance and in helping people buy essentials, and to reduce the relative importance of aid for social programs.

The decisions reached by the administration on the pattern of outlays for fiscal 1975 have been constrained by two major choices. First, faced with an economic outlook that promised both inflation and growing unemployment, the administration chose a "compromise" target for outlay growth of $30 billion over the previous year, believing that this rate of expansion would minimize the risk of aggravating price stability and employment problems. Second, the administration chose to expand outlays for national security purposes by about $7 billion, and proposed to augment the combat readiness of military forces, to accelerate weapon modernization, and to expand research and development for nuclear weapons. These choices presage a growing defense sector for the rest of the decade. (See Chapters 4 and 5.)

Given these two fundamental decisions, only about $23 billion in outlay growth could be allocated to the nondefense portion of the budget. Over $19 billion of that total is predicted by the administration to be needed for automatic increases in certain programs that involve prior government commitments and for pay raises in civilian agencies. For the automatically increasing programs, about $17.5 billion is allocated to the two income support spending categories, with most of the increase going to social security; to aid for the aged, blind, and disabled; and to an expanding food stamp program. There is every reason to believe that these cash and in-kind programs will continue to grow throughout the decade. (See Chapter 7.) If the administration's proposal for national health insurance is enacted, these spending categories will account for a growing share of future federal outlays.

Hence, only $3 billion to $4 billion were available after these fiscal policy and defense decisions had been made and the automatic increases accounted for. Almost all of this is destined for pollution, energy, and transit projects. Outlays for pollution control programs of the Environmental Protection Agency are to rise by $1.5 billion, mainly as a result of growing federal payments to discharge contracts signed with localities in previous years. The administration has proposed an acceleration of energy research and development that will result in an additional $0.5 billion in outlays in 1975. Finally, as a first step in what may become a major new federal responsibility, a small increase in outlays is being requested for urban mass transit. (See Chapter 6 for further discussion of these last two issues.)

The fiscal 1975 budget proposed by the administration contains almost no increases in spending for social grant programs in the areas of education, urban development, manpower, and health. After correcting for inflation over the past three years, the budget actually implies a substantial fall in the real level of federal activity in these areas. Should the administration's proposals be accepted, the relative share of aid for social programs in federal spending would decline over the rest of the decade. (For a more detailed discussion of the distribution of spending in the 1975 budget, see Chapter 2.)

On the revenue side, federal receipts could expand very rapidly between now and 1980 because of economic growth and inflation. As prices and incomes rise, taxpayers move into higher tax brackets. Under the graduated income tax, this upward shift increases the share of national income flowing to the government. When we project federal receipts (under the assumption of full employment) and compare them to projected outlays based on the administration's fiscal 1975 budget program, we find a surplus that would reach $39 billion by fiscal 1980. Naturally, such a surplus of receipts over expenditures will never come about: either taxes will be cut, new programs started, or old ones expanded. (These projections are discussed in Chapter 9.) So, although the fiscal 1975 budget process seems narrowly constrained by the short-run economic outlook and by automatic expansion of programs like social security, there is much wider room in future budgets for exercising choice in national priorities.

How Do Budget Proposals Become Budget Outlays?

There are a great many intermediate steps in both the legislative and the executive branches before a budget proposal results in the actual expenditure of funds by the federal government. Before undertaking a detailed examination of the current proposal, a review of these intermediate steps will provide a clearer picture of what actually happens to the budget, especially, as has been the case recently, when Congress and the administration are at odds over specific programs.

When the administration's budget proposal is submitted to Congress, two separate legislative activities ensue: authorization and appropriation. If some of the proposed programs have not been authorized by law or if legislative authority for existing programs runs out, a bill authorizing the establishment of each specific program must be enacted by both houses of Congress and signed by the President. Once sanctioned by law, outlays for that program can then be undertaken only after another round of legislative activity, known as the appropriations process.

The administration's budget proposal is split into thirteen parts and the appropriations bills are parceled out for consideration by thirteen appropriations subcommittees—first in the House of Representatives and then in the Senate. These appropriations subcommittees hold hearings and ultimately "mark up" (make final decisions on) an appropriations bill, which is then approved by the full appropriations committee and finally by each house of Congress. When the House and Senate bills differ, a compromise is reached in a conference committee composed of representatives of each house of Congress, and the conference report is then considered and voted on by both houses. Finally, the President must sign each appropriations bill before it can become law.

An appropriation law creates *budget authority*,[4] which is the legal

4. Not all budget authority is created by an appropriation law. For some programs Congress votes *contract authority or authority to spend debt receipts and other types of budget authority* in the regular authorizing statutes. These provisions create a legal basis for spending similar to an appropriation but outside the regular appropriations process.

basis for executive branch agencies to undertake spending activity in a specific area. Budget authority is analogous to Congress' putting money into the executive branch's checking account. Normally, the entire sum appropriated is not handed over to an agency; the Office of Management and Budget apportions budget authority to spending agencies, usually on a quarterly basis.

Once an agency's "checking account" has been stocked with the appropriate budget authority and it is able to spend dollars for that purpose, it can incur *obligations*. These are commitments by the agency to make payments such as those for salaries, wages, and interest. Often, the obligation takes the form of a contract for the purchase of supplies, equipment, buildings, land, or research services.

Obligations are liquidated by *outlays*. That is, once the service contracted for in the obligation stage is performed, the government pays its bills. Thus outlays are analogous to withdrawals from the government's checking account. *Outlays* in any year may derive from the *budget authority* of a previous year as well as that of the current year, and the *obligation* that committed the government may have taken place shortly before the outlay (as in the case of payroll expenses) or many years before (as in the case of outlays for aircraft carriers).

Since not all budget authority enacted is obligated or spent immediately, at any moment the government has *balances of budget authority*, akin to the balance in its checking account. Some of these balances may already be obligated or committed (*obligated balances*), but the remainder (*unobligated balances*) is not.

In analyzing the level and allocation of government activities in this book, the amount of *outlays* is the measurement most used. But it is clear that under certain circumstances this rate of withdrawal from a checking account gives a misleading picture of the current and future activity of a program. For example, a program may be incurring very few obligations, but its outlays may be at a high level because of past activity. In this case, outlays would overstate current activity. Alternatively, outlays for a program may be low, but the government agencies may be incurring high levels of obligations and accumulating a large backlog of unspent balances of budget authority; in this case, outlays would understate activity levels. Thus, when outlays do not seem to be pointing in the direction of actual changes in program activity levels, we introduce some of these alternative measures of government activity.

The lags between budget authority, obligations, and outlays in certain programs have given rise to considerable public discussion and litigation over how much discretion the executive branch should have in regulating the pace at which it carries out the programs approved by Congress and signed into law by the President. Although the word *impoundment* refers in a general way to budget authority which has not been spent, there is no broad agreement on its exact meaning. The failure of the executive branch to obligate funds that Congress has authorized over a period of time can be due to a number of reasons, some of which everyone would agree are an appropriate exercise of the managerial function of the administration, some of which are not. There appears to be no single aggregate measure that can untangle these sources of failure to implement programs. Each program must be studied on a case-by-case basis. (See Appendix A for a further discussion of impoundment.)

2. The 1975 Federal Budget

OUTLAYS PROPOSED BY THE ADMINISTRATION for fiscal 1975 are $40.4 billion higher than it originally proposed for fiscal 1974. This increase (which is net of financial adjustments) amounts to a 15 percent rise—in one fiscal year—and is due to several factors.

First, there was an "overrun" of $10.8 billion in outlays for fiscal 1974 as now estimated above the original proposal. Only a small part of the 1974 spending increases can be attributed to congressional restoration of major program reductions proposed by the administration. More important were automatic increases due to inflation in such expenditures as interest payments, greater-than-expected participation in such programs as food stamps, and bigger benefits voted by Congress for social security and other programs aiding individuals.

Second, outlays are to increase between fiscal 1974 and fiscal 1975 by about $30 billion dollars. Most of the extra spending is for income support programs, for both cash and in-kind assistance. This, viewed as a yearly change, was uncontrollable—under existing laws benefit increases have to be paid. Beyond the uncontrollable items, there was a major expansion of the defense budget. The administration plans only modest increases in spending for domestic programs except for income support.

The most important characteristics of the budget changes in the 1974–75 period in terms of priorities are the following:

• The defense budget seems poised for a turnaround from a steadily declining share of the budget to substantial real increases for 1975 and future years.

• Liberalized benefit levels and growth in the number of beneficiaries have resulted in very large increases in outlays for cash income maintenance and programs helping people buy essentials.

• The administration's efforts to hold down the growth of grant programs in such fields as education, manpower, health, and urban community development have been at least partly successful. In many of these areas, federal aid in real terms has declined.

• Decentralization of decision making in social programs, an administration initiative, has been partially successful. Through general revenue sharing and the consolidation of categorical assistance programs, state and local governments have been given a larger role in determining the allocation of public expenditures.

This chapter reviews, in some detail, the principal changes in the 1974 and 1975 budgets, emphasizing for the latter the changes in aid to social programs. The defense budget changes are reviewed in detail in Chapter 4, and income support programs are the main focus of Chapter 7.

What Happened to Last Year's Proposals?

In January 1973 the Nixon administration presented a very unusual budget proposal to Congress. Faced with what the administration (and most others) expected to be a buoyant economy in fiscal 1974, its proposal was to slow down the rate of growth of federal outlays by recommending that many programs be substantially cut or even eliminated. From the administration's point of view there was little choice but to cut back existing programs. A tax increase had been ruled out by campaign promises and a dislike of big government. The administration argued that if it were to let expenditures rise at a "normal rate," the result would be an overly expansionary fiscal policy, sure to lead to excessive price increases. Given these constraints, the target for federal outlays was set at $268.7 billion, only $19 billion above the previous year, and the administration slashed at a broad range of programs to reach this target.

The proposed program reductions of $16.9 billion were spread over most of the ten categories of federal spending shown in Table 2-1.

Table 2-1. Federal Budget Outlays for Fiscal Year 1974, as Proposed in January 1973 and as Estimated in February 1974, by Major Category

Billions of dollars

Category	Program cuts proposed in January 1973 (1)	January 1973 outlay request for fiscal 1974[a] (2)	February 1974 estimate of outlays for fiscal 1974 (3)	Amount of change, 1973–74 (4)
Defense, space, foreign affairs	3.0	88.4	88.9	0.5
Cash income maintenance	1.8	82.0	84.5	2.5
Helping people buy essentials	1.8	26.8	29.1	2.3
Aid for social programs	4.9	16.0	17.8	1.8
Investment in physical environment	1.9	14.3	15.2	0.9
Revenue sharing	0	6.6	6.7	0.2
Direct subsidies to producers	1.6	5.8	4.6	−1.2
Net interest	0	18.7	21.3	2.6
Other programs	0.9	19.6	20.9	1.3
Subtotal	15.9	278.2	289.0	10.8
Financial adjustments	1.0	−9.5	−14.3	−4.8[b]
Total	16.9	268.7	274.7	6.0

Sources: *The Budget of the United States Government, Fiscal Year 1975*, and issues for 1974 and 1973; and authors' estimates. Detail may not add to totals because of rounding.

a. After cuts from column 1.

b. See page 21, note 1.

Fourteen billion dollars of this total cutback were in domestic programs. The largest absolute—and largest percentage—reduction was proposed in aid for social programs, mainly "categorical" grants-in-aid to state and local governments for specific programs in education, health, urban community development, manpower, social services, community action, and area and regional development. The administration contended that many of these programs were ineffective or overcentralized. In addition to the cuts, the administration renewed its previous proposals to consolidate a number of categorical programs into special revenue sharing grants. Proposed outlays for these block grants were lower than those of the programs they were meant to replace.

Columns 3 and 4 of Table 2-1 give the administration's February 1974 estimates of spending in fiscal 1974 and the change from the original estimate. It is important to note that outlays are now expected to be $10.8 billion higher than the administration originally had hoped. This spending increase was pulled down to $6.0 billion by financial adjustments in the budget statement; however, for most purposes, the $10.8 billion increase is the most meaningful index of change.[1]

Added Spending: Activity or Inflation?

The increase in federal spending of nearly $11 billion over the original proposal does not imply an enlargement of government activity. When the administration's budget was presented in January 1973, it was expected that prices would increase about 3 percent during the calendar year. As it turned out, the broadest price index—the implicit price deflator for the gross national product—rose 7.1 percent from the fourth quarter of 1972 to the fourth quarter of 1973. Thus just to cover the unanticipated higher costs of goods and services and maintain the real level of federal government activity would have required about a 4 percent increase in the original proposal of $268.7 billion. That inflation adjustment works out approximately to the $11 billion that was added to fiscal 1974 outlays. In other words, the President's original total expenditure proposals, adjusted for unanticipated inflation, were more or less realized.

Whether the growth in federal spending led to an accelerated price spiral is a question investigated in Chapter 3, but it is generally accepted that much of the inflation can be accounted for by growing demand for farm products, the impact of devaluation on the prices of imported goods, and higher petroleum prices imposed by the oil-exporting countries—forces that are largely independent of fiscal activity. Moreover, federal outlays in fiscal 1974 are expected to grow rapidly, primarily in the last half of the fiscal year, at the tail end of what is expected to be the period of highest inflation. It is implausible, therefore, to attribute present-day inflationary problems to the post-budgetary rise in spending.

What Caused the Added Spending?

Although the $10.8 billion overrun of federal outlays in fiscal 1974 seems, in some spending categories, to offset the administration's

1. Financial adjustments of $4.8 billion stem primarily from an increased estimate of rents for drilling rights on the outer continental shelf. Such rents, received by the federal government, are counted in the budget as negative (that is, a subtraction from) outlays. Thus, when rents rise, recorded outlays fall. For most analytical purposes, in which higher outlays are associated with higher economic activity, such financial transactions are removed from the outlay totals.

original proposed cuts, congressional reversal of the proposed reductions accounts for only a part of the outlay increase.

Table 2-2 breaks down the budget increase of $10.8 billion by

Table 2-2. Fiscal 1974 Outlays: Change in Budget Estimates, by Source and Category, January 1973 and February 1974

Billions of dollars

Source of change and category affected	Amount of change
Primarily due to change in prices and unemployment	**2.5**
Net interest	2.6
Unemployment compensation	0.1
Farm income stabilization	−1.7
Civilian retirement[a]	1.2
Food stamps (increase in bonus)	0.3
Primarily due to incorrect estimates in uncontrollable programs	**2.2**
Disaster relief	0.2
Medicare	−0.4
Medicaid	0.6
Food stamps (increase in participation)	0.5
Veterans' readjustment benefits (GI bill)	0.7
Postal service	0.6
Primarily due to congressional action on domestic programs	**3.8**
Related to proposed cuts	2.3
Social programs (education, manpower, urban community redevelopment, area and regional development, and social services)	(1.6)
Medicare (cost-sharing)	(0.5)
Veterans' pension reform	(0.2)
Unrelated to proposed cuts	1.5
Social security benefits	(1.0)
Food programs (other than food stamps)	(0.2)
Veterans' medical benefits	(0.3)
Department of Defense (including military assistance) program adjustments	**0.5**
Lower appropriation	−1.7
Southeast Asia withdrawal	−1.2
All other (including supplemental appropriation)	3.4
Other, net	**1.8**
Environmental Protection Agency construction grants	0.4
Rural electrification loans moved from budget	−0.5
Pay raise advance	0.3
Small business assistance	0.4
Health and scientific research	0.4
Miscellaneous, net	0.8
Total	**10.8**

Sources: Authors' estimates, using basic data in *The Budget of the United States Government, Fiscal Year 1974*, and *Fiscal Year 1975*.

a. Adjustments in military retirement included under Defense below.

major source of change. The largest increases were $2.6 billion for government interest payments (due to higher interest rates), $1.2 billion for increased costs of civilian retirement programs (due to higher benefits and higher participation), and $1.0 billion for social security benefits (mainly due to higher benefit levels voted in 1973). Apparent underestimates in the original 1974 budget account for another $2.2 billion, and defense outlays for $0.5 billion, despite a reduction in congressional appropriations.

In fact, outlay increases *unrelated* to the congressional reversal of administration proposed cutbacks explain about $8.5 billion of the $10.8 billion adjusted outlay increase in 1974. However, Congress explicitly rejected proposed cutbacks in federal grants-in-aid for social programs and restored part of the funds taken out by the administration. About $1.6 billion was added to outlays in grants for education, health, community activities, and area economic development programs. Although the restoration of funds did not offset all the proposed cuts (see Table 2-1), congressional action did maintain outlays for these grant programs at approximately the same real level as in the previous two years. Later in this chapter, we show that the increases in outlays probably overstate the actual growth of these programs.

The effects of the administration's cutback program are difficult to ascertain in areas other than social grant programs. Proposed legislative changes to reduce benefits to recipients of Medicare and veteran pensions by about $1 billion were rejected. Many of the proposed reductions, variously estimated at from $7 billion to $9 billion, were illusory—that is, "cuts" were proposed from spending levels that never would have materialized.[2] Finally, a number of proposed outlay reductions, estimated at from $1 billion to $2 billion, resulted from a slowing down in the implementation of programs. These slowdowns were given the code name "impoundment" in public discussion of the budget, but that term is ambiguous (see Appendix A).

2. In Appendix B of *Setting National Priorities: The 1974 Budget* (Brookings Institution, 1973), an attempt was made to eliminate those proposed outlay cuts that would have occurred anyway. The result was that, rather than the $16.9 billion claimed by the administration, revised cutbacks were estimated at $12.2 billion. Another study by the U.S. General Accounting Office (see "Statement of Elmer B. Staats," testimony before the Subcommittee on Consumer Economics of the Joint Economic Committee on Budget Reductions, April 18, 1973; processed) characterized as unambiguously "substantive" only $9.0 billion in cuts and could find only $7.5 billion in cuts that clearly reduced outlays.

Table 2-3. January 1973 and February 1974 Estimates of Obligations Incurred and Outlays for Fiscal Years 1972–75

Billions of dollars

	Estimates, January 1973		Estimates, February 1974	
Fiscal year	Obligations incurred	Outlays	Obligations incurred	Outlays
1972	243[a]	232[a]	243[a]	232[a]
1973	272	250	262[a]	247[a]
1974	275	269	295	275
1975	...	...	312	304

Sources: *The Budget of the United States Government, Fiscal Year 1975*, pp. 293, 328; *Fiscal Year 1974*, pp. 329, 334.
a. Actual.

Although slowdowns do seem to have reduced outlays in 1974, most of this is explained by a reduced rate of federal activity in fiscal 1973. Table 2-3 shows obligations incurred and outlays for the fiscal years 1972–75 as originally envisioned by the administration in the budget document of January 1973 and as estimated in February 1974. When the administration presented its budget plan in early 1973, it anticipated a $29 billion increase in obligations between fiscal years 1972 and 1973 and proposed to hold down the increase in obligations for 1974 to $3 billion. Instead, obligations rose $19 billion in fiscal 1973, $10 billion less than had been estimated a year before. Only a small part of this slowdown in 1973 obligations can be explained by changes in budget authority voted by Congress for fiscal 1973—most was the result of executive branch action that delayed the *obligation* of funds. However, by 1974 the backlog of previously voted budget authority, congressional unwillingness to reduce budget authority,[3] and the administration's apparent desire to avoid another confrontation over slowdowns in carrying out programs resulted in an enormous increase of $33 billion in estimated obligations between 1973 and 1974. Not all of this increase was reflected in the outlay increase in fiscal 1974. Rather, the hump in obligations in 1974 made it inevitable that outlays for fiscal 1975 would rise. Thus, the principal slowdown in program implementation occurred in fiscal 1973, and the effects of that slowdown have resulted in lower outlays in 1974 than would otherwise have been the case. In addition, the 1973 slowdown caused

3. Budget authority for 1974 in the original administration proposal was $288 billion; it is now estimated at $311 billion for the same year. But over half of this increase is in contract authority for mass transit, highways, and pollution control that will not result in obligations until sometime in the future.

a bunching of obligations in fiscal 1974, whose outlay impact will be felt in large part in 1975.

TO SUMMARIZE, the increase in outlays of $10.8 billion in fiscal 1974 between the original proposal and the current estimates was due to a number of factors.[4] Nearly half of the increase can be explained by automatic changes in outlays as a result of unanticipated inflation and unemployment and by underestimates of expenditures in other programs. Independent congressional action accounted for most of the rest. With the exception of reversing part of the administration's proposed reductions in federal grants for social programs, congressional activity was for the most part unrelated to the cuts proposed. Slowdowns in the rate at which authorized programs got under way—one of the kinds of reductions proposed by the administration—probably resulted in some reduction in outlays.

The 1975 Budget

As the federal budget for fiscal year 1975 was reaching its final stages of preparation in January 1974, the administration was facing a very different economic picture than it had the year before. Unemployment was rising, partly because of a previous slowing in the growth of the economy and partly because of the energy crisis. At the same time, the prospect of a price spiral in the calendar year 1974 was fairly certain. The wholesale price index had spurted by 18 percent in 1973, and not all the increase had yet been passed on to the consumer.

Since the trends in employment and prices pointed in opposite directions, the determination of a proper fiscal posture for the federal government was particularly difficult. The 1975 federal budget should become more expansionary to offset worsening unemployment, but less expansionary to help curb inflation. These opposing tugs, combined with greater uncertainty than usual as to the accuracy of economic forecasts, resulted in a compromise outlay target for fiscal 1975.[5]

4. It now appears that outlays in fiscal 1974 may not reach the level estimated by the administration. Data released in April 1974 incorporating federal spending through three-quarters of fiscal 1974 indicate that federal outlays in the fiscal year will be "significantly below the path implied in the Administration's budget document." *Survey of Current Business*, Vol. 54 (April 1974), p. 3.

5. Whether this compromise is compatible with the administration's forecast of a mild slowdown in economic activity in the first half of calendar year 1974 is discussed in Chapter 3.

Table 2-4. Estimated Federal Budget Outlays and Change from Previous Year, by Major Category, Fiscal Year 1975

Dollar amounts in millions

Category	Outlays, 1975	Change from 1974	
		Amount	Percent
Defense, space, foreign affairs	$ 96,073	$ 7,197	8.1
Cash income maintenance	98,189	13,736	16.3
Helping people buy essentials	33,217	4,116	14.1
Aid for social programs	18,219	465	2.6
Investment in physical environment	17,342	2,133	14.0
Revenue sharing	6,807	84	1.2
Direct subsidies to producers	3,723	−907	−19.6
Net interest	21,982	647	3.0
Other programs	22,980	2,103	10.1
Financial adjustments	−14,087	211	1.5
Total	**304,445**	**29,785**	**10.8**

Sources: *The Budget of the United States Government, Fiscal Year 1975; The Budget of the United States Government—Appendix, Fiscal Year 1975; Special Analyses, Budget of the United States Government, Fiscal Year 1975.*

The budget for fiscal 1975 requests federal outlays of $304.4 billion, an increase of $29.8 billion, or 11 percent, over the previous year's spending total. Table 2-4 shows the breakdown of the spending increase by expenditure categories. Cash income maintenance programs and those related to defense, the two largest expenditure items, show the largest absolute increase, with income maintenance programs running higher than defense for the first time in history. Spending for defense, space, and foreign affairs is projected to rise by about 8 percent, while the civilian budget, taken as a whole, will rise by 12 percent over the previous year's outlays. The defense category accounts for less than one-quarter of the total outlay increase.

Just to outline these broad changes, however, gives a misleading picture of how the decisions on the 1975 federal budget were made and what their longer-term effects will be. In Table 2-5 we have therefore broken down this change in outlays into two broad components—those expenditure items that are mandatory and those that are more or less at the discretion of the government.

Mandatory Expenditures

Mandatory programs are those in which recipients are entitled to certain benefits, such as social security, or in which outlays are fixed

Table 2-5. Estimated Change from Previous Year in Federal Budget Outlays for Mandatory and Discretionary Programs, by Major Category, Fiscal Year 1975

Category	Mandatory programs		Relatively discretionary programs	
	Amount of change (millions of dollars)	Percent change	Amount of change (millions of dollars)	Percent change
Defense, space, foreign affairs	604	10.8	6,593	7.9
Cash income maintenance	13,736	16.3	0	0.0
Helping people buy essentials	3,764	14.5	352	11.5
Aid for social programs	192	6.0	273	1.9
Investment in physical environment	0	0.0	2,133	14.0
Revenue sharing	84	1.3	0	0.0
Direct subsidies to producers	−434	−13.3	−473	−34.6
Net interest	647	3.0	0	0.0
Other programs	297	16.5	1,806	9.5
Financial adjustments	0	0.0	211	1.5
Total	**18,890**	**12.4**	**10,895**	**8.9**

Sources: Same as Table 2-4. Pay raises for federal employees are classified under relatively discretionary programs. Such raises in the Defense Department are in the first spending category; for civilian agencies, pay raises are in "other programs."

under a previously enacted law, such as general revenue sharing, or in which current outlays merely satisfy certain contracts already entered into, as in the case of interest on Treasury bonds. In these instances, once benefits and entitlements are legally established, outlays are not determined by the current budgetary action of the executive or legislative branches: they are "uncontrollable" by the government.[6] Thus, for example, social security outlays depend both on how many eligible people die, retire, become disabled, or become entitled to survivors' insurance and on the benefit schedules already legislated. The executive branch *estimates* outlay requirements, and Congress examines their reasonability. Neither body decides whether to undertake the outlays, only the amounts likely to be involved.

In looking at the decisions actually underlying the 1975 budget

6. The Office of Management and Budget's concept of "open-ended programs and fixed costs" corresponds to our definition of mandatory programs. In addition to these programs, they classify as "relatively uncontrollable" outlays stemming from prior-year contracts and obligations. (See *The Budget of the United States Government, Fiscal Year 1975,* Table 14, pp. 318–19.) In fiscal 1974, uncontrollables included pay increases as well. (See ibid., *Fiscal Year 1974,* Table 7, p. 333.) We have chosen the term "mandatory programs" to cover the narrower concept of uncontrollability and avoid confusion with the Office of Management and Budget's classification scheme.

proposal, the first step then is to take the estimated increase in mandatory programs "off the top." As Table 2-5 indicates, $18.9 billion of the $29.8 billion total increase in outlays had to be set aside for mandatory program increases. Apart from small increases for military retirement pay and interest on the federal debt, almost all of these are in cash income maintenance programs and in programs that provide in-kind assistance to needy individuals. These two categories account for 90 percent of the increase in mandatory programs. The largest single outlay increase is for the old-age, survivors', and disability programs under social security. In fiscal 1975, these outlays are estimated at $64 billion, an increase of about $9 billion over the previous year. This 16 percent rise is due mainly to benefit increases, effective in March and June 1974, resulting from the Social Security Amendments passed by Congress in December 1973.

Another $3.5 billion increase in outlays for mandatory programs is accounted for by the supplemental security income (SSI) and food stamp programs. SSI is a federal program started January 1, 1974, providing uniform cash payments to low-income aged, blind, and disabled recipients. The program replaces state public assistance programs, although some states will continue programs to supplement SSI. The growth of federal spending in this area is due to three factors. First, the SSI is federally supported in full, whereas the state programs were federally funded only in part. Second, the benefit level in SSI is higher than in many of the state programs. Finally, SSI will provide benefits for many people who either did not qualify or, for some other reason, did not receive benefits under state programs.

Outlays for the food stamp program are expected to increase by nearly 80 percent over the period 1973–75. The 1975 federal outlay of almost $4 billion for this program, which will provide partial subsidies on food purchases for an estimated 16 million persons in fiscal 1975, are about the same as federal expenditures for the more renowned aid to families with dependent children (AFDC) program. The high expansion is in part due to the larger number of recipients— eligibility requirements have become less restrictive in recent years and the program will be available in all counties for the first time in mid-1974—and in part to the increased subsidy per recipient. (See Chapter 7 for a more detailed discussion of recent changes in social security, SSI, food stamp, and related programs.)

Mandatory programs in fiscal 1975 will constitute over 55 percent

Table 2-6. Change from Previous Year in Federal Budget Outlays for Discretionary Programs, Two Different Classifications of Federal Pay Increases, Fiscal Year 1975

	Change	
Classification of pay increase and category of outlay	Amount (millions of dollars)	Percent
Pay increases considered relatively discretionary		
Defense, space, foreign affairs	6,593	60.5
Nondefense	4,302	39.5
Total	**10,895**	**100.0**
Pay increases considered mandatory		
Defense, space, foreign affairs	4,893	56.9
Nondefense	3,702	43.1
Total	**8,595**	**100.0**

Source: Same as Table 2-4.

of federal spending.[7] In the past five years outlays for these programs have doubled, while total federal expenditures have risen by about 50 percent. Thus, to an increasing extent each year, budgetary decision makers find their choices preempted by this growth in mandatory programs resulting from increases in participation and more or less automatic benefit level increases.

Relatively Discretionary Programs

Only $10.9 billion, 37 percent of the projected outlay increase for 1975, was available for other programs after the amounts for mandatory program increases had been set aside. Table 2-6 shows how the administration proposes to allocate this part of the budget over which it has more control.

We should note first that pay raises for federal employees, amounting to $1.7 billion in the Department of Defense and $600 million in civilian agencies, have been included among the relatively discretionary outlays. While the administration and Congress have some choice over the starting date and extent of a pay increase, the federal payroll rise is on the borderline between mandatory and discretionary pro-

7. Under the broader definition now used by the Office of Management and Budget, uncontrollables will constitute 74 percent of 1975 outlays.

grams. For this reason, Table 2-6 also shows the allocation of outlays with mandatory programs redefined to include these pay raises. In any event, given the decision on pay increases, only $8.6 billion was available after adjusting for mandatory programs.

DEFENSE SPENDING

About 60 percent of the increase in controllable outlays are slated for defense, space, and foreign affairs, representing about an 8 percent increase in that sector's relatively discretionary programs. Manpower costs continue to dominate defense spending, as they have for several years. The share of the total defense budget accounted for by payrolls and other expenditures related to the compensation of personnel, which stood at about 40 percent in 1967, now seems to have leveled off at slightly above 55 percent. The steep rise in the wages of defense employees can be linked to the 1967–68 decisions to make federal salaries—military and civilian—comparable to those in the private sector. This legislation resulted in large military pay raises in 1969 and 1970 and additional comparability increases every year since then. Further increases in military pay, particularly for lower-ranking personnel (which were passed in 1971 to facilitate the decision to abolish the draft and move to an all-volunteer military system) have contributed to a smaller degree to the higher cost of manpower.

Whatever the cause, manpower costs have accelerated dramatically and continue to rise every year. In 1975, the administration is requesting $34 billion to pay a military and civilian work force in the Defense Department of about 3.2 million people. This manpower pool is almost 15 percent smaller than the defense work force in 1964—the last year before the Vietnam-associated buildup—but the payroll is more than double the 1964 total of $15.8 billion. The administration argues that the pay raises for Defense Department employees, combined with increases in the prices the military must pay for goods and services, is solely responsible for the increase in national security outlays.

Unfortunately, examination of the one-year change in outlays for defense can be a misleading indicator of trends in the military side of the budget. This is especially true in viewing the changes between fiscal 1974 and 1975 because the administration submitted an unusually large supplemental request for 1974 funds (over $6 billion) at the time it presented its budget. It then programmed two-thirds of the outlays that would result from that request for use in fiscal

Table 2-7. Department of Defense Military Budget, by Alternative Measure, Fiscal Years 1972–75

Dollar amounts in billions

Measure	Actual		Estimated		Growth, 1972–75 (percent)
	1972	1973	1974	1975	
Outlays	$75.2	$73.3	$78.4	$84.6	12.5
Obligations incurred, net	76.2	76.4	85.3	90.9	19.3
Budget authority	75.1	77.6	82.7	91.0	21.2
End-of-year balance of obligated budget authority	24.0	26.9	33.8	40.2	67.5

Sources: *The Budget of the United States Government, Fiscal Year 1975*, and *Fiscal Year 1974*.

1974. This makes the outlay increase from 1974 to 1975 look small. Moreover, since nearly one-third of the defense budget is in procurement, research and development, and construction—forms of spending implying lengthy delays between the obligation of funds and their actual expenditure—outlays often lag considerably behind real changes in activity levels.

Table 2-7 shows several measures of change in the Department of Defense military budget (which constitutes almost 90 percent of the money allocated for defense, space, and foreign affairs) for the past four years. A comparison of the fiscal 1972–75 growth rates in various measures of Defense activity levels shows that, while outlays have indeed exhibited only modest increases so far, a sharp increase can be expected in the future. *Obligations incurred*—which represent the commitment of federal dollars—will have risen more than half again as fast as outlays over the 1972–75 period. Once such obligations are incurred it is only a matter of time before outlays are made. Similarly, *budget authority*, which represents the amount of money the U.S. Treasury puts aside in the Defense checking account, will have risen nearly twice as fast as outlays over the four years. Finally, the end-of-year balance of budget authority that is already obligated—the Defense checkbook balance already spoken for—has grown over five times as fast as defense outlays in the 1972–75 period. The growth of these obligated balances for major equipment, construction, and research and development stands as a rough measure of the succeeding years' outlays. Thus a sharp near-term rise in defense outlays may be expected, barring an unlikely reduction in operating costs.

Actually, then, the new defense budget constitutes the first step of an important change in the U.S. defense posture, and the administration requests a sizable addition to budget authority to pay for it. After adjusting for pay and price increases and for the timing of the supplemental budget request, a real increase of nearly 6 percent has been proposed in budget authority for baseline defense programs. This sharp rise in baseline authority has been requested primarily because the administration now seems to be taking a much stiffer view of defense requirements than it did last year. As the United States withdrew from Southeast Asia, it scaled down the overall size of its general purpose forces. Numbers of U.S. Army divisions, ships, and aircraft all have declined sharply from their peaks in 1968. The administration's view now is that these decreases in U.S. military capability have gone as far as, or even a little farther than, they can without jeopardizing the nation's security. These matters are discussed further in Chapters 4 and 5.

DOMESTIC SPENDING

Given the increase in mandatory programs, the rise in the federal pay scale, and also the decision to raise defense outlays, the administration had a very small margin for other domestic programs. Specifically, of the $29.8 billion outlay increase, only $3.7 billion was available for relatively discretionary domestic programs. However, while $3.7 billion is only 1.2 percent of the total proposed 1975 outlays, it represents a 9.5 percent increase over similar 1974 discretionary domestic programs. In other words, it appeared possible for the administration, within all the constraints listed above, to increase outlays in the remaining domestic programs by enough to compensate for inflation. Most of these domestic programs are for aid to social programs and investment in the physical environment.

The administration is not proposing an across-the-board expansion of domestic programs for 1975. Table 2-8 shows the domestic programs to which the administration gives major emphasis in its 1975 budget proposal. There are three significant increases, accounting for most of the available controllable budget margin. First, outlays for grants for sewage treatment facilities (water pollution control and abatement) are increased by over half. Outlays in this Environmental Protection Agency program derive primarily from obligations incurred in previous years. Since obligations increased fivefold between

Table 2-8. Estimated Changes from Previous Year in Federal Budget Outlays for Relatively Discretionary Domestic Programs, by Category, Fiscal Year 1975[a]

Dollar amounts in millions

	Change, 1974 to 1975	
Category and program	*Amount*	*Percent*
Helping people buy essentials	**$ 352**	**11.5**
Higher education student aid	389	30.2
Child nutrition and school lunch	475	52.1
Surplus commodity distribution (phaseout)	−512	−59.1
Aid for social programs	**273**	**1.9**
Education	381	8.4
Manpower training and employment	−119	−4.0
Health services	50	2.1
Urban community development	173	9.0
Community activities	−376	−61.5
Area and regional development	164	7.7
Investment in physical environment	**2,133**	**14.0**
Water pollution control and abatement	1,435	56.0
Urban mass transit	212	43.4
All other	486	4.0
Direct subsidies to producers	**−473**	**−34.6**
Small business loans	−279	−37.2
Other	−194	−31.5
Other programs	**1,206**	**6.3**
Acceleration of energy research	461	n.a.
Veterans' medical care and other	622	17.4
All other	123	n.a.
Financial adjustments	**211**	**n.a.**
Total	**3,702**	**9.5**

Sources: Same as Table 2-4.
a. Pay increases are not included in the figures in this table.
n.a. Not applicable.

1972 and 1974,[8] the outlay increase for this program in 1975 really did not require any current action. Thus, over one-third of the available $3.7 billion discretionary outlay increase is not so discretionary after all.

Two energy-related initiatives are proposed. One is a 40 percent hike in federal aid to urban mass transit. This increase is for the exist-

8. This rapid increase in obligating funds is, nevertheless, much slower than the rate of increase in contract authority voted by Congress. The failure of the administration to obligate all the funds authorized has led to charges of impoundment. See Appendix A for further discussion.

ing federal assistance program, providing funds only for capital investments (for example, the purchase of buses and commuter railroad cars). After the budget was submitted, the administration proposed a new program to finance operating as well as capital expenses, which will involve additional outlays. The other energy-related proposal is an expansion of research and development into future nuclear and other energy sources. The outlay increase shown in Table 2-8 shows only part of the acceleration of this program; the remainder, mainly research in nuclear energy, is accounted for in defense, space, and foreign affairs. (See Chapter 6 for further discussion of the new transit program as well as the increased energy research budget.)

Finally, the budget shows a substantial increase in outlays to help people buy essentials. One proposal is for increased outlays to pay for appropriations already enacted in the basic educational opportunity grant program, a federal need-based undergraduate grant. In the 1974–75 academic year, the program will be open to qualifying first- and second-year students and the number of recipients will more than double. The fiscal 1975 budget also requests authority to fund all needy undergraduates for 1975–76. The other in-kind assistance program showing substantially larger outlays is child nutrition. Most of the increase stems from the special assistance program which provides free and reduced price school lunches for needy children. Under recent changes in the law, the reimbursement rate for free lunches was raised from 40 cents to 45 cents per meal and for reduced price lunches from 8 cents to 10 cents per meal. Moreover, the scope of the reduced price lunch program was extended to children whose family's income is 75 percent above the poverty level.

The Fate of Aid to Social Programs

Despite congressional unwillingness to accept large cutbacks in social grant programs in the 1974 budget, the administration is again requesting a very tight budget in that category, proposing that outlays for these programs grow only about 2 percent between fiscal 1974 and 1975, much less than the rate of inflation (Table 2-8). Within this aggregate reduction in real services, however, the various assistance categories seem to be moving in disparate fashion. Education and community development programs in *outlay* terms are keeping up with

Table 2-9. Office of Education Budget for Elementary, Secondary, and Vocational
Programs, and Consolidated Education Grants, by Alternative Measure,
Fiscal Years 1972–75

Dollar amounts in millions

Measure	1972	1973	Estimated		Growth, 1972–75 (percent)
			1974	1975	
Outlays	$3,112[a]	$3,192	$3,497	$3,793	21.9
Obligations incurred, net	3,300[a]	3,728	3,702[b]	3,583[c]	8.6
Budget authority	3,307[a]	3,802	3,659[b]	3,583[c]	8.3
End-of-year balance of obligated budget authority	1,451	2,018	2,196[b]	1,987[d]	36.9

Sources: *The Budget of the United States Government, Fiscal Year 1975*, and *Fiscal Year 1974; The Budget of the United States Government—Appendix, Fiscal Year 1975*, and *Appendix, Fiscal Year 1974*.
a. Omits dropout prevention and school library programs.
b. Excludes proposed advanced funding of consolidated education grants.
c. Includes fiscal year 1974 proposed advanced funding of consolidated education grants.
d. Computed by summing the obligated balances in the categorical programs and adding the difference between the end of fiscal year 1974 obligated balance in the advanced funded consolidated grant program and outlays in fiscal year 1975 under that program.

inflation, while community action and manpower programs are being reduced substantially.

The changes in outlays, however, *overstate* the growth in some of these programs. A more accurate view of the trend in activity levels proposed by the administration can be obtained by inspecting changes in some of the alternative measures of program activity.

Education

Table 2-9 presents several measures of activity for the major elementary and secondary education programs of the U.S. Office of Education (USOE).[9] As indicated in the table, outlays for these education programs have grown smoothly and substantially between 1973 and 1975. But when we look at obligations incurred—the rate at which the government is committing itself to make payments—the trend over the same period is actually downward. The reason for these opposing movements can be discerned from inspecting other lines in the table. Between fiscal 1972 and fiscal 1973, Congress increased budget authority for these programs by about $0.5 billion. In

9. These account for more than three-quarters of the education subcategory in aid for social programs. The major omissions are the programs of the Office of Child Development in the Department of Health, Education, and Welfare, and a number of higher education institutional aid programs.

fiscal 1973, although the administration extended its commitments by about $400 million, outlays rose by less than $100 million. This created a huge backlog of end-of-year balances in the USOE checkbook. In 1974 and 1975, the administration is essentially planning to spend out the backlog accumulated in fiscal 1973. Congress is being asked to add less budget authority than in 1973, and USOE plans to slacken the rate at which it makes new commitments over the 1974–75 period. It is clear that under these circumstances, outlays cannot continue their upward course for very long unless Congress adds to the administration's budget authority request. In fiscal year 1974, Congress added about $600 million to the original budget authority request, but that was not enough to equal the previous year's level.

For fiscal year 1975, the administration is requesting a consolidation of a large number of education programs into a special revenue sharing package. In addition, it has agreed to support "advance funding" (to enable school districts to plan ahead) if its consolidation proposals are accepted. Advance funding essentially means that in fiscal 1975, appropriations for two years would be voted, to be used in the school years 1974–75 and 1975–76. Thereafter, Congress would vote for budget authority a year in advance of the school year in which the funds would be committed. Since the budgetary effect of advance funding is to double the total in the initial year, one year of funding is excluded from Table 2-9. It should be repeated that, after these adjustments are made, the budget proposal implies that over the next few years outlays for education grants will be held constant at best, even though the recent trend in outlays is upward.

Urban Community Development

For the last three years the administration has proposed the Better Communities Act, designed to consolidate and replace a number of existing urban-oriented community development programs. The older programs included an assortment of federally assisted projects for slum clearance (urban renewal), demonstration projects (model cities), as well as aid for urban parks, city sewers, rehabilitation of houses and commercial space, and aid in building neighborhood centers and other public buildings.[10] The existing programs are project

10. The program of grants for basic water and sewer facilities developed by the Department of Housing and Urban Development (HUD), which would be consolidated into the Better Communities Act, is included in the tables in this section although it is under the category *investment in physical environment* in other tables in this book.

grants for which states or localities submit a plan to the federal government, which then approves the plan and commits itself to provide funds as the project is being completed. Under the Better Communities Act, the state and local governments will have the final say on project approvals. Funds would be distributed by a formula taking into account population, overcrowded housing, and the number of poor people in the area.

In terms of the federal budget, the proposed demise of the old community development programs and their replacment by a block grant makes it difficult to determine changes in the federal government's activity in this area. In Table 2-10 the administration's estimate of outlays for the period 1972–75 shows a slow rate of increase, with outlays for the new program more than compensating for a decline in old programs between 1974 and 1975. Because of the nature of the projects supported under the older programs—mainly construction of various facilities—the outlays incurred in, say, 1975 reflect completion of projects initiated two, three, four, or more years previously and thus do not properly measure the federal government's current level of support for new undertakings. The amount destined for "new commitments" better reflects the current rate of federal activity; a commitment of funds for the old community development programs means that the federal agency has already approved plans and has, in effect, set aside funds for the project.[11] New commitments, as shown in Table 2-10, have been planned to fluctuate in the 1972–75 period, dropping precipitously in 1974 and then recovering to almost their 1972–73 level by 1975. The reason for the 1974 dry period is that the administration is proposing to undertake very few new commitments under the old programs in that year, and the Better Communities Act funds will not become available for commitment until 1975.

The hiatus in new commitments in fiscal 1974 would allow the administration to limit the government's future outlays for community development programs. As Table 2-10 shows, the balance of budget authority already obligated would reach $5.7 billion by the end of fiscal 1974. In 1975, the administration plans to reduce this balance by about $1.6 billion to finance most of the outlays for the old

11. In the case of some of the old community development programs, the obligation of funds which makes the commitment legally binding occurs at a later date than the commitment itself. When there is such a distinction, we have used the amount committed in our tables.

Table 2-10. Federal Budget for Urban Community Development Programs, by Alternative Measure, Fiscal Years 1972–79
Millions of dollars

	Actual		Projected					
Measure[a]	1972	1973	1974	1975	1976	1977	1978	1979
Outlays	1,988	1,891	2,077	2,214	2,900	3,300	3,200	3,200
Old programs	1,988	1,891	2,077	1,654	1,200	1,100	900	900
New program	0	0	0	560	1,700	2,200	2,300	2,300
New commitments[b]	2,471	2,361	458	2,300	2,300	2,300	2,300	2,300
Old programs	2,471	2,361	458	0	0	0	0	0
New program	0	0	0	2,300	2,300	2,300	2,300	2,300
Budget authority	2,133	2,163	777	2,304	2,300	2,300	2,300	2,300
Old programs	2,133	2,163	777	4	0	0	0	0
New program	0	0	0	2,300	2,300	2,300	2,300	2,300
End-of-year balance of obligated budget authority	5,477	6,632	5,703	5,862	5,200	4,200	3,300	2,400
Old programs	5,477	6,632	5,703	4,122	2,900	1,800	900	0
New program	0	0	0	1,740	2,300	2,400	2,400	2,400

Sources: Same as Table 2-9, and, for old programs, 1976–79, authors' estimates.

a. Old programs are model cities, neighborhood facilities, urban renewal (capital grants), open space, rehabilitation loans, public facilities loans, and sewer and water grants. The new program includes local community development activities under the Better Communities Act.

b. New commitments are total obligations, net of the change in administrative reservations in programs where such reservations are made. In such cases, obligations are measured in the administrative reservations account.

programs in that year, even though no new commitments will be made in 1975 under the old programs.

In fact, were the Better Communities Act to be enacted by 1975, the backlog of obligated balances in the old programs could result in substantial growth of outlays over the next few years, giving the impression of an expanding program. We have illustrated such a possibility in Table 2-10 by assuming that the $4.1 billion in obligated balances in the old programs available at the end of 1975 would be liquidated by outlays of $1.2 billion, $1.1 billion, $0.9 billion, and $0.9 billion, for the years 1976, 1977, 1978, and 1979, respectively. Combined with the administration's plans for spending in the new consolidated program, outlays for urban community development would rise by about $1.3 billion (69 percent) between 1973 and 1979. *But this illustration is entirely consistent with the level of new commitments being frozen at $2.3 billion over the entire 1975–79 period,* a level slightly below the peak reached in 1972.

Congress, of course, must approve these plans, but its ability to control what happens under the old program is in some doubt. Congressional control comes about primarily through voting budget authority, but that does not seem to affect program activity in community development. For example, for fiscal year 1974, Congress appropriated $150 million for the model cities program. The administration's budget indicates, however, that only half of these funds will be committed in 1974 and that the remainder will remain unobligated at the termination of the model cities program in 1975. Indeed, for the seven programs to be consolidated into the Better Communities Act, the administration plans to leave over $1 billion in unobligated balances—voted by Congress, but never committed or spent—in the terminating program accounts. Thus, if Congress wishes to increase federal activity in urban community development, it can either direct the obligation of funds it has already authorized for the old programs, or it can increase the administration's request for funds under the Better Communities Act or other new laws.

Manpower

The decline in outlays for manpower programs is explained mainly by reductions in spending under the Comprehensive Employment and Training Act of 1973 (CETA), another special revenue sharing program.[12] The CETA program consolidates a large number of manpower programs developed in the 1960s, as well as the more recent public service employment program which was designed to provide public jobs in areas with high unemployment rates. In broad program terms, the CETA shifts responsibility for manpower activities from the federal government to the states and localities.

The changes in the level of program activity in the manpower programs, as indicated in the federal budget, are straightforward. As Table 2-11 shows, program activity reached a peak of about $2.5 billion in fiscal 1973 and is scheduled to level off at $2 billion over the next two years.

In fiscal 1973, a boom period in the economy, the public service employment program (then operated under the emergency employment assistance program) accounted for about $1.3 billion of the $2.7 billion in obligations incurred in that year (Table 2-11). By 1975, after the public service jobs program has been fully integrated with the CETA grants to states and localities, the administration estimates

---

12. The manpower activities discussed in this section include only the programs under the Comprehensive Employment and Training Act and the emergency employment assistance program. These account for about half of the outlays for manpower included in the social grants category. The remaining programs are the work incentive program for welfare recipients, federal-state employment service functions, rehabilitation, and some smaller programs.

Table 2-11. Federal Budget for Comprehensive Manpower Programs,ᵃ by Alternative Measure, Fiscal Years 1972–75

Dollar amounts in millions

Measure	Actual 1972	Actual 1973	Estimated 1974	Estimated 1975	Percent change, 1972–75
Outlays	$2,232	$2,491	$2,125	$2,000	−10.4
Obligations incurred, net	2,684	2,688	1,942	2,050	−23.6
Budget authority	2,682	2,798	1,809	2,050	−23.6
End-of-year balance of obligated budget authority	1,460	1,615	1,407	1,456	−0.3

Sources: Same as Table 2-9.

a. Includes comprehensive manpower assistance and emergency employment assistance.

that it will account for $350 million of the $2 billion in obligations incurred in that year. This program will probably employ only 40,000 people, but it will be targeted on areas with high unemployment rates. The exact amount to be devoted to public service employment will rest with state and local sponsors, although the federal government has retained the power to mandate a minimum amount of the CETA funds for this purpose. By raising this minimum it would be possible to direct more money to public employment in certain jurisdictions should the overall employment situation worsen. This is one of the possible alternatives discussed in Chapter 3.

The Real Level of Activity in Social Programs

Over the recent past, inflation has eroded the real level of federal activity in the social grant area. In Table 2-12 we have brought together the data in Tables 2-9, 2-10, and 2-11 on federal obligations for education, community development, and manpower. In 1975, about $1.8 billion more than in 1972 would have to be spent on these programs to maintain the 1972 level of federal activity. Instead, the administration proposes a $0.5 billion reduction in obligations. This means that if the administration's proposals are accepted by Congress the level of federal activity in these areas measured in dollars of constant purchasing power will be about $2.4 billion, or 30 percent, below what it was in 1972. In the manpower programs, the obligation level requested under the budget proposal would have to be doubled in order to restore 1972 activity levels.[13] Moreover, the administration's

13. Most of the increase required to restore the manpower budget to its 1972 real level is to compensate for the reduction caused by the end of the emergency employment assistance program, and thus implies the judgment that public service jobs will be as vital to the economy in fiscal 1975 as in the recession of 1972.

Table 2-12. Federal Budget Shortfall below 1972 Real Level in Obligations for Education, Urban Community Development, and Manpower, Fiscal Years 1972–75

Dollar amounts in millions of current dollars

Program	Change in obligations incurred, 1972–75	Amount of increase needed to keep pace with inflation[a]	Shortfall of obligations below 1972 real level	
			Amount	As percentage of 1975 obligations
Education	$ 283	$ 710	$ −427	−11.9
Community development	−171	656	−827	−36.0
Manpower	−634	475	−1,109	−54.1
Total	**−522**	**1,841**	**−2,363**	**−29.8**

Sources: Tables 2-9, 2-10, 2-11.

a. For the three-year period 1972–75, the price indexes for education, urban community development, and manpower were assumed to increase 22 percent, 27 percent, and 18 percent, respectively. These indexes are based on the Brookings projection model.

requests for social aid seem designed to maintain a fixed level of nominal spending for these programs in the future. As prices increase, therefore, the real level of federal activity will be further reduced. Projections of aid to social programs are further discussed in Chapter 9.

Since most of the money for social grant programs is spent in the form of grants-in-aid to state and local governments, the implications of reduced real federal expenditures in this area are difficult to ascertain. If state and local governments decide to maintain or expand the real level of program activity, the main effect of the reduced federal support is to substitute state and local revenues (or possibly federal general revenue sharing funds) for the federal categorical grants. But both the decline in real levels of grant spending and the relaxation of federal controls on these moneys imply that there is likely to be some reduction in total spending in these program areas.[14]

ONCE THE ADMINISTRATION's outlay target was set by fiscal policy goals, the freedom of choice in the 1975 budget was largely preempted by the growth in mandatory programs, most of which provide income support to individuals. The small margin available after mandatory program growth and payroll increases were set aside was allocated primarily to defense expansion and to realizing past commitments on the EPA pollution control program. Few significant new initiatives

14. See Edward M. Gramlich and Harvey Galper, "State and Local Fiscal Behavior and Federal Grant Policy," *Brookings Papers on Economic Activity* (1:1973), pp. 15–65.

were attempted. Grants for social programs were held down—not as in the request for the previous year by sharp dollar cutbacks—but by allowing inflation to erode real program levels. In addition, even though the administration's 1975 budget message does not make a display of discrediting existing programs, as the 1974 message did, terminations and reductions in many domestic programs are again recommended. Thus the pledges to prevent a tax increase, to maintain a strong national security posture, and to concentrate fiscal policy in an anti-inflationary direction were given high priority, income support programs were allowed to run their course, but aid to social programs were placed farther down the scale of the administration's discretionary choices.

3. The Budget and the Economy

THE FEDERAL GOVERNMENT plays a significant role in the economy because it can use its spending and tax powers to offset fluctuations in private spending and employment. When private demand threatens to fall and lead to higher unemployment, the federal government can offset this pressure by increasing its own spending or by cutting taxes to stimulate private spending. Conversely, if private demand threatens to become excessive and to generate inflation, the government can counteract this pressure by cutting its own purchases or by raising taxes. The federal government's use of its expenditure and tax programs to attempt to achieve the overall price stability and employment goals of the economy—commonly known as fiscal policy—constitutes a first important set of budgetary choices.

The choices facing fiscal policymakers are distinctly unpleasant in 1974. The year began with prices rising as fast as they have ever risen in the postwar period, with industrial production declining, the growth of real output halted, and unemployment climbing sharply. Many of these problems are related to the energy crisis and should prove temporary, but it is most unlikely that either inflation or unemployment will be brought under control by the end of the year. Where it used to be said that policymakers faced a cruel choice between unemployment and inflation, in 1974 it appears that the United States will have neither full employment nor stable prices.

Although there is little that fiscal policymakers can do to alter this

43

gloomy prospect in the short run, there are options open to them over the longer run. For the crucial question in 1974 is the strength of the probable resumption of economic growth in the latter half of the year. If, as the administration forecast indicates, the economy adjusts to the energy crisis, if growth is strong in business investment, exports, and government spending, and if automobile purchases, housing, and inventory investment begin rising—then output should expand at a fairly sharp rate in the second half of the year, which would halt the rise in unemployment. In that event, inflation will present a more serious danger than unemployment, and will require a fairly restrictive fiscal policy. This is essentially what the administration has proposed in its Budget Message.

If, however, growth is not as strong as the administration now anticipates, unemployment will continue to climb. Inflation will still be a problem, but a lesser one, reflecting the delayed effects of earlier price increases rather than the renewed surge characteristic of a booming economy. It would be appropriate in these circumstances to try to slow the increase in unemployment by following a more expansionary fiscal policy than the administration now intends, and to combat any rapidly rising prices with specific measures for the affected industries.

In this chapter we investigate this question of fiscal policy in relation to the 1975 federal budget. After reviewing recent economic events and the outlook for the coming year, we discuss the President's budget proposals. We then examine some measures that might make fiscal policy less restrictive and hence limit the rise in unemployment without unduly aggravating inflationary pressures.

The Economic Events of 1973 and the Outlook for 1974

In order to understand the current economic situation it is necessary to go back to the administration's imposition of controls on prices and wages in August 1971. As shown in Table 3-1, real output rose rapidly from this time until the first quarter of 1973—due largely to very expansionary fiscal and monetary policies at that time. Unemployment declined throughout this period, though lagging somewhat behind the growth in output, from a high of 6.0 percent in mid-1971 to a low of 4.7 percent by late 1973. In fact, the 1971–73 expansion may have proceeded too rapidly—the 7.3 percent average annual

Table 3-1. Rate of Increase in Real Gross National Product, Consumer Price Index, and GNP Quarterly Deflator, and Unemployment Rate, 1971–73

	Percentage change from preceding quarter at annual rates			
Year and quarter	*Real GNP*	*Consumer price index*	*GNP deflator*	*Unemployment rate (percent)*
1971:1	9.1	2.8	5.5	6.0
2	2.9	5.3	4.9	6.0
3	3.6	2.6	2.8	6.0
4	6.6	2.8	1.3	5.9
1972:1	4.9	3.6	5.7	5.9
2	9.5	2.2	1.6	5.7
3	5.8	4.6	2.8	5.6
4	8.1	3.2	3.3	5.3
1973:1	8.7	8.6	6.1	5.0
2	2.4	7.4	7.3	4.9
3	3.4	10.3	7.0	4.7
4	1.3	9.0	7.9	4.7

Sources: *Economic Report of the President, February 1974*, pp. 251, 254, 279, and ibid., *January 1973* p. 223; U.S. Bureau of Labor Statistics, *The Consumer Price Index*, relevant issues.

rate of growth of real output between the fourth quarter of 1971 and the first quarter of 1973 threatened to get out of control and eventually forced a sharp tightening of both fiscal and monetary policies. These policies were effective in markedly slowing the growth rate of total output by the end of 1973.

Inflation

Inflation, which was more or less under control during 1972's Phase II, began to accelerate rapidly at the same time that the government shifted to the looser restrictions of Phase III in January 1973. Economists are, and probably always will be, debating whether the inflation that developed after Phase II demonstrates the virtue of the earlier controls or simply the fact that controls cannot work indefinitely when demand grows rapidly and pressures on manufacturing capacity tighten. Whatever the case, it is clear that price inflation in 1973 was considerably aggravated by two outside forces. First, after many years of relative stability, sudden agricultural shortages caused food prices to soar in late 1972 and 1973. The 1973 consumer price index for food rose at a 21 percent annual rate, the wholesale price of farm products and processed foods and feeds by 27 percent. Second, as a result of two dollar devaluations, prices of imported goods also rose rapidly—at an annual rate of 28 percent between the fourth quarter of 1972 and the second quarter of 1973. When these movements were added to the increasingly tight capacity in major raw materials industries and lingering catchup pressures following the relaxation of price controls, inflation became a very serious problem. Table 3-1 indicates that while the GNP deflator, the most comprehensive price index, increased at an average rate of 3.2 percent in 1972, it was rising at an 8 percent annual rate by the fourth quarter of 1973. Prices for consumer goods were climbing even faster, and both seem likely to continue rising rapidly throughout 1974.

The Energy Crisis

As if this situation were not already bad enough, the energy crisis made it even worse. The Arab oil embargo and production cutback, and the price increase by all petroleum-exporting countries, forced about a 15 percent reduction in petroleum consumption in early 1974 and a sharp rise in the prices of all petroleum products. By April 1974, the price of imported crude petroleum had more than tripled since early 1973, domestic crude prices had also climbed sharply, and retail prices for petroleum products were about 50 percent above their mid-1973 levels. These movements should add about two percentage points to the rate of inflation of the GNP deflator in 1974, and over three percentage points to pre-embargo projections of the rate of consumer price increases. Moreover, a price hike of this magnitude reduces real personal income and consumption demand just like any other $15 billion excise tax. Coupled with the direct decline in automobile sales and production, the effects of the energy crisis alone could lower total output by about 2 percent and increase the unemployment rate by about two-thirds of a percent.[1]

One aspect of the fuel crisis is particularly important here. When

1. These calculations are described in Walter W. Heller and George L. Perry, "The U.S. Economic Outlook for 1974" (release by the National City Bank of Minneapolis, Jan. 8, 1974; processed). In treating the retail price increase for petroleum products like an excise tax, one must allow for any increased investment by petroleum companies. (See Chapter 6 for a full discussion of the energy problem.)

the Arab embargo was first imposed in October 1973, it appeared that there might be serious industrial shortages of petroleum. This would cause producers to cut back production and employment because they could not get enough fuel for their own operations or materials from other producers also short of fuel. Both the allocation program of the Federal Energy Office, which insulated industrial users from the petroleum shortage, and the December price increase by petroleum-exporting countries, which drained large amounts of spending power from the American economy, had altered this prospect even before the end of the embargo in March 1974. Now the 1974 contraction seems to be more like the standard case of overall lack of demand than one of unemployment induced by shortages in strategic materials. However, the other side of the coin is that, regardless of the state of domestic aggregate demand, inflation in 1974 will be much worse because of the world price increase for petroleum products.

The Outlook

The immediate prospect is that output will decline in the first half of 1974 and that both unemployment and the rate of inflation will continue to rise. The Council of Economic Advisers, along with most private forecasters, expects conditions to improve in the second half of the year, but it is by no means clear how much. The council's best guess is that business investment should be rising sharply throughout the year, as suggested by various surveys of business investment plans. Government expenditures at federal, state, and local levels are also expected to rise. Production of automobiles and housing construction, which for different reasons were mainly responsible for the late 1973 downturn, are both expected to increase by the end of the year if there is a strong upturn in car sales and if the late 1973 fall in interest rates generates increased flows of mortgage credit. Net exports will certainly drop in the first half of 1974, but the council believes that the reduction in foreign demand (again largely due to the worldwide impact of the energy crisis) will not be too drastic. If all of these events occur, the current decline will be relatively short, and the overall unemployment rate should not rise above 5.5 percent. But if they do not come about, the economy could remain sluggish for a much longer period and the unemployment rate may well reach 6 percent by the year's end.

The Administration's Fiscal Policy

The administration's Budget Message proposes expenditures of $304 billion and revenues of $295 billion for fiscal 1975. Even though this $9 billion deficit is larger than the corresponding deficit of $5 billion in fiscal 1974, the higher deficit can be accounted for entirely by the fact that the economy is likely to be weaker in 1975. The underlying fiscal policy is actually becoming more restrictive.

The reason for this apparent paradox is that the budget contains many items that are very sensitive to changes in aggregate economic activity. If the level of activity declines, tax revenues decline and unemployment insurance benefits increase, thus leading to a much larger deficit than in some other year when all expenditure programs and tax rates might have been just the same but the overall level of activity higher. Comparing the budget deficits in the two years would then give a very misleading indication of the true impact of fiscal policy on the economy, which in reality would be the same between these two periods.

To get around this difficulty, budget analysts have begun to focus on the so-called full employment surplus. The full employment surplus is calculated by measuring both taxes and expenditures at a standardized full employment rate of activity, thus making these totals independent of the level of economic activity.[2] It is important to do this in fiscal 1975. While the actual budget deficit rises from $5 billion to $9 billion, seemingly a movement toward a more expansionary policy, the full employment surplus changes from a surplus of $4 billion to one of $8 billion, representing a more restrictive budget.

Figure 3-1 shows the full employment surplus by half years over the period 1972–75. Fiscal policy was quite stimulative during the 1972 expansion, and this is reflected in the large full employment deficits in calendar 1972. Then, as a result of a very large increase in social security taxes, the budget became much more restrictive in 1973, with the full employment surplus rising to almost $9 billion by the second

2. For a more complete discussion of the merits and demerits of the full employment surplus as an indicator of the impact of fiscal policy, see Arthur M. Okun and Nancy H. Teeters, "The Full Employment Surplus Revisited," *Brookings Papers on Economic Activity* (1:1970), pp. 77–110.

Figure 3-1. The Full Employment Surplus, National Income Accounts Budget, 1972–75

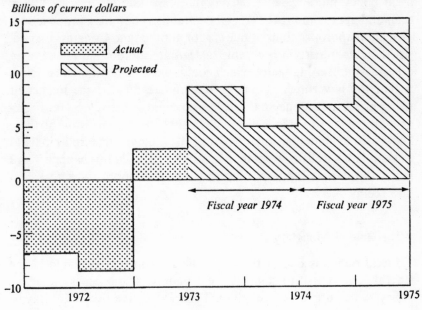

Half years, seasonally adjusted at annual rates

Sources: *Economic Report of the President, Together with the Annual Report of the Council of Economic Advisers, February 1974*, p. 80, for actual data and the U.S. Department of Commerce, Bureau of Economic Analysis, for projections. The data are based on the national income accounts budget, which omits a few asset transactions and timing items that do not immediately affect private income.

half of the year. In all likelihood, this change in budgetary posture had much to do with the concurrent slowdown in activity.

After a brief decline projected by the administration for the first half of 1974 due to a rapid increase in planned expenditures (which may not be realized, see page 25, note 4), the full employment surplus again is slated to rise in the rest of 1974 and 1975. It reaches the level of almost $14 billion by the first half of 1975. If realized, this will represent the tightest fiscal policy since the early sixties. The timing pattern also accounts for the somewhat different descriptions of fiscal policy in the President's *Economic Report*, which indicates no appreciable change in fiscal impact between calendar years 1973 and 1974 (the surplus is close to $6 billion both years), and in the President's Budget Message, which indicates an increasingly restrictive budget between fiscal years 1974 and 1975.

The budget is only a proposal, of course, and it is always possible that present plans will not be realized. One factor which could make fiscal policy more expansionary is that expenditures may be higher than anticipated in fiscal 1975—the administration may propose supplemental appropriations of one sort or another and Congress may resist the cuts in certain programs or legislate more rapid increases in others. An offsetting factor which could make policy more restrictive is that the government typically has underestimated the impact of rising prices and money incomes on revenues—recently by fairly sizable amounts. In Chapter 9 we show that the combination of these factors led to an underestimate of the full employment surplus in fiscal 1974 and may well do so again in fiscal 1975. Should this happen, fiscal policy in the next eighteen months will be even more restrictive than now seems likely.

The Role of Monetary Policy

Fiscal policy is one of the two main instruments available to the federal government to stabilize the economy. The other is monetary policy, which operates through the Federal Reserve Board's ability to influence the monetary reserves of the banking system—and hence the money supply and interest rates on various assets and liabilities. These monetary and credit market variables affect spending demands by altering the costs of financing and the availability of funds facing households and firms in their decisions to buy homes, capital equipment, and consumer goods.

Because the government can influence overall spending demands in these two different ways, a complete picture of how government policy can help stabilize the economy depends on monetary policy as well as on the budget. Unfortunately, it is very difficult to forecast monetary impacts. First, as with fiscal policy, there are methodological difficulties in simply describing monetary policy. Interest rates, the variables which probably most directly influence spending demands, rise and fall with economic activity just like the budget surplus. Bank credit and the stock of money are also influenced by economic activity in the short run, though considered in the longer run they probably do provide a much better indication of the posture of monetary policy. But even if observers could agree on these quantity variables as indicators of monetary policy, it would still be difficult to predict the policies to be followed by the independent Federal Reserve. The Council of Economic Advisers can only suggest that a rate of growth of the broadly defined money stock (money plus time deposits) of about 8 percent in 1974 "would be consistent with our expectations concerning the increase in money GNP during 1974."[3] It is up to the Federal Reserve Board to determine whether this policy actually will be followed.

In view of these difficulties, it seems unlikely that actions of the central bank will greatly alter the stabilization picture which comes from simply examining fiscal policy. If the money supply was to grow at the rate envisioned by the council in 1974, which is quite high by historical standards, it would barely keep pace with inflation. Thus the supply of money in real terms might not rise at all during the year. This would be a fairly restrictive monetary policy, one which is unlikely to exert a significant expansionary force in 1974.

Fiscal Policy Options for 1974

Even though it may appear strange for the administration to be planning an increasingly tight fiscal policy just as the economy is beginning to slide downward, there is one obvious reason for doing so. That reason is—as we have said—inflation. Whereas in the sixties prices did not begin to rise sharply until the overall unemployment rate fell to the neighborhood of 4 percent, in the seventies prices are rising sharply even when the economy is operating at much higher rates of unemployment. This makes pursuit of a vigorous antirecessionary policy much more risky than it was in the past.

There are several possible causes of present-day American inflation —or really the fact that inflation develops at such high rates of unemployment. A first difficulty, already mentioned, lies with the escalating worldwide commodity price increases in the past two years. These rates of increase have been most rapid for food and fuel, but are also notable for many basic industrial materials. A second difficulty concerns the changing composition of the labor force—the increasing proportion of women and teenagers who, because of higher rates of job turnover and undoubtedly some job discrimination, have higher rates of unemployment and thereby raise the overall average unem-

3. *Economic Report of the President, Together with the Annual Report of the Council of Economic Advisers, February 1974*, p. 32.

ployment rate at any level of inflation.[4] A third factor involves expectations. Even modest inflation accompanying efforts to reduce unemployment can penalize workers who have made wage bargains under the assumption of price stability. This forces workers to renegotiate wage contracts to catch up, firms to increase prices, and so forth, until inflation is accelerating rapidly. The latter factor could become extremely important in the next year, because if workers' wages respond to recent price increases for food and fuels, and then industrial prices respond to this growth in wages, the United States may find itself in an inflationary spiral which could last for many years.

Any Solutions?

Whatever the cause of present-day inflation, there are no ready-made solutions. The classical remedy of putting the economy through a recession stiff enough to kill the inflation implies a fearful cost in terms of unemployment. Policies to improve the structure of labor markets—and hence to reduce the wage pressures generated at any level of unemployment—have so far not met with any resounding success, though there are those who believe that these policies would prove helpful if tried on a larger scale.[5] Policies to control prices and wages pursued in Phases I and II appear to most observers to have been moderately successful, but they would have more difficulty in coping with the current inflation.

While inflation is a very serious problem at the present time, it may not get any worse if measures are taken to stimulate the economy and keep the unemployment rate below 6 percent. First, as mentioned above, the current inflation is largely due to shortages of petroleum and other internationally traded commodities, not excessive aggregate demand. Second, certain labor markets are likely to be so depressed in 1974 that it is hard to see how moderately expansionary policies could generate inflationary pressures in these markets. Third, personal tax cuts might conceivably be used to compensate workers for the price rises that have already occurred and hence moderate wage pressures. Thus, although past experience dictates a none-too-sanguine view of measures that purport to improve the unemployment-inflation rela-

4. The Council of Economic Advisers makes much of this phenomenon. See also George L. Perry, "Unemployment Flows in The U.S. Labor Market," *Brookings Papers on Economic Activity* (2:1972), pp. 245–92.

5. See Charles C. Holt and others, *The Unemployment-Inflation Dilemma: A Manpower Solution* (Urban Institute, 1971).

tionship, there may nevertheless be some scope for selective but non-inflationary budgetary expansion in 1974 to limit the anticipated rise in unemployment.

What Strategies?

There are basically two strategies for dealing with unemployment without seriously aggravating inflation. The first, more pessimistic but less risky, approach accepts the reduction in private employment and merely tries to cushion its effects through unemployment insurance or a public employment program. The second, more optimistic but more risky, strategy attempts to prevent the rise in unemployment from occurring by discretionary fiscal measures. Although some income support measures could be expanded rapidly, most expenditure programs are not easy to use for stabilization purposes, and the usual remedy is to cut federal income or social security taxes on households. For either strategy, the guiding principle might be to try to protect those least able to deal with present-day economic difficulties—low-income families that tend to lose their jobs first in times of unemployment and that are most hurt by rapid increases in prices. This consideration, along with the demonstrated difficulty of ever altering a policy once it is intiated, would suggest that if antirecessionary measures are taken, they should be those which would also have desirable effects on the income distribution.

STRENGTHENING UNEMPLOYMENT INSURANCE

The first strategy for dealing with the prospective rise in unemployment is simply to recognize its inevitability and try to protect unemployed workers from the consequences. The present unemployment insurance program, enacted in the Great Depression, is the key element in this strategy. Accordingly, the administration has recently proposed liberalizing amendments which will raise unemployment benefits in certain states and also slightly increase the coverage of the program.

The unemployment insurance system is a combined federal-state program. States assess a tax on employers within their state and deposit the money in a federal trust fund. Benefits are paid out of this fund, but states are free to set payment levels by varying the percentage of previous wages covered and the maximum benefits paid. States are also required by federal law to pay benefits for twenty-six weeks and, by the Employment Security Amendments of 1970, to pay an additional thirteen weeks of benefits in all states whenever the national unemployment rate among insured workers exceeds 4.5 percent for three consecutive months, or in individual states whenever the state-insured unemployment rate is above 4 percent and has increased by 20 percent over the corresponding period two years before.

There are two main weaknesses with this system. First, many states have set either their percentage of previous wages covered or their maximum benefit payments so low that there is in fact not much protection for unemployed workers. In 1973, for example, the average weekly benefit for all unemployed workers was only $58.50, less than the poverty standard for a family of four. A full 40 percent of all beneficiaries in the system received benefits of less than half of their previous wages. In May 1973, the administration proposed legislation to correct this defect by requiring states to pay workers benefits equal to 50 percent of previous wages, up to a maximum of at least two-thirds of the average weekly wage of covered workers in the state. This proposal would liberalize benefits, but only for workers in those states where benefits are least generous relative to wages. As such, it reduces the cost of unemployment for those who bear the heaviest burden. Since only the lowest benefits are increased—and only to levels which are still meager relative to wages—it also minimizes the risk that liberalizing benefits might encourage workers to forgo paid employment for the sake of unemployment insurance.[6]

A second problem with the present system is that coverage is incomplete. Again in 1973, unemployment insurance covered only 38 percent of the total number of unemployed workers.[7] In part this incomplete coverage is because some occupations are still not covered (such as domestic and farm workers, though the administration's 1973 proposal recommends extending coverage to some in the latter group). In part it is because the program does not cover the relatively small percentage of unemployed workers who have been unemployed more than twenty-six weeks. But the main cause is that the large number of

6. An argument that this labor force withdrawal is important was made by Martin Feldstein in "The Economics of the New Unemployment," *The Public Interest*, No. 33 (Fall 1973), pp. 3–42.

7. Coverage is a little better in high unemployment years when unemployment consists more of experienced workers. In 1971, for example, when the overall unemployment rate was 5.9 percent, the program covered 43 percent of the total number of unemployed.

unemployed workers with less than fourteen to twenty weeks of previous work experience are not covered by unemployment insurance.
While it may be stretching the insurance concept to cover these workers
in the present system, the serious prospects of rising U.S. unemployment in the period ahead increases the need to protect those poor and
inexperienced workers who are particularly vulnerable to declines in
employment opportunities. In Chapter 7 we discuss some of the ways
this might be done through income support programs.

PUBLIC EMPLOYMENT

A second measure which could be used to lessen the adverse consequences of unemployment is public employment. Public employment was also first introduced in the United States in the Great Depression but it has not been used very heavily in the postwar period.
However, there were several small public-employment measures as
part of the antipoverty program in the mid-sixties, and the now ex-
pired emergency employment assistance program was established in
1971 to deal with high unemployment. As was mentioned in Chapter
2, Congress recently passed the Comprehensive Employment and
Training Act which consolidates a number of separate manpower programs into a special revenue sharing grant, which includes a $350 mil-
lion authorization for public employment programs for local jurisdictions where the unemployment rate exceeds 6.5 percent for three
consecutive months. Senator Jacob K. Javits has recently proposed
amending this act to establish a much larger—$4 billion—fund for
public employment.

The idea behind public employment is quite simple. There are unemployed workers on the one hand and jobs that must be done on the
other. Why not use those unemployed workers to fill these jobs and
make everybody better off?

Although a large public employment program will increase
consumer incomes and stimulate aggregate demand just like any
other government expenditure program, there is one consideration
that might make it a better form of expenditure in a period when both
unemployment and inflation threaten simultaneously. The present
program is designed so that funds can be targeted to certain local
areas or labor markets which may have been particularly hard hit by
the slowdown in production. Since these local labor markets are already very depressed, one would not expect a moderately sized public

employment program to generate inflation in that market. This could be an important factor in 1974, given the uneven incidence of declines in employment caused by the energy crisis.

Both the 1971 emergency employment assistance program and the present program have expanded employment by making grants to government units for the purpose of hiring unemployed workers. Although this arrangement creates possible delays in hiring and also raises doubts as to whether local jurisdictions really have increased employment or have merely received federal money to employ workers they would have hired anyway, the 1971 act has apparently performed well on both counts: money was spent quickly and employment was increased. While it is estimated that almost half of this increase would have occurred even in the absence of the program, there was still a significant expansion in job opportunities, including those for disadvantaged workers.[8] Given this generally favorable experience, it seems likely that a similar program could also be useful at the present time. One new departure which might prove especially interesting in light of the energy shortage would be to hire workers for public transportation jobs—in either urban bus companies or rail transportation operations—that substitute for the private automobile.

There is much to be said for public employment, but there is also one potential problem. Recent labor market research indicates that present-day U.S. unemployment reflects not so much a lack of total numbers of jobs, but a lack of good jobs.[9] It seems to be relatively easy for workers, especially youths, to get "dead-end" jobs which they soon quit, and relatively hard for them to find jobs that enable or encourage them to develop a permanent employment attachment. Any public employment program that tries to deal with unemployment should also deal with this more basic structural question. But in providing attractive jobs, public employment can become quite costly —paying fairly high wages with high capital and overhead costs. It is hard to see how any program at the $350 million level could directly hire more than, say, 40,000 workers. Even if a program of this size

8. See Sar A. Levitan and Robert Taggart (eds.), *Emergency Employment Act: The PEP Generation* (Olympus, 1974); and National Planning Association, "An Evaluation of the Economic Impact Project of the Public Employment Program" (NPA, January 1974; processed).

9. See, for example, Feldstein, "Economics of the New Unemployment," and Robert E. Hall, "Why Is the Unemployment Rate So High at Full Employment?" *Brookings Papers on Economic Activity* (3:1970), pp. 369–402.

were concentrated on a limited number of areas, it could make only a marginal difference in unemployment conditions.

TAX REDUCTION

The alternative approach would be to act before unemployment develops and to try to ward off threatened increases by cutting taxes in anticipation of the rise in unemployment. There are many possible types of tax reduction. Suggested measures include a reduction in social security tax rates, introducing exemptions and deductions into the social security tax system, providing an optional tax credit into the personal income tax, or simply increasing the personal income tax exemption. While all of these measures are basically motivated by a desire to limit the prospective rise in unemployment, the reasons range from the idea that the government should cut personal taxes in return for a "social contract" that wage earners will not try to catch up for past price increases with increased wage demands, to the idea that households should be compensated for the redistribution of income in favor of oil companies (measures to increase taxes on oil companies are discussed in Chapter 6).[10]

The most regressive federal tax in the United States today is the social security tax. The combined employer-employee payroll tax rate is now 11.7 percent (5.85 percent is paid by the employer, 5.85 percent by the employee) on wage and salary income up to $13,200, with no tax at all on wages above that level. Although there is some uncertainty as to whether the employer's portion of this tax retards the growth in wages or accelerates the growth in consumer prices, the tax is highly regressive either way—payroll taxes as a percent of income are roughly twice as high on workers who make $5,000 a year as on those who make $25,000 a year and four times as high as on those who make $50,000 a year. These taxes have become so large that they now almost completely offset the progressivity of the federal income tax; in 1973 a worker with three dependents earning $10,000 a year paid a higher fraction of his earnings in income and payroll taxes combined than did a similar worker earning $25,000. Since payroll tax rates could go even higher under currently contemplated

10. The first argument is from "Statement of George L. Perry" before the Joint Economic Committee, February 20, 1974 (processed); the second from "Statement of Charles L. Schultze" before the Senate Committee on Appropriations, March 20, 1974 (processed).

schemes for financing national health insurance (see Chapter 8), this tax might be a good one to reduce.

Paradoxically, even though they are the most regressive of federal taxes, social security taxes are also probably the least unpopular. People seem to relate social security taxes they pay to benefits they will ultimately receive, and hence they are less inclined to view this tax as a tax and more inclined to view it as saving than, say, income or excise taxes. Even if there is a special tax that is earmarked for social security benefits, however, there is no intrinsic reason that the social security tax has to be regressive, or cannot be cut in a way which makes the overall tax system more progressive. A simple reduction in social security tax rates, with an offsetting transfer from general revenues into the social insurance trust fund, would be one measure that would make the overall tax system more progressive; as an alternative, there could be a straightforward introduction of deductions and exemptions into the social security tax system.[11]

A second approach would be to cut personal income taxes. Senator Walter F. Mondale has proposed an optional $200 tax credit which could be used instead of the $750 personal exemption; Senator Edward M. Kennedy has proposed increasing the dollar value of this exemption from $750 to $850 in 1974 and $900 in 1975. While both measures compensate households for the inflation which has taken place since previous exemption levels were established, the Mondale proposal is focused more on low-income people because it recognizes the fact that increases in the exemption are worth more to high-income people with high tax rates. The optional credit avoids this difficulty by ensuring that the exemption is worth at least $200 to everybody. To illustrate how important this difference is in reducing tax burdens for lower-income groups, under the present tax system a family of four begins paying personal income taxes when their income reaches $4,300 a year, $571 below the poverty standard for such a family; under the Kennedy proposal they would begin paying taxes

11. For a more complete discussion of the social security system, see Joseph A. Pechman, Henry J. Aaron, and Michael K. Taussig, *Social Security: Perspectives for Reform* (Brookings Institution, 1968). A more recent paper by Aaron argues that the benefit side of the system does not offset the regressivity of tax rates, because of the higher mortality rates and earlier entry into the labor force of low-income people. See "Demographic Effects on the Equity of Social Security Benefits" (paper presented at the International Economic Association Conference on the Economics of Public Services, Turin, Italy, April 1974; processed).

at $4,700, still lower than the poverty standard; while under the Mondale proposal they would not begin paying taxes until income reached $6,247, $1,376 above the poverty standard.[12]

Table 3-2 compares these four possible tax cuts according to the benefits received by various groups in the income distribution. Plan One reduces the employee portion of social security taxes by 1 percentage point (from 5.85 to 4.85 percent), and the somewhat higher tax rate on self-employed workers by 1.5 percent (from 8.05 to 6.55 percent). This change reduces revenue by $6.7 billion in 1974 and $7.2 billion in 1975. Plan Two retains the present social security rate structure but introduces a low-income allowance for the first $650 of earnings and allows a $400 personal exemption, which would operate like the present personal income tax system. It reduces revenues by $7.1 billion in 1974 and $8.0 billion in 1975. Plan Three is the Mondale plan, which reduces revenues by $5.9 billion and $5.7 billion in 1974 and 1975; and Plan Four is the Kennedy proposal, which reduces revenues by $4.0 billion and $6.3 billion in the two years. These revenue changes, ranging from $4 billion to $8 billion, would all prevent the full employment surplus from rising during fiscal 1975, but themselves would probably be responsible for a reduction in the unemployment rate of only about 0.25 percent below what it would otherwise be (say, from 5.75 to 5.50 percent). They are, therefore, very moderate expansionary measures.

Although the revenue implications are similar for all four plans, the distributional implications clearly are not. Plan One, the social security tax rate cut, gives 8 percent of the benefits to those with incomes below $5,000 and another 47 percent of the benefits to families with incomes between $5,000 and $15,000. The low-income allowance and personal exemption in Plan Two direct these social security cuts even more to low- and middle-income families, giving 20 percent to families below $5,000 and 48 percent to those between $5,000 and $15,000. The Mondale plan gives somewhat less to the first group, because they pay small amounts of income tax and thus would not benefit from this credit, but more to the second. The Kennedy plan gives less to both groups than all other plans. On distributional grounds, then, the

12. On April 21, 1974, Senators Kennedy and Mondale agreed on a compromise tax cut plan that would raise the personal exemption to $825 and introduce an optional $190 tax credit. We were not able to compute what the precise impact of this plan would be before this book went to press but, in general, it would reduce taxes about as much as the two original proposals and have intermediate effects on the income distribution.

Table 3-2. Distribution by Income Class of Revenue Losses for 1974, and Amount of Loss for 1974 and 1975, under Four Tax Reduction Plans

Tax reduction plan	Percentage distribution of tax reduction in 1974							Revenue loss (billions of dollars)	
	Adjusted gross income class in thousands of dollars								
	0–5	5–10	10–15	15–20	20–25	25 and over	All classes	1974	1975
Plan One[a]	7.9	18.6	28.7	21.3	11.3	12.2	100.0	6.7	7.2
Plan Two[b]	19.5	23.2	25.0	16.1	7.7	8.4	100.0	7.1	8.0
Plan Three[c]	12.2	39.1	35.9	11.6	1.0	0.1	100.0	5.9	5.7
Plan Four[d]	5.2	19.9	26.4	19.9	11.3	17.3	100.0	4.0	6.3

Source: Estimated from the Brookings file of 1970 individual income tax returns with data projected to calendar years 1974 and 1975 income levels.
a. In Plan One, the social security employee tax would be reduced 1 percent, the tax on self-employed workers 1.5 percent.
b. In Plan Two, a $650 low-income allowance and a $400 personal exemption would be introduced into the social security rate structure.
c. In Plan Three, the worker would have an option of electing a $200 credit for each exemption or a $750 exemption, whichever yielded the lower tax.
d. In Plan Four, the personal exemption would increase to $850 in 1974 and $900 in 1975.

social security low-income allowance combined with an exemption and the optional tax credit seem superior to the other proposals.[13]

One argument sometimes made against any of these tax cuts is that they erode the federal tax base and make it that much more difficult to finance desirable expenditure programs in the future. While this is a valid concern, our long-run projections in Chapter 9 indicate that it should be possible to make such tax cuts and still undertake a reasonably broad array of new programs. In a more fundamental sense, measures that introduce long-needed changes in the government's effect on the distribution of income should always rank high on a list of budgetary priorities.

THE ADMINISTRATION'S PLAN of a full employment surplus rising from $5 billion in 1974 to $14 billion in the first half of 1975 is a fairly restrictive fiscal policy. It is based on two judgments: that a substantial economic rebound is likely to occur after midyear and that relaxing fiscal restraint now would cost more in the way of increasing inflationary pressure than it would gain by shortening the intervening period of high unemployment. The case for providing more budgetary stimulus rests on two different judgments about the economy and the risks ahead: that the second half rebound expected by the administration is not assured and that moderately lower unemployment would not add significantly to inflationary pressure. Thus the administration's fiscal policy risks the possibility of a long period of high unemployment, while the alternative posture risks an overstimulation of the economy. In the end the choice is partly based on a forecast of the economic outlook, partly on an evaluation of the social costs of higher unemployment and inflation.

13. Both the Mondale and Kennedy proposals (Plans Three and Four) could be targeted more to the poor if the tax credit or unused exemption were actually rebated to people whose income and tax liabilities were very low. Such proposals are often made in connection with welfare reform. See Chapter 7.

4. The New Look in Defense

THIS YEAR'S DEFENSE BUDGET and the administration's accompanying statements defining the nation's military requirements point to major changes in U.S. defense policy and military strategy. They may turn out to be the most far-reaching changes since 1961, when the new Kennedy administration sought to reformulate defense goals and restructure forces. To finance this new approach, the President proposes the second largest real increase in obligational authority for U.S. baseline (or peacetime) forces in more than a decade.

This cost increase is not readily apparent from the data presented in the budget. Estimated outlays of $85.8 billion and requested obligational authority of $92.6 billion exceed the figures for fiscal 1974 by less than the amount necessary to offset the effects of inflation.[1] However, if the data are reorganized so as to show the discretionary changes in baseline forces proposed for 1975, the budget request indicates that total obligational authority for these forces, in constant dollars, will increase by $4.3 billion, or 5.8 percent. In addition, our projection of the cost of the new defense posture indicates that obligational

1. There is always some ambiguity as to what is or is not included in estimates of the defense budget. The estimates in this chapter comprise all expenditures administered by the Department of Defense, including funds for military assistance. They exclude approximately $1.5 billion spent on military programs by the Atomic Energy Commission and many smaller defense-related expenditures by other civilian agencies that, though not considered here, are related to the present requirements of national security. These expenditures, along with outlays for space and international affairs, are included in the defense category used in Chapters 1, 2, and 9.

authority for defense will rise by an average of 3.9 percent a year, in real terms, over the rest of this decade. As a result, by 1980, military baseline expenditures could amount to $103 billion in constant dollars of fiscal 1975 purchasing power, and overall military expenditures including retired pay and support of other nations could be $113 billion. If so, the claim made by national security on the nation's resources is likely to remain virtually constant at about 6 percent of projected gross national product (GNP), marking the end of a six-year decline in the defense share of the nation's resources.

In terms of force structure and military preparedness, the implications of the new defense proposal are even more dramatic. In the administration's view, the fiscal 1975 budget is the first of an era when budgets will be designed specifically to meet the nation's military requirements over the "long haul."

Some proposals would improve capabilities quickly:

• More Army combat units and Navy warships in fiscal 1975, reversing a five-year decline.

• Larger inventories of ordnance, spare parts, and equipment; speedup of maintenance schedules; and assignment of more men to combat units to heighten the readiness of general purpose forces.

• Accelerated modernization schedules of some weapon systems to improve battlefield performance.

Other proposals would more radically affect the U.S. defense posture, but only over a number of years. They reflect changes in current assumptions that determine the proper size and structure of U.S. forces, and the most desirable characteristics of new weapon systems:

• *New criteria for determining the size and composition of strategic nuclear forces.* These are still at issue. Some initiatives, especially in the strategic research and development program, could increase spending in the late 1970s, and in the 1980s if they result in changes in the structure of U.S. strategic nuclear forces. Most important of these programs are those to improve the capability of existing Minuteman land-based ballistic missiles and to begin to develop a successor to Minuteman. Other suggested changes will reduce costs. For example, the building schedules for the new Trident strategic submarine and missiles and the new B-1 bomber have been extended, and the possibility has been raised of less expensive substitutes for these systems later on. Also, air defense forces are being sharply pruned, resulting in sizable future savings.

• *New emphasis in the general purpose forces and strategic mobility forces on improving the readiness of military units.* U.S. preparedness to engage in short conflicts is to be increased and will take precedence over the capability to fight prolonged wars. Thus manpower is to be shifted from support elements to combat units. Reserve forces will be reorganized, reduced in size, and prepared for more rapid mobilization and deployment. Programs to enlarge the capacity of strategic airlift forces to deploy forces promptly during the early stages of a conflict are also in progress.

• *Renewed emphasis in weapon acquisition programs and manpower policies on moderating the long-term upward trend in costs per unit of combat capability.* Programs begun during the past five years to develop less expensive ships and aircraft are now being extended to new kinds of military equipment. Other weapon development programs that might result in very high-cost systems are being reconsidered, and measures to reduce the growth in manpower costs are at least in view.

Clearly the administration believes that the United States requires greater combat capabilities, both immediately and over the long term. To underwrite this requirement, it proposes not only to obtain greater efficiency from existing forces, but also to set in motion programs that will call for higher defense budgets, even into the eighties. What prompted this new look at defense?

For one thing, there is a new secretary of defense, James R. Schlesinger. While many of the changes incorporated in the new defense posture have long been advocated inside and outside the Pentagon, they are now being given a more sympathetic hearing.

The state of the economy also had an impact on defense decisions. At least $1 billion to $1.5 billion—and possibly as much as $4 billion—were not cut from the defense request in December because of the presumed effect of this additional obligational authority on the nation's economic health.

A third factor was the war in the Middle East. A number of lessons have been drawn from the war, most of which concern the relative effectiveness of various kinds of weapons, the impact of new technologies on the dynamics of the battlefield, and the importance ascribed to the "readiness" of military forces.

The war also affected broader policy decisions. It demonstrated the limits of détente, underscored the importance of military force in international politics, gave a certain reality to what had become increasingly abstract conceptions of direct military threats to the United States or to its allies, and dramatized the advances in military capabilities achieved by the Soviet Union during the past ten years. In these ways, the war helped to create a political climate favorable to proposals for sizable increases in defense spending.

But the most important factor of all has been the administration's concern that long-term trends in the U.S. defense posture were conveying the wrong signals to the Soviet Union and to U.S. allies alike. In the administration's view, the defense of the Western democracies —and thereby protection of U.S. national security—requires the United States visibly to maintain at least parity with the USSR in strategic nuclear power, to contribute to the maintenance of favorable military balances in Europe and in Asia, and to ensure free access to the seas. While the extent of the Soviet advance in weapons quality and force levels may be disputed, there is little question that Soviet military capabilities have improved relative to those of the United States since 1964. The administration's concern is that the change in the relative military balance has gone as far as, or perhaps even further than, it can without negative political consequences and undue security risks.

Much in the new defense posture is intended to halt or to reverse this trend in the relative military balance, and it is primarily for this reason that defense spending is slated to rise significantly. The administration has expressed the hope that on-going negotiations with the Soviet Union—on mutual force reductions in Europe and on further limitations of strategic weapons—will permit future reductions in defense spending. In its opinion, however, the best way to ensure the success of the negotiations is to make clear to the USSR what will happen if they fail. Additional unilateral reductions in U.S. capabilities or even a standpat posture, it is argued, would erode Soviet incentives to reach new agreements.

Politically, therefore, the new budget is designed to signal Soviet leaders that the United States is prepared to move only as far, and only at the same pace, as the USSR toward measures of arms control and more cooperative mutual relations. In the meantime, the new defense posture indicates that the United States is prepared to undertake whatever measures are necessary to maintain, and perhaps even to improve, its relative military position, both immediately and in the future. And, militarily, the new defense posture is intended to permit the President to act more promptly, with greater force, and with greater confidence than he could at present should the two super-powers once again confront each other during a crisis.

All of this suggests a considerable reshuffling of forces and a fairly extensive redesign of the nation's military stance. Why are they neces-sary? And are they worth the cost? The long-run reforms now envi-sioned—such as reductions in manpower assigned to headquarters staffs—could result in reduced military costs in the future. The key questions, however, relate less to these reforms than to the admin-istration proposals that would increase force levels, improve combat readiness, change planning criteria for strategic forces, and thus raise defense spending despite the savings from measures proposed to in-crease efficiency. Basically, these questions concern the relationship between the U.S. military posture and foreign policy requirements: In the absence of the changes specified by the new defense posture, in what ways and to what degree would U.S. military forces be inade-quate for the challenges facing the nation now and in the foreseeable future?

In 1970, for example, after reviewing future defense needs under the newly formulated Nixon Doctrine, the administration decided that 13 Army divisions would be sufficient to meet the requirements posed by the nation's security objectives and military strategy. Apparently, 13 divisions are no longer considered sufficient. How has the inter-national environment changed in the past four years to justify this shift in requirements?

The purpose of this and the following chapter is to clarify these issues. This chapter focuses on the administration's defense decisions and their rationale. After examining the size of the increase in defense obligational authority requested for fiscal 1975, decisions affecting general purpose forces, strategic nuclear forces, and strategic mobility forces are examined in detail. Changes in the defense posture as they pertain to each force type are discussed, and the implications of spe-cific decisions on the structure and cost of U.S. military forces are projected for the decade.

Chapter 5 examines some of the critical assumptions that underlie the new defense posture in greater depth, including such issues as the role of strategic nuclear weapons and the prospective military bal-

Table 4-1. Modifications in the Original Fiscal Year 1974 Department of Defense Budget

Total obligational authority in billions of dollars

Event and date	Amount	Change
Initial request (January 1973)	85.0	...
Net change incorporated in amended request (September 1973)	...	−2.5
Amendment for emergency aid to Israel and Cambodia (November 1973)	...	+2.4
Reductions made by 93rd Congress, 1st Session (December 1973)[a]	...	−4.0
Enacted by Congress (93 Cong. 1 sess.)	80.9	...
Supplemental requests, total (February 1974)	...	+6.2
To finance pay raises	...	+3.4
For increases in fuel prices	...	+0.5
For incremental costs of operations during the Middle East war	...	+0.2
For increases in U.S. force readiness and modernization	...	+2.1
Final 1974 budget if supplemental request is approved in full	87.1	+2.1

Sources: U.S. Department of Defense, News Releases 44-73, January 29, 1973, and 43-74, February 4, 1974; unpublished data from the Office of the Secretary of Defense (Comptroller); *The Budget of the United States Government, Fiscal Year 1975.*

a. Includes $400 million reflecting the Congress' decision not to enact certain legislation—primarily recomputation of retired pay and authorization for certain enlistment bonuses.

ances in Europe and on the high seas. We conclude our review of defense issues by summarizing the major choices facing the nation in its consideration of the defense budget.

How Large an Increase Has Been Proposed?

In fiscal year 1974, the initial defense budget proposal was modified by an extraordinary number of amendments and supplemental requests. As a result, there is some confusion about the actual size of the budget for that year and how it differs from the fiscal 1975 proposal. Table 4-1 summarizes the changes already made or proposed in the fiscal 1974 Defense Department budget in terms of total obligational authority (TOA).[2]

2. The financial data in this chapter are generally given in terms of total obligational authority, which is similar to "budget authority," as defined in Chapter 1. It is the amount requested from Congress, modified by certain financial adjustments. TOA for defense rarely differs from budget authority for defense by more than $1 billion. Obligational authority is a better indicator than outlays of the fiscal consequences of decisions about activity levels in defense because about one-third of the outlays in any one year reflect decisions taken in prior years to obligate funds.

Five separate events contributed to fluctuations in total obligational authority for defense after the fiscal 1974 budget was submitted in January 1973. TOA had to be increased by $3 billion because the rate of inflation was greater than had been allowed for and because devaluation of the dollar increased the dollar cost of U.S. military expenditures abroad. The Middle East war added another $4.5 billion ($2.2 billion for military aid to Israel and $2.3 billion to augment the readiness of U.S. armed forces and to pay for U.S. operations connected with the crisis). TOA was reduced by $1.3 billion because the United States ended its combat involvement in Southeast Asia. And Congress cut another $4.0 billion from the administration's request. Action on pay raises added to the confusion. Initially, the fiscal 1974 budget included an allowance for pay increases anticipated during calendar years 1973 and 1974. These funds were omitted when the Defense Department amended its request in September 1973, and had to be requested again in the form of a supplement to the fiscal 1974 budget this past February.

Comparing the final request for fiscal 1974—$87.1 billion—to the total obligational authority requested for fiscal 1975—$92.6 billion—reveals an increase of $5.5 billion, an amount wholly accounted for by pay and price increases. Such a comparison, however, fails to bring out the fiscal impact of recent decisions on the size, structure, and quality of baseline U.S. military forces. For this purpose, two kinds of adjustments are necessary.

First, the effects of changes in payments to retired military personnel (retired pay), the incremental cost of the war in Southeast Asia, and military assistance programs—particularly, the uncommonly large emergency aid to Israel—should be excluded. These costs bear little relation to the on-going U.S. defense effort.

Second, adjustments need to be made to the fiscal 1974 supplemental request. Two-thirds of the supplemental total of $6.2 billion is for purposes traditionally considered by Congress, and administratively sanctioned by the executive branch, as justification for supplemental requests:

• $3.4 billion to finance increases in military and civilian pay rates already approved by the Congress;

• $0.5 billion to pay for increases in fuel prices beyond those already incorporated in the fiscal 1974 request;

• $0.2 billion for incremental costs incurred by U.S. forces during the Middle East war.[3]

However, the remaining $2.1 billion is for initiatives to improve future U.S. military capabilities. Inventories are to be increased, the amount of time spent on equipment maintenance and overhaul reduced, airlift capacity expanded, a new base constructed in the Indian Ocean, and some modernization programs accelerated. While the perceived need for these measures partly stems from events occurring during fiscal 1974, the funds are not required to meet expenses incurred during that year. Only a small portion of these funds would be spent during fiscal 1974; for that matter, a large portion of the request would not actually be obligated until fiscal 1975.

In effect, the readiness package of $2.1 billion in the supplemental request represents new decisions to increase activity levels in defense rather than the fiscal effects of past decisions, and therefore can appropriately be treated as part of the fiscal 1975 defense program.[4]

If the components of the supplemental request are redistributed,

3. Rules governing the submission of supplemental budget requests are specified in Office of Management and Budget, "Circular No. A-11" (rev., June 22, 1973; processed). This document specifies that supplemental requests are expected to meet one of the following criteria: (a) existing laws make such payments mandatory; (b) "an emergency situation arises that requires unforeseen expenditures for the preservation of life or property"; (c) increased workload is uncontrollable; or (d) new legislation requires additional funds.

4. Such an assessment of the fiscal 1974 supplemental request is contentious. The Defense Department disagrees, while the Congressional Research Service, the Joint Economic Committee, and others have made similar adjustments when comparing the fiscal 1974 and 1975 defense requests. In opposing such a readjustment, the Defense Department argues that in any fiscal year extraordinary events occur which cause reevaluation of immediate defense needs. In fiscal 1974, the major such event was the Middle East war. Usually, desirable changes in the defense posture made evident by these extraordinary events can be financed by reprogramming obligational authority enacted for other purposes. In fiscal 1974, however, this source of fiscal flexibility was eroded because price increases far exceeded the inflation rate computed in the initial defense request. Aside from fuel price increases which are covered in fiscal 1974 in another part of the supplemental budget, prices are said to have risen by $4.1 billion, and thus to have reduced the real value of the fiscal 1974 defense appropriation by that amount. The Defense Department argues, therefore, that the $2.1 billion which is under dispute is in fact a partial offset to this shortfall in the fiscal 1974 appropriation and therefore should properly be treated as a supplemental to the 1974 budget rather than as an addition to the fiscal 1975 request. The fact remains, however, that the readiness supplemental is designated to be used to procure specific weapons in greater quantities, or to carry out other defense activities at greater rates than were envisioned in the original fiscal 1974 request. Thus, the readiness package will not be used to pay the higher costs of past requests (such as is the case for the supplemental requested for fuel), but will be used to finance improvements in the defense posture.

Table 4-2. Department of Defense Budget for Baseline Forces,
Fiscal Years 1974 and 1975

Total obligational authority in billions of dollars

	Amount	
Category of request	1974	1975
Enacted by 93rd Congress, 1st Session	80.9	...
Supplemental request in 1974 budget	4.1	2.1
Initial request in 1975 budget	...	92.6
Total	**85.0**	**94.7**
Deductions for non-baseline components		
Retired pay	5.2	6.0
Incremental cost of the war in Southeast Asia	1.6	1.9
Support of other nations	4.1	2.0
Total obligational authority for baseline forces, current dollars	**74.0**	**84.8**
Allowance for pay and price increases	...	6.5[a]
Total obligational authority for baseline forces, fiscal year 1974 dollars	**74.0**	**78.3**

Sources: Department of Defense, News Release 43-74, February 4, 1974; unpublished data from the Office of the Secretary of Defense (Comptroller). Detail may not add to totals because of rounding.

a. This figure is $1.4 billion greater than the allowance actually incorporated in the fiscal 1975 budget. The increase reflects an April 1974 revision by the Defense Department to the rate of inflation expected during fiscal 1975.

it can be seen that the fiscal 1975 defense program shows an increase of $10.8 billion in obligational authority for baseline forces. Table 4-2 indicates that $6.5 billion of this increase is attributable to the effects of inflation. In these terms, the budget envisions a real increase of 5.8 percent in obligational authority for baseline forces.

This increase may turn out to be an underestimate. The $6.5 billion allowance for pay and price increases reflects a revised estimate by the Department of Defense of the rate of inflation expected during fiscal 1975. It is $1.4 billion greater than the allowance for inflation actually incorporated in the 1975 budget proposal, meaning that the real value of the goods and services to be purchased in fiscal 1975 will be that much less than envisioned in February 1974 when the budget was submitted to Congress. The administration may decide to absorb this reduction. Alternatively, it could amend its 1975 budget proposal or request a supplemental to the 1975 budget to compensate for this greater than expected inflation, and thereby maintain defense activities at the levels initially planned. In the latter case, the new budget would propose a real increase in total obligational authority for base-line forces of 7.7 percent.[5]

Components of the 1975 Defense Budget

Changes in the defense budget are perhaps better understood if the components are rearranged according to function. This is done in Table 4-3 which, for comparative purposes, also presents similar data for fiscal 1964 (the year prior to major U.S. involvement in the Vietnam war), fiscal 1968 (the peak war year), and fiscal 1974. In this table (and in those that follow), support and overhead costs, such as the cost of recruiting, training, and personnel health care, are allocated to the different combat missions.

When pay and price increases are taken into account, the fiscal 1975 request nearly matches the total obligational authority for defense enacted in 1964. It is about three-fourths the size of the budget at the height of U.S. involvement in Southeast Asia.

Baseline forces will cost about 5 percent less, in dollars of constant purchasing power, than they did in either 1964 or 1968. The baseline portion of the budget is divided into three functional categories:

General purpose forces consist of ground combat units (Army and Marine Corps), tactical aircraft (based on land and at sea), and most Navy ships. Obligational authority for general purpose forces is to increase by $1.9 billion, in real terms, in fiscal 1975, raising TOA for these forces nearly 10 percent above its level in fiscal 1964. Over the past ten years, general purpose forces have increased their share of the baseline budget at the expense of strategic nuclear forces, as shown below:

	Percentage of baseline obligational authority		
Fiscal year	*Strategic nuclear forces*	*Strategic mobility forces*	*General purpose forces*
1964	33	3	64
1968	27	4	69
1973	24	3	73
1974	21	3	76
1975	21	4	75

5. The allowances for pay and price increases cited above pertain only to baseline forces. Adding the effects of inflation on retired benefits, incremental costs of the war in Southeast Asia, and the cost of military assistance programs would raise the initial budget allowance to $5.8 billion and the revised allowance to $7.5 billion.

Table 4-3. Distribution of Department of Defense Total Obligational Authority, by Functional Category, and Outlays, Selected Fiscal Years, 1964–75

			Estimate	
Category	1964	1968	1974	1975
Total obligational authority in billions of current dollars				
General purpose forces	30.4	36.6	56.6	63.4
Strategic nuclear forces	16.1	14.4	15.4	18.3
Strategic mobility forces	1.8	2.4	2.0	3.1
Subtotal for baseline forces	**48.3**	**53.4**	**74.0**	**84.8**
Incremental cost of the war in Southeast Asia	...	19.3	1.6	1.9
Retired pay	1.2	2.1	5.2	6.0
Support of other nations	1.1	0.8	4.1	2.0
Total	**50.6**	**75.6**	**85.0**	**94.7**
Outlays in billions of current dollars				
Total	50.8	78.0	79.1	86.2
Total obligational authority in billions of 1975 dollars				
General purpose forces	58.1	61.1	61.5	63.4
Strategic nuclear forces	29.7	23.4	16.7	18.3
Strategic mobility forces	3.5	3.8	2.2	3.1
Subtotal for baseline forces	**91.3**	**88.3**	**80.4**	**84.8**
Incremental cost of the war in Southeast Asia	...	31.2	1.8	1.9
Retired pay	2.4	3.6	5.7	6.0
Support of other nations	1.7	1.2	4.4	2.0
Total	**95.4**	**124.3**	**92.3**	**94.7**
Outlays in billions of 1975 dollars				
Total	95.7	127.6	85.9	86.2

Sources: Data for 1964 and 1968 are derived from Department of Defense, unpublished computer tabulation (1974). The costs of strategic nuclear forces are the sum of the strategic forces program, half of the intelligence and communications program (program III of the Five-Year Defense Program), one-tenth of the National Guard and Reserve program (V), four-tenths of the research and development program (VI), and a percentage of the three support programs—central supply and maintenance (VII), training, medical, and other general personnel activities (excluding retired pay) (VIII), and administration (IX)—which varied each year in direct proportion to the ratio of operating costs between strategic and all other forces. The costs of strategic mobility forces are the sum of the airlift and sealift program, 5 percent of program III, 5 percent of program V, 1 percent of program VI, and a variable percentage of the three support programs VII–IX. The costs of baseline general purpose forces were taken as Department of Defense total obligational authority less the cost of strategic nuclear forces, strategic mobility forces, the war in Southeast Asia, support of other nations, and retired pay. Data for 1974 and 1975 are derived by the authors according to the methodology for budget projections used in Edward R. Fried and others, *Setting National Priorities: The 1974 Budget* (Brookings Institution, 1973), Chapter 9. Note that the categories used this year differ from those in previous editions of *Setting National Priorities*. Also note that in this table, and in all those to follow, the $2.1 billion readiness supplemental (see Table 4-1) is included with the totals for fiscal 1975, and deducted from official estimates for fiscal 1974. Detail may not add to totals because of rounding.

Strategic nuclear forces, which consist of land-based interconti-nental ballistic missiles, ballistic missiles launched from submarines, manned bombers and associated tanker aircraft, air and missile de-fenses, and warning and surveillance systems, absorb about one-fifth of the total defense budget. In fiscal 1975, their cost will increase by $1.6 billion, in dollars of constant purchasing power, to $18.3 billion.

This amount is still less than two-thirds the total obligational authority enacted for strategic nuclear forces in fiscal 1964, when the United States was building up its land-based and submarine-launched missiles and when it still maintained a large number of bombers and air defense forces, which were retired later in the 1960s.

Strategic mobility forces absorb about 4 percent of the defense budget. They consist primarily of long-range cargo aircraft. A sharp increase in obligational authority ($0.9 billion) has been proposed this year.

Costs not pertaining to baseline forces will account for 10 percent of the budget in fiscal 1975, down from about 30 percent in 1968: a trend mainly reflecting the steep decline in the incremental cost of the war in Southeast Asia. This decline now seems to have come to an end, however, and a real, if small, increase in Vietnam spending has been proposed for fiscal 1975. But the war certainly is no longer a major element in total defense spending. Funds now allocated for Vietnam and the increase requested for fiscal 1975 are to be used primarily to pay for indigenous manpower and to supply equipment to the South Vietnamese armed forces, and to pay about 6,000 American civilian advisers. Some $500 million is to be used to meet the incremental costs of maintaining U.S. Air Force units in Thailand and Guam and U.S. Navy ships in the South China Sea.

Retired pay, another non-baseline component of the budget, is becoming an increasingly important element in defense costs. The costs of retirement benefits have increased two and one-half times, in real terms, since fiscal 1964. They now account for 6 percent of the defense budget.

Support of other nations, the third non-baseline component, includes military assistance programs and the accompanying costs incurred by U.S. forces. With the exception of the emergency aid to Israel last year, this category has fluctuated very little.

Implications of the 1975 Budget for Forces and Costs

U.S. postwar military strategy rests on two fundamental assumptions: (a) strategic nuclear forces alone cannot deter the full range of threats to vital U.S. interests; and (b) the nation's security interests are best served by the maintenance of sizable military forces outside the western hemisphere—in Europe, in the Atlantic and Pacific

Oceans, and in a few nations of East Asia. Planning for strategic nuclear forces is based on a special set of assumptions concerning how best to deter the outbreak of nuclear war and to maintain other U.S. security objectives (see Chapter 5).

The size and shape of general purpose and strategic mobility forces are determined in a formal sense by an assessment of U.S. requirements to fight one major war in Europe or Asia and at the same time retain some forces to be used as a reserve or to meet the needs of a limited contingency. Two scenarios serve, for planning purposes, to determine such force requirements. A European scenario envisions an attack against Western Europe by the Soviet Union and its allies in the Warsaw Pact. In this scenario, the U.S. objective would be, in conjunction with its NATO (North Atlantic Treaty Organization) allies, to defend Western Europe successfully for an initial period without resorting to nuclear weapons. "Initial" is not defined precisely in official documents, but sixty to ninety days is probably a reasonable assumption. In the Asian scenario, the U.S. objective would be to help South Korea, Japan, or other U.S. allies defend themselves, if attacked, for an indefinite period of time. Statements associated with the new defense budget pay far more attention this year to the European scenario than in previous years and almost no attention to Asian contingencies.

Decisions about U.S. military forces also depend on other and more complex factors. Forces are maintained as much to deter aggression as they are to fight wars. Moreover, military forces also serve important political functions—with regard to relations between the United States and the Soviet Union and China, as well as with regard to relations between the United States and its allies. Decisions concerning U.S. military forces may be influenced as much by the perceived consequences of change for these important political objectives as by the requirements posed strictly by military planning contingencies. In fact, military and political purposes may sometimes conflict. A change in the force structure which improves war-fighting capabilities may adversely affect either the deterrent potential of U.S. forces or their political impact. For example, it can be argued that deployment of ballistic missile defenses, which would improve U.S. capabilities to fight a nuclear war, would also cause an escalation in the arms race and introduce new uncertainties in U.S.–Soviet relations, thereby making a nuclear conflict somewhat more likely. Finally, a host of other factors—domestic politics, organizational and individual interests, and bureaucratic inertia, to name a few—all play important roles in decisions concerning U.S. military forces.

We now turn to a detailed examination of the decisions affecting the baseline components of the defense budget and their implications for forces and costs over the remainder of the decade, beginning with the three components of general purpose forces. In examining these sections, readers should be aware that: (a) unless otherwise stated, all cost comparisons are given in dollars of constant fiscal 1975 purchasing power; (b) all descriptions of fiscal 1974 and 1975 costs assume a redistribution of the fiscal 1974 supplemental request as described on page 69; and (c) projections of costs beyond fiscal 1975 simply extrapolate the consequences of continuing present policies—they do not attempt to predict the actual amounts that will be expended.

Ground Combat Forces*

Ground combat forces are the most costly component of the defense budget, accounting for nearly one-third of the total obligational authority allocated to baseline functions. The fiscal 1975 request for ground combat forces is $25.8 billion, only slightly larger than the amount authorized last year. At the end of fiscal 1975, active ground combat forces will consist of 16⅓ Army and Marine divisions, 3 separate brigades, and an assortment of support units. Reserve manpower assigned to ground combat functions will comprise 8 full divisions, 24 separate brigades or regiments, and numerous support elements. All told, there are about 944,000 men and women on active duty and 620,000 reservists in ground combat units.

The new defense posture contemplates important changes in the structure and readiness of ground combat forces. In fiscal 1975, the first steps will be taken toward shifting Army manpower from support to combat categories. Sizable reductions will be made in reserve forces. The new budget also emphasizes programs to augment inventories of ground combat equipment, to modernize the U.S. industrial base for the production of armaments, and to increase the general technological sophistication of U.S. ground force weaponry. These changes, when coupled with continuing major modernization programs in armor, helicopters, and air defenses, indicate a determina-

* Prepared with the assistance of Jeffrey Record.

tion to squeeze more ready combat power from existing forces and to enhance the survivability of U.S. forces on battlefields increasingly dominated by new technologies.

The recent war in the Middle East gave greater urgency to these long-discussed improvements in ground combat capabilities. The war demonstrated an extraordinarily high rate of consumption of equipment and munitions. Expenditures on both sides of ammunition, missiles, and even major items of equipment such as tanks and aircraft far exceeded previous estimates of the rates likely in this type of conflict. Defense officials therefore reexamined U.S. stockpiles and are now pressing for higher inventory levels and for the establishment of production facilities for selected high-consumption items that can be activated quickly during emergencies.

The war was the first in which ground forces, both armored and infantry, employed large numbers of antitank missiles. While, on balance, tanks themselves remained the principal antitank weapon system, the results suggest that armored vehicles may be more vulnerable than previously believed unless accompanied by infantry and supported by artillery. During the early phases of the war, Israel relied almost exclusively on tank guns for defense against opposing armor, while the Arab armies were equipped with a variety of Soviet-made antitank missiles. The results were disastrous from Israel's viewpoint; some 200 tanks were lost during the first few days of combat, more than 10 percent of the entire prewar inventory. Israel's disadvantage in antitank missiles was overcome only by a shift in armor tactics and by the diversion of most of its air force to support ground troops.

The war also caused some rethinking with regard to the ability of ground forces to operate in the absence of friendly control of the skies above the battlefield. The massive use by the Arab armies of mobile surface-to-air missiles was a significant innovation in land combat. It demonstrated that ground forces equipped with an adequate number and appropriate mix of mobile air defenses—both radar-directed guns and missiles—could make at least limited territorial advances against superior air forces.

While the Middle East war occurred too late in the budget cycle to exert an overriding influence on programs for ground combat forces in fiscal 1975, its long-run effect could be significant. The war may lead to a further shift in U.S. planning away from the tank itself as the primary antitank weapon to a less costly vehicle-mounted, or even hand-carried, antitank missile. Similarly, the relatively small number of technologically sophisticated missiles now protecting ground combat forces are likely to be replaced by greater numbers of less complex and relatively inexpensive air defense systems. Moreover, a judgment that advances in technology are now favoring defensive capabilities at the expense of the primary offensive arms—armor and tactical aircraft— would be particularly telling for the future structure and size of U.S. ground forces. Such an evaluation could lead to basic changes in the military posture adopted by NATO, in the design of armored vehicles, and in the mix of different kinds of military units within Army divisions. But if such changes are made, their effect will not be felt for several years.

In the meantime, the 1975 budget provides for relative stability in total manpower assigned to ground combat forces, but also for important changes in the Army's force structure. The Army will gain 12 new battalions—the basic independent combat unit—an increase of about 8 percent:

• Five of the battalions will form a new armored brigade, assigned to the 1st Cavalry Division. Formation of the new armored brigade will permit creation of a new kind of combat organization from elements now assigned to the 1st Cavalry. This new unit, called an "air cavalry combat brigade," will be highly mobile and heavily dependent on helicopters.

• Four more battalions will be used to bolster one or two other divisions which at present are under strength. These additions will bring all active Army divisions, except the 25th Division in Hawaii, up to full readiness.

• The remaining three new battalions are ranger units, which would be used primarily for minor contingencies.

In total, 17,000 people will be added to Army combat forces at the expense of various support forces. About one-third will come from reductions in headquarters staffs both in Washington and overseas and the remaining two-thirds from personnel cuts in Army strategic air defense units, intelligence and communications, and training programs.

Defense spokesmen have indicated that they intend to continue the shift of personnel from support to combat functions. But it is uncertain how far ground combat forces can be increased without expanding total manpower levels or how long it will take to implement

**Table 4-4. Distribution of Manpower in Ground Combat Forces,
End of Selected Fiscal Years, 1964–80**

Description	1964 actual	1974	1975	1980[a]
Total manpower (thousands)[b]	1,125	941	944	944
Army	972	782	785	785
Marines	153	159	159	159
Number of divisions	19⅓	16	16⅓	18
Army	16⅓	13	13⅓	15
Marines	3	3	3	3
Manpower in divisions (thousands)	309	256	261	288
Army	261	208	213	240
Marines	48	48	48	48

Sources: *Annual Defense Department Report, FY 1975*, Report of the Secretary of Defense James R. Schlesinger to the Congress on the FY 1975 Defense Budget and FY 1975–1979 Defense Program (March 4, 1974); Department of Defense, "Manpower Requirements Report for FY 1975" (February 1974; processed); unpublished data from the Department of Defense.

a. Assumes constant manpower levels from fiscal 1975 to fiscal 1980, and the creation of 1⅔ division equivalents during that same period.

b. End of fiscal year strengths including all Army forces, and Marine forces except personnel assigned to Marine air wings.

such changes. Table 4-4 describes the potential distribution of manpower for ground forces by 1980. Army spokesmen mention 16 divisions as an objective, the number maintained in fiscal 1964, but this may be overly ambitious. In our judgment, it seems feasible to add another 1⅔ divisions by the end of fiscal 1980, bringing the total to 15, without significantly increasing total manpower or requiring unrealistic reductions in support functions. This would involve a shift of about 54,000 men from the support units to division forces (including initial support increments) after fiscal 1975 and would increase the percentage of total Army manpower in divisions to 30.5 percent— a modest goal compared to the 80 percent figure characterizing the Soviet Army.[6]

Sizable reductions are planned for reserve ground combat forces. Authorized paid drill strength for the Army Reserve is slated to decline 6.5 percent from the level attained at the end of fiscal 1974. The ultimate magnitude of these reductions is uncertain, but a recent study suggested that all reserve forces (including tactical air and naval forces as well as ground combat units) could be reduced by as much

6. To achieve this staggering proportion, however, the Soviet Army makes considerable sacrifices in force readiness, sustainability, the quality of its equipment, and the comfort of its personnel.

as 300,000 men without eliminating any of their essential purposes.[7] In the meantime, equipment, training, and levels of readiness are being improved, and reserve units, at the battalion level, are being designated for affiliation with active Army divisions for training and for deployment in the event of mobilization.

Obligational authority for procurement, research and development, and construction for baseline ground combat forces is proposed to increase $500 million, or about 10 percent, in 1975. Much of this increase is requested for the procurement of ammunition and modernization of ammunition production facilities. Including the supplemental request for fiscal 1974, funds for ammunition procurement are proposed to rise by more than 50 percent. Moreover, the modernization program for ammunition production facilities is just getting under way. The full program will cost $4.1 billion and will be completed in the mid-1980s. The acquisition of antitank missiles also has been stepped up sharply.

Despite reductions in the size of support and reserve elements and slowdowns in major weapon acquisition programs, the drive to increase U.S. ground combat capabilities implies a sizable increase in spending for these forces, close to 4 percent per year over the remainder of the decade. If so, aside from price increases, ground combat forces would cost $5.1 billion more in fiscal 1980 than the amount requested this year.

These cost implications are summarized in Table 4-5. The projection assumes a constant ground combat force of 944,000 people but a shift from 16⅓ to 18 Army and Marine divisions by fiscal 1980. In the absence of more specific information, reserve manpower is held at levels planned for the end of fiscal 1975.

Nearly half the increase ($2.4 billion) will be needed to fund real growth in the price of military and civilian manpower. Pay rates are assumed to increase 3 percent per year above price increases in order to assure comparability with the wage increases typically experienced in the private sector. But the projection also assumes that no additional pay increases are necessary to assure continuance of the all-volunteer service. Another one-third of the increase in the cost of ground combat forces ($1.8 billion) will be used for the acquisition of major systems and for modernization of ammunition production

7. Martin Binkin, *U.S. Reserve Forces: The Problem of the Weekend Warrior* (Brookings Institution, 1974), pp. 35, 62–63.

Table 4-5. Projected Costs of Ground Combat Forces, by Category,
Fiscal Years 1974–80ᵃ

Total obligational authority in billions of 1975 dollars

Category	1974	1975	1976	1977	1978	1979	1980
Major system acquisitionᵇ	0.8	1.0	1.4	1.3	1.8	2.3	2.6
Other investmentᶜ	4.9	5.2	5.1	5.2	5.2	5.3	5.3
Direct operating costsᵈ	9.8	9.9	10.2	10.6	11.0	11.4	11.8
Indirect operating costsᵉ	9.7	9.7	9.8	9.9	10.1	10.2	10.3
Subtotal	**25.3**	**25.8**	**26.6**	**27.0**	**28.1**	**29.2**	**30.0**
Allowance for cost growth	...	...	0.1	0.2	0.2	0.4	0.5
Allowance for new initiatives	...	...	...	0.1	0.2	0.3	0.4
Total	**25.3**	**25.8**	**26.7**	**27.3**	**28.5**	**29.9**	**30.9**

Sources: Figures for fiscal years 1974 and 1975 are derived by the authors from data appearing in: U.S. Department of Defense, News Release 43–74, February 4, 1974; *Annual Defense Department Report, FY 1975; The Budget of the United States Government, Fiscal Year 1975—Appendix;* Department of Defense, "Program Acquisition Costs by Weapon System: Department of Defense Budget for Fiscal Year 1975" (1974; processed); various authorization and appropriation hearings before the House and Senate committees on the Department of Defense budget for fiscal year 1974, and statements by Department of Defense officials on the fiscal year 1975 budget; unpublished data from the Office of the Secretary of Defense (Comptroller). Detail may not add to totals because of rounding.

Figures for fiscal years 1976–80 are projections by the authors based on data appearing in the documents listed above and on the basis of various statements by administration officials as to future U.S. defense policies.

a. Excludes incremental costs of the war in Southeast Asia.

b. Includes research and development, procurement, and military construction costs directly associated with major systems.

c. Includes research and development, procurement, military construction, and family housing traceable to ground combat forces other than that covered in note *b.*

d. Includes military personnel and operations and maintenance appropriations for active forces funded in program II of the Five Year Defense Program (FYDP), plus all military personnel and operations and maintenance appropriations for reserve ground combat forces.

e. Includes a share of indirect support costs such as communications, training, logistical support, and administration (programs III, VII, VIII, and IX of the FYDP) proportionate to the direct operating costs of ground combat forces. Ratios between direct and indirect operating costs are computed by military service and therefore differ among the different types of forces.

facilities. In fiscal 1980, three of the five Army major modernization programs are likely to be near their peak requirement for obligational authority. The balance of the increase is accounted for by real growth in the cost of equipment and by initiatives likely to appear toward the end of the decade. The latter could result either from new weapon programs, such as precision-guided artillery projectiles, or from a decision to expand to 16 Army divisions even if it is necessary to raise manpower levels.

Tactical Air Forces*

Changes in the new defense posture will affect tactical air forces, the second component of general purpose forces, only in minor ways

* Prepared with the assistance of William D. White.

for the next few years. Some research and development programs have been accelerated in order to improve tactical strike capabilities at night and under adverse weather conditions or in the presence of concentrated air defenses. Inventories of spare parts, weapons, and the accoutrements of electronic warfare will be enlarged, and the depot modernization program will be stressed. Only minor changes in force levels are contemplated for the near future, however. The Air Force will operate 69 tactical fighter and attack squadrons this year, an increase of one over last year. The Navy will operate 15 aircraft carriers at the end of fiscal year 1975, an increase of one from the number at the end of fiscal 1974. Previous plans to retire two older carriers have been postponed. Marine Corps tactical air force levels remain unchanged at three wings. Reserve squadrons will decrease by one.

While the tactical air force structure is relatively stable, all components are undergoing extensive modernization programs. And herein lies the crux of the problem facing U.S. planners with regard to tactical air forces, as well as much of the potential impact of new directions in the defense posture. Problems in modernizing tactical air forces stem for the most part from rapid growth in the real unit cost of aircraft. The question is how, in light of escalating costs, existing forces can be modernized at a reasonable pace without an accompanying steep decline in the number of aircraft maintained in the U.S. inventory, the elimination of certain performance standards now demanded of U.S. tactical fighters, or increases of 100 percent or more in investments for tactical air power. The answer is that they cannot; one or more of these consequences will have to be accepted. And the answer to the logical next question—which ones?—depends on the outcome of current debates within the Department of Defense.

The civilian leadership in Defense typically has favored accepting modifications in the performance of some aircraft and some increases in spending, but not decreases in force levels. This is indicated by the emphasis now being placed on developing lower-cost aircraft as alternatives to the very expensive designs currently being acquired. The military services, however, seem to have opposed both relaxing performance standards in order to lower costs and reducing force levels. They argue that it is necessary to replace virtually all existing aircraft with technologically advanced, multipurpose, and consequently very expensive designs.

The Navy faces the worst modernization problem.[8] The number of aircraft carriers will decline to 12 by around 1980, simply by virtue of the age of existing carriers and the long lead times necessary to build new ones. In order to maintain 12 carriers indefinitely, moreover, the Navy soon must begin to replace the 7 vessels commissioned from 1955 through 1961. Because of fiscal constraints, these new ships are not likely to be supercarriers like the *Nimitz*, joining the fleet in fiscal 1975, which cost more than $1 billion. According to Secretary Schlesinger, future carriers will be much smaller than the *Nimitz* and possibly not nuclear-powered; they will cost about $600 million apiece.

Plans for Navy aircraft modernization also require reconsideration. The announced goal of the Navy's primary aircraft acquisition program, the F-14, is 16 squadrons, which will cost over $8 billion (including Phoenix missiles) and meet less than one-half of Navy and Marine Corps requirements for fighter aircraft. If the F-14 were to be used to replace all Navy and Marine tactical fighter, attack, and reconnaissance aircraft, the cost of the complete program would increase to $35 billion, making it the most costly weapon program ever undertaken. And even if the rate of F-14 procurement were doubled, modernization would not be completed until fiscal 1988, at which time the cycle would have to be repeated with a new design because by then the first F-14s would be at least as old as existing Navy aircraft.

The first step in developing an alternative to the F-14 is proposed in the 1975 budget: to spend $34 million to study the characteristics of a lower-cost fighter aircraft (VFX). What will replace the Navy's attack and reconnaissance aircraft is unclear, however. And the Navy cannot indefinitely avoid choosing between procuring less expensive designs, reductions in tactical air strength, and the massive expenditures necessary to utilize a modified version of the F-14 in these roles.

The Air Force faces a similar problem but of lesser magnitude. The cost of its new high-performance fighter, the F-15, is also rising

8. Estimates of the cost of tactical air forces in this book are higher than those in previous editions of *Setting National Priorities* because the costs of acquiring and operating the Navy's aircraft carriers have been shifted from naval forces to tactical air forces. While the new estimates reflect the relative costs of these two kinds of general purpose forces more accurately, they probably still understate the cost of Navy tactical air power, as they do not include any portion of spending associated with the carriers' escort and support ships.

sharply.[9] The Air Force could replace all its fighter and reconnaissance aircraft with the F-15 for $22 billion by 1984. However, the A-10, a relatively inexpensive aircraft specialized for ground attack, will probably be introduced into operational squadrons by 1977.[10] The Air Force also is developing two prototype lightweight fighters and has plans for a third design similarly specialized for air-to-air combat over the battlefield. The key question is whether these lower-cost aircraft prove to be substitutes for the F-15 in some tactical functions or additions to total force levels. One sign in this regard is the treatment now accorded the A-10. Last year it appeared that several A-10 wings would be added to the Air Force structure. Now it appears that such an increase is unlikely; some of the A-10s will go immediately to the reserve forces, others will replace A-7s in the active force structure. Whether this change in Air Force planning portends that other less expensive specialized aircraft now being developed will replace more expensive multipurpose systems in the future—and if so, to what degree—remains to be seen.

Another Air Force acquisition deserving mention is more than $500 million in the 1975 budget to purchase 12 airborne warning and control systems (AWACS). Until this year, the system was being developed primarily for the defense of the United States from bomber attacks. The program called for the purchase of 42 aircraft, 25 of which were to be used for bomber defenses. The primary mission of AWACS today is said to be to provide highly survivable, mobile, long-range warning and command and control for tactical air operations. With the shift of missions, however, only 8 aircraft were deleted from the number planned to be acquired, not the 25 that might have been expected, with no reduction in total program cost. Thus, *in its tactical aspect,* the AWACS program shifted suddenly from a plan to purchase 17 aircraft at a unit acquisition cost of about $55 million each to a planned purchase of 34 aircraft at $68 million apiece.

Our projection of the costs of tactical air forces is shown in Table 4-6. Modest increases are expected in obligational authority for the remainder of the decade. In fiscal 1980, TOA for tactical air is likely to be about $4 billion more than the amount requested for fiscal 1975.

9. After adjusting for greater than anticipated inflation, the unit cost of the F-15s procured in fiscal 1975 will be 30 percent more than the Defense Department projected last year ($12.4 million versus $9.5 million per aircraft).

10. The A-10 also has experienced considerable cost growth in real terms, 16 percent, since fiscal 1974. Unit acquisition costs now are expected to reach $3.1 million.

**Table 4-6. Projected Costs of Tactical Air Forces, by Category,
Fiscal Years 1974–80[a]**

Total obligational authority in billions of 1975 dollars

Category	1974	1975	1976	1977	1978	1979	1980
Major system acquisition[b]	5.0	4.2	4.3	4.0	4.2	5.2	5.0
Other investment[c]	5.4	5.3	5.8	5.9	5.9	6.0	6.0
Direct operating costs[d]	6.7	7.0	7.3	7.4	7.6	7.7	7.9
Indirect operating costs[e]	6.7	6.5	6.6	6.8	6.9	7.1	7.2
Subtotal	23.8	23.0	24.0	24.1	24.6	26.0	26.1
Allowance for cost growth	...	...	...	0.1	0.1	0.2	0.2
Allowance for new initiatives	...	...	0.1	0.1	0.3	0.6	0.8
Total	23.8	23.0	24.1	24.3	25.0	26.8	27.1

Sources: Same as Table 4-5. Detail may not add to totals because of rounding.

a. Excludes incremental costs of the war in Southeast Asia.

b. Includes research and development, procurement, and military construction costs directly associated with major systems.

c. Includes research and development, procurement, military construction, and family housing traceable to tactical air forces other than that covered in note *b*.

d. Includes military personnel and operations and maintenance appropriations for active forces funded in program II of the Five Year Defense Program (FYDP), plus all military personnel and operations and maintenance appropriations for reserve tactical air forces.

e. Includes a share of indirect support costs such as communications, training, logistical support, and administration (programs III, VII, VIII, and IX of the FYDP) proportionate to the direct operating costs of tactical air forces. Ratios between direct and indirect operating costs are computed by military service and therefore differ among the different types of forces.

The projection assumes that the number of Navy carriers and air wings declines to 12 by 1980: an inescapable trend. Air Force force levels are assumed to remain constant. The projection further assumes completion of the F-14, F-15, and A-10 programs as now described, and procurement of new, and lower-cost, aircraft carriers beginning in fiscal 1977. The allowance for new initiatives would be used to pay for necessary aircraft modernization programs not yet publicly specified.

Naval Forces*

Initiatives in the new defense posture do not appear to affect naval general purpose forces much, but some short-term changes are proposed. Inventories of spare parts, equipment, and other war reserves will be augmented. Ships are to be overhauled and aircraft maintained on accelerated schedules, thereby reducing the portion of the force which is not available for combat at any one time. And the previously scheduled retirement of a few older ships has been postponed, so as to avoid near-term reductions in the availability of combat forces.

* Prepared with the assistance of Jerry A. Kotchka.

As a result of the base closings announced in 1973, the Navy did make proportionately larger manpower reductions than the other services, but the bulk of the reductions in the Navy's shore establishment appears to be over. Some reductions are said to be planned in headquarters staffs, but these have not shown up in the manpower breakdowns as yet. Substantial cuts, about 12,000 military personnel, will be made in the size of training programs, but these are caused in large part by the reduced number of recruits now entering the service.

It is in ship design and construction that the Navy's initiatives are most significant. The modernization problem confronting tactical air forces has already been encountered with respect to Navy ships, and the outline of a reasonable solution now seems clear. The Navy emerged from World War II with a large fleet of brand new ships; the average age of the fleet was only five years in 1946. By the late 1960s, the fleet had reached a peak average age near eighteen years, and a large number of vessels were due for retirement. But in the interim, warships became larger, more complex, far more sophisticated technologically, and acquired additional functions; as a result, their price tags soared. It was soon apparent that the cost of replacing World War II ships on anything near a one-for-one basis would be astronomical; besides, it was not evident that wartime force levels should be maintained. Thus the Navy confronted the familiar choice between sizable cuts in force levels, reductions in the capabilities of some warships, or impossible budgets. The policy adopted to solve this problem was to accept lower force levels but to contain the size of the reduction by instituting a weapons acquisition strategy known as the hi-lo mix.

Essentially, the Navy began to build two kinds of ships. It continued to buy some very expensive multipurpose units, incorporating the latest advances in military technology and capable of holding their own against the most sophisticated opponents. These vessels, which constitute the high end of the mix, primarily are designed to fill requirements posed by scenarios envisioning conflict with the Soviet Union. On the low end, ships were designed for one specific function or they were retained as multipurpose vessels, but only in situations where relatively unsophisticated military technologies would be brought to bear against them; thereby their performance requirements could be relaxed. These ships are meant to fill the military and

Table 4-7. Projected Costs of Naval Forces, by Category, Fiscal Years 1974–80[a]

Total obligational authority in billions of 1975 dollars

Category	1974	1975	1976	1977	1978	1979	1980
Major system acquisition[b]	2.8	3.2	3.4	3.5	3.6	3.2	3.6
Other investment[c]	2.7	3.5	3.6	3.6	3.7	3.7	3.8
Direct operating costs[d]	3.5	3.9	4.0	4.2	4.4	4.5	4.7
Indirect operating costs[e]	3.3	3.9	4.0	4.1	4.3	4.4	4.7
Subtotal	**12.4**	**14.5**	**15.0**	**15.4**	**15.9**	**15.8**	**16.8**
Allowance for cost growth	...	...	0.1	0.3	0.5	0.6	0.6
Allowance for new initiatives	...	...	...	...	0.1	0.2	0.2
Total	**12.4**	**14.5**	**15.1**	**15.7**	**16.5**	**16.6**	**17.6**

Sources: Same as Table 4-5. Detail may not add to totals because of rounding.

a. Excludes incremental costs of the war in Southeast Asia.

b. Includes research and development, procurement, and military construction costs directly associated with major systems.

c. Includes research and development, procurement, military construction, and family housing traceable to naval general purpose forces other than that covered in note *b*.

d. Includes military personnel and operations and maintenance appropriations for active forces funded in program II of the Five Year Defense Program (FYDP), plus all military personnel and operations and maintenance appropriations for reserve naval forces.

e. Includes a share of indirect operating costs such as communications, training, logistical support, and administration (programs III, VII, VIII, and IX of the FYDP) proportionate to the direct operating costs of naval general purpose forces. Ratios between direct and indirect operating costs are computed by military service and therefore differ among the different types of forces.

diplomatic purposes of naval forces which require keeping larger numbers of ships in the force.

What has happened during the past seven years is that the number of naval vessels has dropped steadily. There were 976 commissioned ships in the U.S. Navy in 1968; there will be a low of 508 ships by the end of fiscal 1975. During this period, most of the World War II ships will have been retired and some high-cost units introduced. Now, however, larger numbers of both high-cost and the new low-cost vessels are beginning to make their appearance and naval force levels will begin to rise, leveling off near 600 by 1980. The trend in combatant force levels already has been reversed; the number of warships and submarines in the fleet will increase by 12 during fiscal 1975.

Our projection of the future costs of naval forces is shown in Table 4-7. Operating costs will increase moderately, reflecting both the increase in pay rates and, more important, the fact that the increasing number of vessels will necessitate increases in total manpower. We estimate that an additional 15,000 men will have to be assigned to ships' complements by fiscal 1980; moreover, 40 percent of this increase will be for highly trained, very expensive, and hard-to-retain personnel associated with nuclear-powered submarines.

The primary impetus for continued real growth in the cost of naval forces, however, comes from the shipbuilding program and from other investments to improve the Navy's weapons, sensors, and electronics. And it is the rate and extent of these programs that constitute the main issues in naval general purpose forces.

The projection makes the following assumptions regarding the Navy's shipbuilding program:

• In addition to the new primary aircraft carriers included in the costs of tactical air forces, we assume that the acquisition of 8 sea control ships will be fully authorized by fiscal 1980. These relatively small ships, which will carry helicopters and vertical or short takeoff and landing aircraft (V/STOL), are designed primarily to protect military and civilian convoys in areas not threatened by sophisticated air forces. The program is controversial and has been delayed by Congress. Concern centers on the desirability of building a carrier whose potential is limited by the pace of advances in V/STOL technology, on the question of whether existing air-capable platforms could not perform these kinds of missions, and on certain design specifications of the ship itself.

• An extensive escort building program is incorporated. For the low end of the Navy mix, the projection assumes complete funding for 50 small escort ships (patrol frigates) and 30 patrol hydrofoil boats carrying surface-to-surface missiles (PHM). For the high end, the projection completes the 30-ship *Spruance*-class destroyer program, completes funding for the 2 nuclear-powered frigates authorized by Congress last year and provides obligational authority for 4 more of these ships toward the end of the decade, and begins to provide obligational authority for a new conventionally powered air defense destroyer—the DGX—in fiscal 1976.

• The attack submarine program will cost less than previously projected. A new force level objective (90 versus 105) and a lower construction rate (5 every two years instead of every year) have been announced. The possibility that future submarine construction may include a less expensive alternative to the present *Los Angeles* class has also been raised. These changes reflect fiscal constraints, a large backlog at the only three U.S. shipyards capable of building these vessels, and possibly problems in manpower recruiting and retention.

• A small program is funded at about $300 million per year to modernize the U.S. force of support and other auxiliary ships. These vessels have been neglected in shipbuilding programs since 1967 but receive increased attention in fiscal 1975.

In all, obligational authority for naval forces, which is requested to rise by a very substantial 17 percent in fiscal 1975, is likely to continue to rise by nearly 4 percent per year between fiscal 1975 and 1980, reaching a total near $18 billion at the end of the decade.

Strategic Nuclear Forces*

Planning for strategic nuclear forces is in considerable flux. The consequences of important policy changes for forces and costs remain uncertain at the present time, pending final decisions on the most appropriate criteria to determine the structure and size of the nation's strategic forces and the outcome of negotiations with the Soviet Union. Generally, though, the new policies imply a 9 percent increase in obligational authority for strategic forces in fiscal 1975 and steady increases for the remainder of the decade. Compared to the projections of the fiscal consequences of the administration's policy in *Setting National Priorities* last year, the new look in strategic forces implies lower spending for the next few years but greater costs at the end of the decade and into the 1980s.

Short-term changes in strategic nuclear forces run contrary to those in general purpose forces. Offensive components—bombers and missiles—are to remain at virtually constant levels. Nor are significant changes planned in the readiness of strategic forces, because strategic forces have always been kept at very high readiness levels. In fact, some savings will be achieved by reducing the number of personnel assigned to older model B-52 bomber squadrons.

Forces used to defend the United States against attack by bombers are to decline substantially in number, continuing a trend begun more than ten years ago. The new budget proposes to phase out all surface-to-air missiles in strategic roles by the end of the fiscal year and to make additional cuts in interceptor aircraft leading to a force of 12 active and reserve squadrons in fiscal 1976. Programs also are under way to consolidate military and civilian radar systems. Most systems now used exclusively by the military will be eliminated by fiscal 1979. The strategic role for the Army's new surface-to-air missile (SAM-D) was discarded last year; and this year, as noted above, emphasis in

* Prepared with the assistance of Alton H. Quanbeck.

development of the airborne warning and control system (AWACS) has shifted to tactical missions.

These changes in air defense forces reflect two factors. The decision to forgo defending the United States from the Soviet Union's large missile force (as specified in the 1972 treaty limiting the deployment of antiballistic missiles) made large expenditures to defend the nation against the USSR's much smaller force of strategic bombers seem pointless. This reasoning is reinforced by the Soviet Union's continuing failure to develop a major force of modern long-range bombers. Remaining air defenses are aimed chiefly at maintaining surveillance over U.S. air space and preventing unauthorized overflights.

Another change that will reduce obligational authority for strategic forces in the near term is a slowdown in the two largest modernization programs: the B-1 bomber and the Trident submarine and missile, both designed to maintain the U.S. nuclear retaliatory capabilities for the next several decades. The B-1 slowdown reflects problems now appearing in developing the aircraft and its avionics, and a slowdown in the Trident construction rate was directed by Congress in fiscal 1974. Perhaps more important, there are now two new competitive programs in the offing. Relatively small requests are included in the fiscal 1975 budget to develop (1) a smaller, cheaper strategic submarine utilizing an existing nuclear reactor design (SSBN-X) and (2) a cruise missile that could be launched from a far less sophisticated and less expensive aircraft than the B-1. Both programs could provide considerable savings in the future, depending on the size of the portion of the planned purchase of Trident and B-1 for which they are substituted.

On the other hand, the prospect of more fundamental change in U.S. strategic planning is reflected in other research and development initiatives which, while small at present, could imply large expenditures toward the end of the decade. These doctrinal changes and their implications for the structure of U.S. strategic forces are discussed at length in Chapter 5. We limit discussion here to possible effects on strategic hardware and costs.

In essence, the new initiatives are of two kinds. One, a greater emphasis on flexibility in strategic targeting and expanding the options available to the President in time of crisis, has few cost implications. The changes in strategic targeting are already being made, and the major system change to facilitate this new flexibility—the installation of the command data buffer system at all Minuteman III bases—will not require much more obligational authority. While this new emphasis may require future modifications to command and control systems or to surveillance programs for postattack assessment, its impact on the structure, size, or cost of strategic forces will not be major.

The second and more significant type of initiative pertains to changes that would permit the United States to match projected advances in Soviet strategic capabilities. And the most significant effect of this insistence on "essential equivalence" has been programs to improve the capabilities of U.S. missiles to destroy hardened targets such as missile silos or underground command posts.

The potential of a missile to destroy hardened targets depends on the number, yield, and accuracy of the warheads it carries. The first two factors, in turn, depend mainly on the payload capacity of the missile's propulsion system, or its "throw-weight." Present U.S. missiles have relatively good accuracy but limited throw-weight. All three elements, however, figure in the administration's proposals to improve the ability of U.S. land-based missiles to destroy hardened targets.

First, production of Minuteman III land-based missiles is to be continued at the minimum rate consistent with keeping the production facilities in operation. This step, which will cost $300 million plus Atomic Energy Commission expenditures in fiscal 1975, holds open the option of replacing the 450 single-warhead Minuteman II missiles with the multiple-warhead Minuteman III later in the decade. Obligational authority sufficient to replace 550 Minuteman I missiles with Minuteman III already has been enacted.

Second, various research and development programs are under way to improve the accuracy, yield, and number of warheads on Minuteman. These programs would require close to $200 million in obligational authority in fiscal 1975.

Third, about $40 million is requested to continue development of technologies that could be used in a completely new land-based missile—one that could replace Minuteman in the 1980s. This new missile could be launched from fixed silos like Minuteman but have much greater throw-weight, or it might be launched from aircraft or some kind of land-mobile system. In either case, the cost potential of the program is very large.

As a result of these changes, because of the on-going negotiations

**Table 4-8. Projected Costs of Strategic Nuclear Forces, by Category,
Fiscal Years 1974–80[a]**

Total obligational authority in billions of 1975 dollars

Category	1974	1975	1976	1977	1978	1979	1980
Major system acquisition[b]	3.7	4.0	4.5	5.5	6.3	6.5	6.4
Other investment[c]	3.8	5.3	5.5	5.8	6.3	6.6	6.8
Direct operating costs[d]	4.2	4.2	4.0	4.0	4.0	4.1	4.2
Indirect operating costs[e]	5.0	4.8	4.6	4.6	4.6	4.7	4.8
Subtotal	16.7	18.3	18.5	20.0	21.2	21.9	22.2
Allowance for cost growth	...	...	0.2	0.4	0.5	0.7	0.7
Allowance for new initiatives	...	...	0.1	0.2	0.3	0.4	0.5
Total	16.7	18.3	18.8	20.6	22.0	23.0	23.4

Sources: Same as Table 4-5. Detail may not add to totals because of rounding.

a. Excludes incremental costs of the war in Southeast Asia.

b. Includes research and development, procurement, and military construction costs directly associated with major systems.

c. Includes research and development, procurement, military construction, and family housing traceable to strategic nuclear forces other than that covered in note *b*.

d. Includes military personnel and operations and maintenance appropriations for active forces funded in program I of the Five Year Defense Program (FYDP), plus all military personnel and operations and maintenance appropriations for reserve strategic forces.

e. Includes a share of indirect operating costs such as communications, training, logistical support, and administration (programs III, VII, VIII, and IX of the FYDP) proportionate to the direct operating costs of strategic forces. Also includes civil defense appropriations of $86 million. Ratios between direct and indirect operating costs are computed by military service and therefore differ among the different types of forces.

for strategic arms limitations with the USSR, and because most of the new initiatives are considered hedges that might lead to full-scale development and procurement of new systems rather than fixed programs, the future costs of strategic forces are quite uncertain. Our projection is shown in Table 4-8.

The projection assumes that strategic force levels, with the exceptions of the further reductions in air defense forces described earlier, remain constant through the remainder of the decade.

Regarding modernization programs, the projection assumes that: (a) procurement of the B-1 bomber begins in fiscal 1977 and of a new tanker aircraft in fiscal 1980; (b) the remaining 450 single-warhead Minuteman missiles are replaced by Minuteman IIIs and development of a follow-on land-based system is funded at a moderate rate, but no procurement money is authorized for the new system in this decade; (c) the Trident submarine is built at a rate of 2 per year until the initial program objective of 10 is reached, at which time the smaller strategic submarine will enter production; (d) development and procurement of Trident I missiles are funded at a rate sufficient to ensure the outfitting of Trident submarines and the backfitting of Poseidon submarines beginning in fiscal 1979; (e) development of the Trident II missile is initiated but no˙procurement is authorized in this decade; (f) strategic cruise missiles are not procured during the decade; and (g) about $250 million is spent annually on missile defense research, but no deployments are authorized beyond the one-site Safeguard system.

The allowance for new initiatives is designed to compensate for some of the uncertainties as to the future cost of present research programs and represents a conservative estimate of incremental costs should decisions be taken to begin procurement of strategic cruise missiles, advanced land-based missiles, or new missile or air defenses before 1980.

Overall, obligational authority for strategic forces is projected to increase at an average rate of 5 percent per year for the rest of the decade. The largest jump in costs will occur in fiscal 1977 and 1978, as both the B-1 bomber and Trident missiles enter production. The cost increase rate could either taper off or increase further at the end of the decade, depending on decisions concerning new land-based missiles.

Strategic Mobility Forces*

Strategic mobility forces constitute an important element in U.S defense strategy. They are used to move small amounts of men and equipment to distant parts of the world to deal with minor contingencies and also to provide timely and sizable matériel assistance to allies. But their primary use—and the rationale on which decisions about the size and structure of these forces are based—is to reinforce U.S. troops in Europe in the event of a major attack by the Warsaw Pact countries. A demonstrated ability to move large numbers of U.S. ground combat forces, perhaps one-quarter of a million men (7⅔ divisions), to central Europe in as little as thirty days is considered essential both to retain allied confidence in U.S. capabilities and to deter Soviet aggression.

After decisions to expand airlift capacity significantly were reached in the early and mid-1960s, little attention was paid to strategic mo-

* Prepared with the assistance of Martin Binkin.

bility forces until this year. Indeed, defense officials evidently believed that existing airlift and sealift forces were sufficient for at least the remainder of the decade. These forces now consist of 4 active squadrons of C-5A and 13 active squadrons of C-141 cargo aircraft augmented with reserve crews, about 30 active sealift vessels, and commercial aircraft and privately owned merchant vessels that could be mobilized at the discretion of the President.

Initiatives in the supplement to the fiscal 1974 budget and in the 1975 budget, however, indicate the administration's dissatisfaction with present mobility capabilities. It is not the capacity of the force to move cargoes over a long period that is questioned, but its ability to move large quantities of men and equipment in the early stages of a conflict. According to Secretary Schlesinger, decisions made at the end of the last decade—to acquire 4 rather than the previously planned 6 C-5A squadrons and not to acquire a fleet of fast deployment logistics ships—have made it impossible to get as many U.S. forces to Europe in the crucial early weeks of a conflict as prudence would suggest is desirable. Consequently, he has proposed measures that would reduce by nearly 60 percent the time required to move a force of several divisions, their initial support increments, and their equipment to Europe. Under these programs, the average time to deploy a division would be reduced from nineteen to seven days.

Although the urgency associated with implementation of these programs, as indicated by inclusion of $169 million for these purposes in the supplemental request to the fiscal 1974 budget, has not been fully explained, the factors that prompted them are apparent. The shift clearly reflects greater emphasis within the Defense Department on planning for an intense conflict of several weeks' duration in Europe rather than a longer war. Many have long argued for such a move, based mainly on the appraisal that Soviet forces were structured to gain a quick victory. The administration now seems to have accepted the thesis that the first thirty days of a conflict in Europe are likely to be decisive.

Other factors contributing to the decision include the on-going negotiations with the Soviet Union for mutual troop reductions in Europe, and pressures originating in Congress for unilateral U.S. reductions should the negotiations fail. Demonstrating an improved capacity to move large numbers of men and their equipment to

Europe at the very onset of a crisis would, it is argued, help ease the political consequences of U.S. troop withdrawals from the continent.

The October war in the Middle East, on the other hand, did not contribute to the decision to augment mobility forces. The U.S. ability to supply Israel promptly and in sufficient quantities, once the decision to do so was made, may indeed have been crucial in determining the outcome of the crisis. But the requirements for strategic airlift capacity generated by this kind of contingency are well within present capabilities. The need for increased airlift capacity rests on the assessment of demands posed by the possibility and character of a major conflict in Europe.

Three programs have been proposed to improve the lift capacity of existing aircraft.

First, the potential wartime utilization rate of C-5A and C-141 aircraft is to be raised 25 percent by increasing maintenance personnel and stocks of spare parts and by increasing the ratio of active-duty crews to aircraft from 2.0 to 2.75. This program would cost $130 million for additional spare parts, plus $200 million each year in greater operating costs.

Second, certain aircraft modifications are to be made to increase the volume of cargo which can be carried by the fleet of C-141s by 30 percent, and also to add in-flight refueling equipment to the aircraft, thereby making the planes less dependent upon foreign bases for long-range missions. The total cost of the program is estimated at $450 million.

Third, a program is suggested to modify 110 wide-bodied commercial jets (Boeing 747s and Douglas DC-10s) now in service so that they can accommodate military cargoes. The entire set of modifications, including financial inducements to encourage the airlines to participate in the program, is estimated to cost about $10 million per aircraft—a total of $1.1 billion. In addition to direct cash payments, possible financial incentives include low-interest loans, investment tax credits, tax-free sinking funds, and increased rates of allowable depreciation.

To finance these three programs, the proposed fiscal 1975 budget requests a sharp increase in obligational authority for strategic mobility forces. If approved, TOA for these purposes would rise more than 40 percent from its level in fiscal 1974. Moreover, strategic mobility would require slightly higher obligational authority for the re-

Table 4-9. Projected Costs of Strategic Mobility Forces, by Category, Fiscal Years 1974–80[a]

Total obligational authority in billions of 1975 dollars

Category	1974	1975	1976	1977	1978	1979	1980
Major system acquisition[b]	0.0	0.4	0.3	0.3	0.3	0.3	0.2
Other investment[c]	0.6	0.7	0.7	0.7	0.7	0.7	0.7
Direct operating costs[d]	0.7	1.0	1.1	1.1	1.1	1.2	1.2
Indirect operating costs[e]	0.9	1.0	1.0	1.1	1.1	1.1	1.1
Subtotal	2.2	3.1	3.1	3.2	3.2	3.3	3.3
Allowance for cost growth	...	...	...	...	...	...	0.1
Allowance for new initiatives	...	...	...	...	0.1	0.2	0.2
Total	2.2	3.1	3.1	3.2	3.3	3.5	3.6

Sources: Same as Table 4-5. Detail may not add to totals because of rounding.

a. Excludes incremental costs of the war in Southeast Asia.

b. Includes research and development, procurement, and military construction costs directly associated with major systems.

c. Includes research and development, procurement, military construction, and family housing traceable to strategic mobility forces other than that covered in note *b*.

d. Includes military personnel and operations and maintenance appropriations for active forces funded in program IV of the Five Year Defense Program (FYDP) plus all military personnel and operations and maintenance appropriations for reserve strategic mobility forces.

e. Includes a share of indirect operating costs such as communications, training, logistical support, and administration (programs III, VII, VIII, and IX of the FYDP) proportionate to the direct operating costs of strategic mobility forces. Ratios between direct and indirect operating costs are computed by military service and therefore differ among the different types of forces.

mainder of the decade. On average, TOA for strategic mobility would increase 3.0 percent per year between fiscal 1975 and 1980.

This projection is summarized in Table 4-9.

The Overall Defense Budget

The overall financial implications of the new look in defense are summarized in Table 4-10. It should be reemphasized that the projection merely extrapolates the costs of continuing present policies; it is not a forecast of what in fact will happen. The projection shows that total obligational authority requested for baseline forces, already 5.5 percent higher than the amount enacted for fiscal 1974, will increase steadily for the remainder of the decade. By fiscal 1980, TOA for baseline forces will reach $102.6 billion in 1975 dollars, an average annual increase of 3.9 percent. Ground combat and strategic nuclear forces will be the largest contributors to this trend, each requiring $5.1 billion more in TOA in fiscal 1980 than in fiscal 1975. The relative increase in strategic nuclear forces is sharper than that for ground

Table 4-10. Projected Department of Defense Total Obligational Authority, by Mission Category, and Outlays, Fiscal Years 1974–80

Mission category	1974	1975	1976	1977	1978	1979	1980
Total obligational authority in billions of 1975 dollars							
Ground combat forces	25.3	25.8	26.7	27.3	28.5	29.9	30.9
Tactical air forces	23.8	23.0	24.1	24.3	25.0	26.8	27.1
Naval general purpose forces	12.4	14.5	15.1	15.7	16.5	16.6	17.6
Strategic nuclear forces	16.7	18.3	18.8	20.6	22.0	23.0	23.4
Strategic mobility forces	2.2	3.1	3.1	3.2	3.3	3.5	3.6
Subtotal for baseline forces	**80.4**	**84.8**	**87.8**	**91.1**	**95.3**	**99.8**	**102.6**
Retired pay[a]	5.7	6.0	6.4	6.7	7.0	7.3	7.6
Incremental cost of the war in Southeast Asia[b]	1.8	1.9	1.7	...	...	...	...
Support of other nations[c]	4.4	2.0	1.9	3.3	3.1	2.8	2.6
Total for Department of Defense	**92.3**	**94.7**	**97.8**	**101.1**	**105.4**	**109.9**	**112.8**
Amount included in above total for real increases in pay[d]	...	...	1.3	2.6	4.0	5.5	7.1
Outlays in billions of 1975 dollars[e]							
Total for Department of Defense	**85.9**	**86.2**	**90.3**	**94.6**	**100.4**	**106.4**	**110.8**
Total obligational authority in billions of current dollars							
Assuming 3 percent annual price increases[f]	85.0	94.7	100.7	107.3	115.2	123.7	130.8
Assuming 5 percent annual price increases[f]	85.0	94.7	102.7	111.5	122.0	133.6	144.0
Outlays in billions of current dollars							
Assuming 3 percent annual price increases[f]	79.1	86.2	93.2	100.8	110.2	120.2	128.8
Assuming 5 percent annual price increases[f]	79.1	86.2	95.2	105.0	117.0	130.1	142.0

Sources: Tables 4-5 through 4-9, and estimates derived as explained in notes *a* to *f*.

a. The cost of retired pay in constant dollars is calculated, in each year, by multiplying the Defense Department's projected number of retirees by the average level of benefits in fiscal 1975; with the exception that benefits paid to the projected number of new retirees are inflated at 3 percent per year after fiscal 1975.

b. Incremental costs of supporting U.S. forces in Southeast Asia, about $500 million in fiscal 1975, are assumed to be reduced to zero by fiscal 1977. From that point on, the cost of military assistance to South Vietnam is included in "Support of Other Nations."

c. Support of other nations is assumed to decline gradually for the rest of the decade as the Korean program comes to an end. The sharp increase in fiscal 1977 occurs because of the inclusion of aid to South Vietnam at that point.

d. Each mission category projection assumes a real pay increase of 3 percent corresponding to the average increase in productivity in the private sector.

e. Outlays are assumed to rise each year by the amount of the increase in TOA, plus an additional amount so as to reduce the gap between outlays and TOA to $2 billion by fiscal 1980.

f. Data for fiscal 1974 and 1975 represent actual price experience; not the stated assumption.

combat forces, however. A breakdown of the growth in TOA by mission for fiscal year 1975 and for the period 1975–80 is shown below:

Mission category	Increase in obligational authority (billions of dollars)		Average annual increase (percent) 1975–80
	1975	*1975–80*	*1975–80*
Ground combat forces	0.6	5.1	3.7
Tactical air forces	−0.8	4.1	3.3
Naval forces	2.1	3.1	4.0
Strategic nuclear forces	1.6	5.1	5.0
Strategic mobility forces	0.9	0.5	3.0
Baseline total	**4.4**	**17.8**	**3.9**

When the estimates of retirement pay and of the future obligational authority for military assistance programs (including those to South Vietnam) are taken into account, total obligational authority for the Department of Defense is projected to increase to $112.8 billion, in constant 1975 dollars, by fiscal 1980. Increases in pay beyond those necessitated by price rises account for about 40 percent ($7.1 billion) of this $18.1 billion rise in defense obligations. In terms of outlays, the increase in defense spending will be greater. Assuming that the fiscal 1975 gap of $8.5 billion between obligational authority and outlays is reduced to $2 billion by the end of the decade, defense expenditures, in dollars of constant purchasing power, are likely to reach more than $110 billion by the end of the decade. This would mean an average increase of nearly 5.2 percent per year, or about one point more than the expected annual rate of real increase in the gross national product.

Thus the new look in defense, because of its drive to increase the combat potential of U.S. general purpose forces, its maintenance of a rapid pace in weapons modernization, its emphasis on force readiness, and its initiatives in strategic nuclear weaponry, implies higher spending for U.S. military forces, even apart from the predictable effects of price increases. If present policies are continued, this trend will hold over the remainder of the decade and, in all likelihood, will extend well into the 1980s. What might cause this projection to be modified?

One possibility would be for the Defense Department to undertake

further measures to reduce the cost of acquiring and maintaining each
unit of military capability. Greater efficiency would make it possible
to build and maintain the military forces required by the new defense
posture at lower cost. A second possibility would be for Congress, or
the administration in subsequent years, to revise the military requirements implicit in the defense posture either upward or downward.
An upward reassessment would stem from a belief that the international situation was posing greater threats to U.S. security than in
the past—in either a political or a military sense—and that, consequently, even greater combat capabilities were required. A downward
revision of defense requirements might stem from a more modest
definition of U.S. objectives abroad, a less troubled view of the international environment and Soviet military capabilities, or a down-
grading of the perceived utility of military forces to achieve political
objectives. Such a reassessment would mean that reductions in forces
or modernization rates could be made without undue risk and that the
cost reductions implied by the reforms envisioned in the new defense
posture could be used for nonmilitary purposes rather than for
greater combat capability. The next chapter discusses some major
issues involved in these choices.

5. Assessing U.S. Military Requirements

PRESSURES FOR A LARGER DEFENSE BUDGET stem mainly from the administration's concern that under the existing guidelines U.S. military forces will not be able to meet the challenges likely to face the nation in the decade ahead. Assessments of the international environment in the 1980s—what threats will be posed to national security, and how U.S. military forces can help to safeguard the nation's interests—have led to this concern.

Judgments on the adequacy of U.S. military forces depend on projections of the military balances in four separate arenas. One, the balance in Northeast Asia between U.S. and allied forces and those of China and North Korea, no longer seems so important. Relations with China have improved markedly and U.S. interests in Asia are viewed from a narrower perspective than in the past. There is a broad consensus, too, that U.S. forces now in the region are at least adequate for the largely political purposes of U.S. deployments there.[1] In each of the other three arenas, however—the balance in strategic nuclear capabilities, the balance of ground and tactical air forces in

1. The military balance in Asia and alternative U.S. force structures for that region were discussed in Edward R. Fried and others, *Setting National Priorities: The 1974 Budget* (Brookings Institution, 1973), pp. 361–73.

Europe, and the worldwide balance of naval power—there is sufficient ambiguity about U.S. needs to permit widely divergent views.

In this chapter, we examine measures that could reduce the cost of defense manpower, thereby leading to lower defense budgets even without reductions in requirements for combat capabilities. We then describe those aspects of the three military balances that are highlighted by this year's budget decisions. And we address the fundamental choices facing the nation on the future size and composition of the defense budget.

Reducing the Cost of Defense Manpower

For at least ten years, the United States has been moving toward a higher-priced defense structure, one in which the costs of supporting a single unit of military force in the field have grown steadily. Two major trends—a sharp increase in the unit cost of military equipment, and the rising price of defense manpower—are the major causes. The steps being taken to alleviate problems associated with the cost of military hardware are discussed for each type of military force in Chapter 4. The other trend—rising manpower costs—has been due to two factors. One is the efficiency with which manpower is utilized—how many people it takes to acquire, operate, direct, and sustain each combat unit. The second is the price paid for each employee of the Defense Department, both military and civilian.

More Efficient Use of Manpower

Inefficiency in the utilization of manpower has been discussed extensively in previous editions of *Setting National Priorities* and elsewhere.[2] These inefficiencies still persist, but the Defense Department has introduced some measures that might mitigate their effect or, at least, prevent their aggravation. Manpower efficiency is generally measured by the ratio of manpower in combat units to manpower in support elements, more popularly termed the relationship of "teeth to tail." The analogy is somewhat misleading. "Tail" or support elements should not automatically be equated with inefficiency. The rifleman on the frontlines must be recruited, paid, fed, clothed, and kept healthy; his equipment must be acquired, stocked, maintained, and

2. See Martin Binkin, *Support Costs in the Defense Budget: The Submerged One-Third* (Brookings Institution, 1972).

repaired. These functions require support units. Compared to the situation in the 1950s, the new technologies and resulting greater capability of U.S. general purpose forces, the higher state of readiness in which military units are now maintained, and the improvements in military living conditions all quite legitimately required a shift in the balance between combat and support manpower. The question is whether this shift has gone too far.

The 1975 defense budget proposal has contradictory implications for the efficient use of manpower.

On the side of *greater efficiency*, there has been a review of headquarters and their staffs. Resulting reductions in manpower assigned to these command echelons for the most part are being translated into increased combat capabilities. For example, the Air Force reported that reductions in headquarters and other support manpower has meant that it can retain three airlift squadrons previously scheduled to be inactivated. The Navy, which through fiscal 1974 is to reduce its headquarters billets some 25 percent from their 1969 peaks, plans only relatively small reductions in the future. The Army is making the sharpest cuts in its headquarters personnel. In fiscal 1975, it plans to close seven headquarters and pare other staffs, which will reduce their number by 5,900 people—18 percent of the headquarters personnel authorized in 1974. These manpower savings will be used to help create the additional brigade and extra battalions planned for 1975. For all the military services, manpower reductions in headquarters staffs will amount to 14,000 in 1975, and Secretary James R. Schlesinger has indicated that there are more reductions to come.

On the side of *less efficiency*, the Defense Department seems to be having second thoughts about reducing the number, size, and manpower requirements of military bases. In April 1973, an extensive list of base closings was announced. This cutback affected 219 bases, of which 40 were to be closed completely. It implied cost savings of $375 million per year and manpower reductions or reassignments of almost 43,000 people. At the time, it was also announced that further closings were being contemplated. Speculation as to the extent of additional base closings focused on the number necessary to meet former Deputy Secretary of Defense David Packard's 1971 estimate that justifiable base closings could save at least $1 billion per year.[3] Now, however, indications are that few, if any, additional base closings should be ex-

3. *Washington Post*, December 14, 1971.

pected—a change that probably resulted from the outcry raised by Congress when the last set of closings was announced and from concern about the effect of further base closures on a weak economy. Whether this stance will be maintained in the future remains to be seen.

The Rising Pay Bill

The second aspect of the manpower cost problem, the rising price of personnel, has been the major cause of recent increases in defense spending. Between fiscal years 1968 and 1975, spending for baseline forces increased by approximately $30 billion in current dollars, two-thirds of which went for rising personnel costs. In 1975, military and civilian payrolls, the payment of benefits to military retirees, and other costs associated with personnel compensation will consume more than 56 percent of baseline defense outlays. This figure compares with 47 percent in fiscal 1968 and 43 percent in 1964.

Pay comparability. Far and away the most significant factor in this growing manpower bill has been the decision to make the pay of federal employees "comparable" to that of individuals in the private sector. Legislation to accomplish this objective was passed in 1967. Large catch-up pay raises in fiscal 1969 and 1970 and subsequent increases to maintain comparability were the consequence. The comparability legislation accounts for more than two-thirds of the increase in pay and related expenses since 1968.

Change to an all-volunteer force. Another factor contributing to manpower costs was the decision to replace the military conscription system with an all-volunteer armed force. While often blamed for much of the manpower price increase, this factor has actually been relatively unimportant. Because of the comparability pay legislation, the price of defense manpower would have risen substantially with or without the later (1971) decision to end the draft. Pay increases, enlistment bonuses, and other costs incurred in moving to an all-volunteer military service have not accounted for more than 10 percent of the rise in the price of manpower since 1968.

Grade creep. A third factor is the higher grade structure that now characterizes both the civilian and the uniformed manpower pools. Table 5-1 shows the upward movement in the distribution of defense manpower among the civilian and military grades.

Much of this trend can be attributed to the war in Southeast Asia.

Table 5-1. Trends in the Distribution of Grades among Civilian and Military Defense Personnel, Selected Fiscal Years, 1960–74

Category	1960	1964	1968	1972	1974
Percentage of enlisted men					
Lowest three grades	49	41	38	27	29
Fourth, fifth, and sixth grades	44	52	54	62	60
Seventh grade and higher	7	7	8	11	10
Percentage of officers[a]					
First lieutenant (lieutenant junior grade) and below	33	33	36	26	29
Captain (lieutenant) through lieutenant colonel (commander)	62	62	59	68	65
Colonel (captain) and above	5	5	5	6	6
Number of enlisted men per officer	6.9[b]	7.0	7.5	6.1	6.2
Percentage of civilian employees					
GS-6 and below	57	50	49	43	n.a.
GS-7 to GS-12	37	42	42	46	n.a.
GS-13 to GS-18	6	8	9	11	n.a.
Average grade of personnel					
Military, enlisted	3.8	4.0	4.2	4.5	4.3
Military, officers	3.1	3.2	3.2	3.3	3.2
Civilian	6.6	7.2	7.2	7.8	7.4

Sources: Civilian employees, unpublished data from U.S. Civil Service Commission, Manpower Statistics Division, except average grade for 1974, which is from *The Budget of the United States Government—Appendix, Fiscal Year 1975;* military employees, from hearings before the House Committee on Appropriations, various years.

n.a. Not available.

a. Officer ranks in parentheses are equivalent ranks in the U.S. Navy.

b. Data for 1961.

Between 1965 and 1968, the armed forces were expanded sharply. Opportunities for command multiplied and promotions were accelerated. The significant personnel reductions after 1968 tended to affect the lower civilian and enlisted military grades disproportionately. Also, fewer officers were dismissed than would have been required to regain the prewar ratio of officers to enlisted men. These phenomena are not unusual; the same pattern was evident during the force reductions after the Korean war and World War II. However, in those cases, there were later reductions in the more senior grades. As this "grade creep" became more noticeable in the past few years, grade distribution was stabilized and steps taken to reverse the trend. Nonetheless, the present grade structure is still higher than that which characterized the defense work force before the war. The fiscal impact of lowering the grade structure would be significant. A return to the

1964 average for enlisted and civilian ranks and to the 1964 ratio of officers to enlisted men would save $630 million a year, assuming current manpower strengths were maintained.

There is some justification for a higher grade structure. Military equipment is more sophisticated than it was ten years ago and thus requires more highly skilled personnel to operate and maintain it. Recruiting and retaining skilled individuals may require the greater pay and promotion incentives associated with a higher grade structure. But the sizable pay increases already granted to military and civilian personnel may be adequate inducement—which would support a conclusion that the increase in the grade structure is excessive in terms of present needs.

Retired pay increases. A final factor contributing to the higher price of defense manpower has been a sharp increase in the number of military retirees and the higher pay rates at which their benefits are pegged. More than $6 billion, about 6 percent of the 1975 budget, is allocated to the payment of benefits to those who have retired from military service. Ten years ago, there were less than half this number of retirees receiving benefits, and retirement pay consumed $1.4 billion, or 3 percent of the defense budget.

Limiting the Growth of Manpower Costs

Regardless of cause, the rise in the price of manpower, in both absolute and relative terms, has been dramatic. While the rate of increase will not be as sharp in the future, continuing increases in the price of manpower can be expected so long as it is desired to maintain comparability between pay rates in the private and government sectors. The size of the increase will be influenced, however, by two proposals now before Congress that would alter the price of defense personnel, and by proposals for more far-reaching reforms in the military compensation system.

Recomputation of military retired pay, a proposal which would increase manpower costs, has been rejected for the past two years by Congress but will come once again before the legislature in 1974—this time without the support of the Defense Department. The question is whether military retired pay, which is adjusted each year to account for inflation, should also be adjusted whenever there is an increase in active-duty military pay exceeding the allowance for inflation. This was the practice until 1958. A one-time recomputation, primarily to adjust for the large increases in military pay granted in 1969, 1970, and 1971 would cost about $400 million per year in present prices. The cost of legislation calling for recomputation on a regular basis would be considerably higher, averaging over $6 billion a year through the end of the century. It should be noted that no other government retirement plan includes provisions for recomputation.[4]

Reforming the method of computing military pay increases, another measure before Congress, would slow the growth of manpower costs. The proposal aims to correct an anomaly in the formula used to compute military pay raises each year, which results in higher pay increases for military personnel than are necessary to maintain comparability with the private sector.

Calculations of comparability pay and of the incentives needed for an all-volunteer service are based on "regular military compensation," which includes the elements of pay that are viewed as equivalent to monetary income in the private sector. Regular military compensation consists of basic pay (78 percent), quarters allowances (9 percent), subsistence allowances (8 percent), and a tax advantage (5 percent).[5] It does not include special bonuses, fringe benefits (such as commissary and medical privileges), or retirement benefits. In 1967, Congress directed that (1) each year the percentage increase in pay given to federal civilian workers was to be applied to all components of regular military compensation; but (2) the percentage increase, when translated into dollars, was to be added to the basic pay element alone. Therefore, under this system a given percentage increase in federal civilian pay is accompanied by a higher percentage rate of increase in military basic pay, but military allowances—an important component of military compensation for some grades and specialties —are not altered automatically. Military pay rates have now been changed eight times in this manner.

This formula for calculating military pay increases has resulted in several anomalies, all of which have the effect of increasing military pay by more than the criteria of comparability with the private sector would require:

4. Two factors would work toward reducing future pressures for recomputation: a change in the formula by which military pay raises are calculated (see below); and if, as in 1973, the rise in the consumer price index outran the increases in military pay.

5. Military quarters and subsistence allowances, whether in cash or in kind, are not subject to federal income tax. A specific monetary value, based on an assumed average military income, is attached to this element of pay.

- Military personnel who receive quarters and subsistence in kind get an extra increase in basic pay as the cost of these services rises, even though it is the government that pays the higher prices.

- Military personnel receiving cash allowances for food and quarters are understandably compensated for inflation by the extra increase in their basic pay. However, the cash allowances, which are left unchanged by this formula, then seem to be too low, resulting in pressures to increase them. Because of this reasoning, allowances for quarters were increased substantially in fiscal 1972 as part of the volunteer incentive package, and allowances for subsistence were increased in fiscal 1973 to compensate for the rising cost of food. Those receiving cash allowances, therefore, are being compensated twice for the same purpose.

- Other elements of military compensation, such as reenlistment bonuses, separation pay, benefits to retirees, and the government's contribution to social security benefits, are increased by more than is necessary because they are tied to basic pay.

The alternative method of computing military pay raises now before Congress would increase both basic pay and quarters and subsistence allowances by the same percentage as the increase in civilian pay. This is a simple and effective way to fulfill the objectives of the comparability legislation. If the formula were applied to the next pay raise, savings in fiscal 1975 could approach $200 million. Even more substantial savings would result in the future. Assuming annual pay raises of 6 percent, by fiscal 1980 savings would have grown to $1.7 billion per year.

These are staggering consequences from what seems to be a minor quirk in the military pay system. The urgent need to correct it can be brought out in another way. If the proposed formula had been in effect since 1967, in place of the existing system, the 1975 military payroll would be $1.7 billion less than it is, a reduction of almost 10 percent.

More far-reaching reforms in the military compensation system also could result in sizable future savings in the cost of defense manpower. Two major possibilities are:

- To replace the present system—in which military compensation takes the form of wages, allowances, fringe benefits, and payments in kind—with a single salary system. Turning all forms of military compensation into cash payments would not only make comparisons between military and civilian pay scales easier and more accurate but could also magnify the appeal of the present level of compensation for recruiting and reenlistments. Current practices hide many of the tangible benefits of military service, even from those receiving them.

• To align the benefits granted to retired military personnel more closely with those paid under the federal civilian retirement system: a change which would reduce the projected long-range cost of military retirements. A set of proposals was submitted by the administration in 1973, but for the most part Congress has not yet acted on it. While entailing small initial costs, the proposals would save more than $1.5 billion annually by the year 2000. At the same time, consideration could be given to removing the annual cost of benefits paid to military retirees from the Defense Department's budget, as its inclusion overstates what the nation is presently spending for defense. In its place, Defense could be required to contribute to a retirement fund, roughly like a private pension fund, the current costs of future benefits determined on an actuarial basis. Thus only the discounted cost of new obligations would be included in the budget.

Reforms such as these often have floundered because they appeared to penalize active members of the armed services. Individuals who chose a military career, it is argued, did so partly because they were led to expect, explicitly or implicitly, certain kinds and amounts of benefits. A sharp change in those benefits, particularly a change affecting individuals who already had invested considerable time in the military, would not be fair. Consequently, most proposals for major reforms in the military compensation system emphasize longer-term savings rather than measures that would reduce immediate costs. For these reasons, such proposals often do not receive serious attention from Congress or the Defense Department; yet their consequences for the size of future defense budgets are potentially much greater than those involved in debates over weapon systems.

The establishment of the Defense Manpower Commission by Congress in 1973 provides a new opportunity to reevaluate the military compensation system and other factors contributing to the rising price of manpower. The commission is charged with conducting a comprehensive study of the requirements for and utilization of manpower by the Department of Defense. It is to give special attention to (1) the ratio of personnel in support units to those assigned to combat forces; and (2) the pay structure, grade structure, retirement pay, and recruitment of defense manpower. The commission's task is urgent; its recommendations could have a major effect on the magnitude of defense spending in the future.

The Strategic Balance

The overriding purpose of the nation's strategic nuclear forces is to ensure that they never have to be used. These forces are designed, maintained, and deployed so as to deter potential adversaries from initiating actions that the United States would consider hostile. Clearly, nuclear weapons cannot be effective in forestalling all unfriendly initiatives directed at this nation or at its friends. Yet U.S. defense policy depends on these forces, in varying degree, for deterrence of a wide spectrum of possible threats: direct attacks on the United States itself or on its allies with nuclear weapons, nonnuclear assaults in Europe or Asia, and even certain forms of political coercion.

Strategic nuclear forces also serve other important functions. The U.S. nuclear arsenal provides awesome destruction potential: a fact that can never be totally ignored by other nations. Even when strategic forces remain in the background, the risks associated with their potential use must have some, perhaps implicit, impact on the decisions of policymakers in other nations. And at other times when the risks of nuclear war are made more explicit by the words of American leaders or by military demonstration—during, for example, the short-lived October 1973 crisis with the USSR—the size and shape of U.S. strategic forces can have a fundamental impact on the outcome of events.

Until recently, U.S. strategic nuclear capabilities clearly were superior to those of any potential adversary. Beginning in 1965, however, Soviet deployments of strategic missiles began to increase substantially. The USSR has since surpassed the United States in the number of deployed land-based intercontinental ballistic missiles (ICBMs) and will soon surpass it in the number of submarine-launched ballistic missiles (SLBMs). These Soviet missiles also tend to be much larger (to have greater throw-weight) than their U.S. counterparts. The United States still has the advantage in strategic bombers and in various qualitative features of strategic missiles—in accuracy, for example, and in the technology of multiple independently targetable reentry vehicles (MIRVs). Nonetheless, the United States no longer holds the vast strategic edge over its adversary it once had. Taking everything into account, now there is probably a situation of rough overall strategic parity.

The 1972 Interim Agreement on strategic offensive forces formalized the Soviet Union's advantage in the number of strategic missile launchers—land- and sea-based—permitted to each side. Presumably, the United States found this provision acceptable because the agreement was temporary (it expires automatically in 1977); because during this period the U.S. lead in weapons technology and in strategic bombers could not possibly be overcome; and because, in any event, the agreement only ratified an existing situation. From the U.S. perspective, the strategic balance is as good as and possibly better than it would have been if the agreement had not been negotiated—the United States had had no plans to increase its numbers of launchers at that time.

The future, however, is not as certain. While the pace of Soviet technological advance in strategic weaponry has not been faster than expected, the breadth of the USSR's present research and development program causes considerable concern. During 1973, the Soviet Union flight-tested four new land-based missiles, three of which carried MIRVs. These tests showed that the Soviets are now placing more sophisticated computing and control mechanisms on board their missiles—an important step toward improving missile accuracy. The USSR has also demonstrated a new submarine-launched missile which is already operational. And the USSR has active research programs on ballistic missile defense, mobile land-based missiles, and air defenses. It continues, however, to pay less attention to long-range bombers.

These developments have led to some debate in the United States about which concepts should guide decisions on the size, composition, and plans for possible use of strategic nuclear forces. The secretary of defense argues that past U.S. strategic doctrine is inadequate in a time of nuclear parity because it does not take full account of the political implications of nuclear weapons. He believes that continued adherence to that doctrine could lead to a further erosion of the U.S. strategic position, since the United States would refrain from developing certain strategic capabilities now potentially available to the Soviet Union. Thus the United States could actually become inferior in some forms of strategic power by the 1980s.

The contrary view is that these potential differences are unimportant. Despite wide-ranging developments in weapon technology, the overall balance of nuclear power remains stable. As a result, the political consequences of imbalances in specific areas—which some fear —are unlikely to occur. The destructive capabilities on each side are massive; both nations deploy far more nuclear power than necessary to destroy the opposing society. Also, the survivability of nuclear forces is high at present; both sides have sufficient forces to ride out a preemptive attack and still inflict massive damage in retaliation. Moreover, neither side can have high confidence in what could be accomplished by its strategic forces in a first strike because they have never been tested in combat. These factors should give pause to any nation that contemplates a nuclear exchange under the impression that the advantage of striking first would outweigh the chances of war being avoided altogether.

The stakes are high in this debate. Changes in nuclear policy could have a major impact on future relations between the United States and the Soviet Union. Inappropriate development of nuclear capabilities could generate large expenditures and lead to a less stable balance of forces. Inadequate development could leave the United States more vulnerable to coercion by foreign nations. Part of the debate focuses on specific requests in this year's defense budget. While the amounts involved are small at present, decisions made now could imply annual variations in defense spending of as much as $3 billion to $5 billion in the late 1970s and the 1980s.

Projecting Superpower Nuclear Capabilities

Table 5-2 compares the U.S. and Soviet strategic arsenals in 1965, 1975, and 1980 on the basis of several measures of strategic capability. The 1980 projection assumes a continuation of present restraints instituted by the strategic arms limitation talks (SALT) agreements, but no additional limits on offensive arms. While this is not the most likely case, it serves to illustrate the relevant points.

Data in Table 5-2 show that in 1965 the United States maintained a major advantage in every index of strategic capability. By 1975, the Soviets will have deployed sufficient forces to take a large lead in the number of missiles and in the payload and equivalent megatonnage deliverable by missiles. The United States will retain its advantage in bombers, however, and if the payload and megatonnage deliverable by bombers is included in the calculations, the Soviet advantages are

Table 5-2. Strategic Nuclear Capabilities of the United States and the Soviet Union, Midyear, 1965, 1975, and 1980

	1965		1975		1980[a]	
Measure of capability	United States	Soviet Union	United States	Soviet Union	United States	Soviet Union
Force levels (number)						
Intercontinental ballistic missiles	854	230	1,054	1,587	1,014	1,409
Submarine-launched ballistic missiles	496	96	656	750	696	906
Long-range bombers	696	140	396	126	391	126
Payload capacity (millions of pounds)[b]						
Total	10.0	3.5	8.2	10.3	6.5	12.4
Missile payload only	2.2	2.0	3.1	9.0	3.0	11.1
Independently targetable warheads (number)						
Total	4,276	516	8,538	2,499	12,274	5,264
Missile warheads only	1,350	326	6,922	2,337	10,278	5,102
Equivalent megatonnage[c]						
Total	5,501	823	3,658	4,355	3,548	7,242
Missile equivalent megatonnage only	1,423	190	1,985	3,993	2,302	6,880

Sources: Authors' estimates derived from (1) International Institute for Strategic Studies, *The Military Balance, 1973–1974* (London: IISS, 1973), and the *1964–1965* issue; (2) Ian Smart, *Advanced Strategic Missiles: A Short Guide* (London: Institute for Strategic Studies, 1969); (3) *ABM, MIRV, SALT, and the Nuclear Arms Race*, Hearings before the Subcommittee on Arms Control, International Law and Organization of the Senate Committee on Foreign Relations, 91 Cong. 2 sess. (1970); and (4) *U.S.–U.S.S.R. Strategic Policies*, Hearing before ibid., 93 Cong. 2 sess. (1974).

a. The 1980 figures assume that the United States carries out its strategic programs as described in chapter 4. For the Soviet Union, it assumes: (a) the deployment of three new kinds of ICBMs beginning in 1976 at the rates observed for present Soviet missiles; (b) no new long-range bombers; and (c) continued deployment of *Delta*-class strategic submarines. Both sides are assumed to observe the restrictions contained in the present SALT agreement on numbers of deployed missile launchers, but to continue to make qualitative improvements in their strategic forces.

b. Since the weight-carrying capacity of missiles and bombers is not directly comparable, this index considers the payload of each system that could be used to carry nuclear weapons, their protective structures, and associated guidance system as the relevant measure.

c. Equivalent megatonnage is a measure of the area destruction capacity of a nuclear arsenal in light of its various components and weapons sizes. It reflects the fact that the size of the ground area which would be destroyed by a nuclear explosion does not increase one-to-one with increases in the size of the nuclear warhead.

reduced sharply. The United States will continue to retain a gross, if declining, advantage in the relative number of independently targetable warheads.

By 1980, the larger size of the new Soviet ICBMs and their mastering of MIRV technology will permit them, under the assumptions used in our projection, to move further ahead in two measures of strategic power. The USSR is likely to have a 25 percent lead in total payload and about double the United States in total equivalent megatonnage. The United States will still retain, however, more than a two-to-one lead in independently targetable warheads.

What does this comparison of future capabilities imply? It indicates that while there will continue to be rough parity in total strategic capabilities, each side will have important specific advantages. The central question is whether the Soviet advantages would have adverse political implications. Secretary Schlesinger and others in the administration believe that they would. Under the concept of "essential equivalence," the secretary has argued that the United States must not permit the USSR to acquire an advantage in any aspect of strategic power, lest it exploit this unilateral advantage for political gain. And the particular asymmetry that causes the secretary most concern is the possibility that Soviet forces will achieve superiority in the future in the potential capability of the two sides' strategic forces to destroy hardened targets—particularly opposing missile silos.

By 1980, the USSR is likely to be able to destroy a substantial number of U.S. ICBMs in a first strike. This Soviet capability will continue to increase in the eighties. As we have noted, Soviet missiles already are larger than their U.S. counterparts and therefore are capable of carrying warheads with larger yields. Moreover, two of the new ICBMs now being tested in the USSR are estimated to have a throw-weight three to five times that of the missiles which they apparently would replace. Besides, in 1980 Soviet capabilities are likely to be limited only by the accuracy of their missiles. In calculating the probability that a missile will destroy a target of a specified hardness, accuracy is far more important than warhead size; a twofold increase in accuracy equates to an eightfold increase in yield. Once the Soviets master the techniques necessary to obtain accuracies closer to those even now available to the United States, they would be likely soon to acquire a capacity to destroy virtually all the U.S. land-based missiles in a first strike.[6]

While the United States also has the capability to destroy Soviet land-based missiles, it can only do so at present by using several of its relatively accurate but small warheads against each silo target. The limited size and number of present U.S. missiles, the greater number

6. Missile accuracy is measured by "circular error probable" (CEP)—the radius of a circle around the missile's planned impact point within which 50 percent of the firings are expected to fall. The CEP usually given for Minuteman is 1,500 feet (approximately 0.25 nautical mile). Soviet CEPs are generally assumed to be more than 0.50 nautical mile.

of missile targets in the USSR, and the problem of "fratricide" would prevent the United States from achieving a near-total first-strike capability against Soviet land-based missiles.[7] These limitations can be overcome, however, by greater missile accuracy, such as that which could be achieved, for example, by building reentry vehicles with terminal guidance systems.

Should an asymmetrical situation develop, it is maintained, the United States would be at great disadvantage. Put briefly, the Soviets could initiate certain kinds of limited nuclear wars to which the United States would not have an exactly corresponding response, and Soviet decision makers might believe that they could take political advantage of this asymmetry—for example, by pressuring U.S. allies for concessions, thus precipitating a crisis whose results would be hard to predict. Moreover, it is feared that if the United States does not respond firmly even to the *potential* unilateral development by the Soviet Union of a first-strike capability against U.S. land-based missiles, Soviet leaders may come to doubt U.S. resolve, and this perception could lead them to behave imprudently during times of international tension. And, finally, there is concern that under such conditions U.S. allies might come to question the credibility of U.S. nuclear guarantees: a development that could lead to a loosening of ties within the alliance and greater pressures in other nations for the development of sizable nuclear capabilities of their own.

Departures in U.S. Strategy

The administration has responded to these projections of future strategic capabilities in several ways. First, the position has been adopted that any follow-on SALT agreements must reduce the imbalance in the number of missiles permitted to each signatory. According to Secretary Schlesinger, some asymmetries would still be acceptable but neither side can be permitted a significant unilateral advantage.

Second, U.S. targeting doctrine and the various software systems through which targets are selected and programmed into the weapon delivery systems have been modified so that, in the event of a nuclear war, a greater number of options for limited strikes would be available

7. Fratricide: The number of warheads that can be effectively targeted against a single missile silo within a short time may not exceed two or three. It is theorized that the performance of warheads arriving later is likely to be degraded by the effects of the earlier nuclear explosions.

to the President. Some of these target lists will be restricted to military targets; others will be directed against particular industries. The option of ordering a full-scale attack against the Soviet population will still be available to the President. To this basic strike plan, however, the menu of options for limited nuclear exchanges directed primarily at military targets has now been expanded.

Third, the administration has initiated a series of research and development programs, which, if continued, would provide the United States with a more efficient capability to destroy hard targets. Only by demonstrating U.S. resolve in this manner, the administration argues, will the Soviets be persuaded to give up their potential first-strike capability against ICBMs, either through further SALT agreements or by unilateral restraint. These research and development programs, which would cost $540 million in fiscal 1975 and much more thereafter, have been described in Chapter 4. They constitute the most controversial departure in U.S. strategic policies.

Three major issues arise in evaluating these proposed advances in the U.S. ability to destroy hard targets.

First, there is the question of the survivability of Minuteman land-based missiles. Some take a more optimistic view than that previously expressed. For example, U.S. Air Force Chief of Staff General George S. Brown recently asserted that Minuteman would not become vulnerable for many years to come. He based this assessment primarily on the USSR's surprisingly slow progress in improving missile accuracy.[8]

Second, there is a question as to how much would be gained from expenditures to improve hard target kill capabilities. There would seem to be little chance that they could significantly reduce the damage the United States would suffer in the event of a nuclear attack, since these programs would affect only the destructive potential of Soviet ICBMs, not its submarine-launched missiles or bombers, and since the Soviet ICBM silos themselves could well have been emptied of their missiles by the time they were struck by American ICBMs. A more valid military reason for improving hard target kill capability would be to provide additional options for limited nuclear wars—to make available additional target sets as it were. But would this be an advantage? If the U.S. purpose were to limit a nuclear war, ICBMs—

8. *Washington Post*, March 23, 1974.

the Soviet Union's main strategic weapon—would seem to be *the last thing* to attack. The loss of some ICBMs would probably be the single event most likely to guarantee launch of the remaining Soviet missiles. Striking other military targets (such as Soviet strategic air defenses if war ensued from a European crisis) would seem to be a far better means of demonstrating resolve and restoring stability without escalating to an all-out nuclear exchange. And almost all military targets other than hardened ICBM silos are already vulnerable to U.S. nuclear weapons.

Third, there is the question of Soviet reaction to these U.S. initiatives. The deployment by the United States of a serious first-strike capability against ICBMs would provide an added incentive for the USSR to strike first in a crisis. Thus the strategic balance would be less stable and the probability of a nuclear exchange would be somewhat greater. The Soviets' likely reaction with regard to their own weapon programs also seems hard to predict. They could ignore the U.S. improvements or shift a greater portion of their missile forces to sea so as to compensate for reductions in the survivability of their own land-based missiles. A more probable reaction, however, would be for the USSR again to accelerate its own ICBM programs. This might involve deploying their new missiles equipped with MIRVs on a faster schedule, building more ICBMs, or—perhaps the most likely possibility—deploying a mobile land-based missile. An extreme reaction would be for them to withdraw from the treaty limiting antiballistic missiles and to step up defensive programs, arguing that the U.S. initiatives indicated the United States was now adopting a war-fighting posture for its strategic forces rather than being interested primarily in the deterrent effects of nuclear weapons. Such a conclusion by the Soviets cannot be ruled out since they only recently seem to have accorded some credibility to U.S. deterrence theory generally, and since they already suspect the motives behind other U.S. weapon programs—particularly those in antisubmarine warfare—which potentially threaten other elements of their strategic forces. Any of the more likely Soviet reactions would cause an escalation in the arms race.

Alternative Strategies

Looking beyond specific decisions in this year's budget, there are a wide variety of longer-term strategies available to cope with the projected development of Soviet hard target kill capabilities. Three possibilities are described below.

Alternative one represents a logical extrapolation of the research and development programs contained in the administration's budget request. It tries to match the Soviet hard target kill potential and thus neutralize political consequences presumed to flow from the otherwise asymmetrical situation. With this strategy, the United States would replace the remaining 450 Minuteman II missiles with larger Minuteman IIIs. Furthermore, the United States would develop and acquire, on a relatively rapid schedule, a new reentry system for all 1,000 Minuteman missiles. This system would include perhaps three maneuvering reentry vehicles (MARVs), each with a greater yield than that of present Minuteman warheads. Most important, MARVs would be far more accurate than existing systems. New terminal guidance technologies make "circular errors probable" (CEPs) on the order of a few hundred feet, or better, not at all implausible. With accuracies of this order, only about two warheads would be required to guarantee a very low survivability for each Soviet missile silo. Thus the United States would match the Soviet first-strike potential, and the political consequences associated with an asymmetrical situation would not be pertinent. The acquisition costs of this alternative are likely to be about $5.8 billion.

Alternative two would seek to negate the Soviet Union's potential to destroy hard targets by eliminating its most important aim points: U.S. land-based missiles. This could be done within a SALT framework by negotiating an agreement which reduced the total number of missiles permitted, but allowed each nation to determine how that total should be divided between land- and sea-based weapons. Or it could be done unilaterally by the United States, in which case the United States would still have two strategic components—bombers and submarines—each independently capable of carrying out most strategic missions.

Under this alternative, deployment of Minuteman III would be halted at 550 missiles. Nearly all U.S. land-based missiles then would be phased out as the USSR achieved the capability of destroying them in a first strike; some ICBMs might still be retained for use in limited warfare. The phase-out would be accomplished gradually, so as to minimize adverse political consequences, and so as to permit replacement of the capabilities represented by these missiles with additional missiles based at sea. The number of strategic submarines that should be acquired to compensate for the phase-out of Minuteman is not certain. At one extreme, the rule of thumb could be adopted that the total number of independently targetable warheads in the U.S. inventory should remain roughly stable. Under this rule, 11 of the new smaller (SSBN-X) strategic submarines, each carrying 16 missiles with an average of 10 warheads apiece, would provide the equivalent of the present Minuteman force. The acquisition costs of such a measure would be about $4.2 billion. This replacement option could not be carried out under the terms of the present SALT agreement because only limited substitutions of submarine- for land-based missiles are now permitted; but, in any case, it would not be possible to carry out this weapon program until after the present agreement expires in 1977 because of the lead time involved in submarine construction.

Alternative three would use direct measures to protect U.S. land-based missiles from a Soviet first strike. This might be attempted by deploying major antiballistic missile defenses, by superhardening U.S. ICBM silos, by replacing Minuteman with mobile land-based systems, or by a combination of these measures. Any such attempt, however, would be very expensive and possibly self-defeating to boot. For example, deployment of the site defense ABM system around the five Minuteman wings would cost between $5 billion and $9 billion. Also, any improvement in Minuteman survivability would probably soon be countered by new Soviet measures to improve their ICBM capability. Moreover, deployment of an extensive ABM system would require abrogation of the 1972 ABM treaty, and upset the stability of U.S.–Soviet relations. Besides, U.S. ABM deployments would probably spur similar deployments on the Soviet side. Consequently, U.S. confidence in the penetration capabilities of all its missiles—ICBMs and SLBMs—could be undermined. Thus, in the name of ICBM survivability, a far less stable situation than the one caused by vulnerable ICBMs alone could be created.

Inclusion of some research and development programs in the fiscal 1975 budget request does not indicate that the administration has irreversibly decided to pursue the first alternative: to replace U.S. land-based missiles with an upgraded system. Secretary Schlesinger has, on the contrary, denied that this is the case, and others in the administration have hinted that they might favor the second alternative: to phase out U.S. land-based missiles. The requests for research and development may have been proposed simply to put pressure on the Soviets to agree to a follow-on SALT agreement that would deny to them the potential unilateral advantage they now hold. If such an agreement is not reached, however, and if the research programs involved in developing the first alternative are carried forward, it will become increasingly difficult to adopt the second alternative in later years.

The Naval Balance

The balance of global naval power between the United States and the Soviet Union has received much attention in recent years primarily because, aside from their potential roles in wartime, navies serve important political functions.

For one thing, both superpowers use their navies as a means of affecting the outcomes of international crises. During the past twelve years, nearly every military confrontation between the United States and the Soviet Union has been expressed through the movement of warships and submarines. Naval forces are more mobile, more flexible, and less disruptive in an economic, political, and psychological sense than other forms of conventional military power. They imply— at least in the short run—a lesser risk of a mutually disastrous general war than strategic nuclear forces. Thus both the United States and the Soviet Union maintain standing naval forces in several regions to demonstrate their interest in and commitments to their respective allies. At times of rising tension they tend to reinforce these deployments, or to move warships closer to the source of tension, so as to demonstrate their concern, to warn potential adversaries, to bolster allied confidence, or to carry out specific military tasks. Lessened tension often is indicated by moving warships away from the confrontation point, by sending the ships into port, or similar actions.

Changes in the relative size and capabilities of the two navies also are viewed as an important indication of long-term trends in the determination and the ability of the superpowers to influence the course of world affairs. This may appear odd in view of the much greater military strength available to the superpowers from their nuclear arsenals. Nonetheless, there is general recognition that any decision to employ nuclear weapons would be irrational or desperate—and that therefore it is the relative capabilities of the superpowers' general purpose forces that will ultimately determine the outcome of their adversary relations.

On the surface, at least, trends in the two navies have run in opposite directions for the past several years. We noted in Chapter 4 that in the late 1960s U.S. naval force levels began to decline sharply as large numbers of ships built during World War II became obsolete. While Soviet naval force levels have also declined of late, since 1967 the Soviet political leadership has been far more willing to deploy its naval forces far from their home waters and to use them to exert influence on the outcome of international crises. This gave the impression that Soviet force levels were rising. Besides, impressive Soviet modernization programs for submarines and surface warships resulted in important qualitative advances in Soviet naval power.[9]

Beginning around 1970, this apparent contrast between a declining U.S. Navy and a growing Soviet naval threat caused U.S. naval officials to issue vigorous public warnings concerning the extent to which Soviet naval capabilities were improving relative to those of the United States. Now that a few years have passed, however, and both the outlines of the U.S. naval modernization program and the near-term limits on Soviet developments have become more apparent, a less stark evaluation may be possible.

Naval Strength in the Eighties

Because of the long lead times and large quantities of various resources involved in building warships, it is possible to predict the approximate size and structure of a navy far into the future. While such a projection, based solely on unclassified material, is unlikely to constitute a fully accurate prediction of the specific number and kinds of ships in the fleet, it is useful in indicating the direction and rough outlines of future naval force developments. A projection of comparative U.S. and Soviet naval strengths in 1980 is summarized in Table 5-3. The following points are most important:

• In aircraft carriers and amphibious assault forces, the United States will enjoy a major advantage, having 12 full-size carriers capable of accommodating modern jet aircraft, and 14 smaller carriers. The USSR will have only 6 carriers, none of which will be capable of handling high-performance jets.

• In major warships (cruisers, frigates, destroyers, and ocean-going escorts), the two superpowers will have compensating advantages: a

9. See Barry M. Blechman, *The Changing Soviet Navy* (Brookings Institution, 1973), for a description of these developments.

Table 5-3. Naval Strength of the United States and the Soviet Union, 1980

	Number		Displacement (thousand tons)	
Measure of strength	*United States*	*Soviet Union*	*United States*	*Soviet Union*
Full-size aircraft carriers	12	0	965	0
Carriers for vertical or short take-off and landing aircraft and helicopters	14	6	348	216
Amphibious warfare ships	56	117	732	220
Cruisers and frigates	38	34	305	354
Destroyers and ocean-going escorts	172	206	880	529
Nuclear attack and cruise missile submarines	86	133	433	623
Diesel attack and cruise missile submarines	0	76	0	166
Smaller surface combatants	43	310	14	97
Mine warfare ships	a	200	a	120
Support ships	46	53	1,116	490

Sources: Authors' estimates based on material appearing in: (a) an enclosure to letter of Admiral Elmo R. Zumwalt, Jr., to Representative Les Aspin (April 1973); (b) John E. Moore (ed.), *Jane's Fighting Ships, 1973–74* (McGraw-Hill, 1973); (c) Robert P. Berman, "Soviet Naval Strength and Deployment" (paper presented at the second conference on Soviet Naval Developments, Halifax, Nova Scotia, October 1973); (d) Michael MccGwire, "Soviet Naval Programmes," *Survival*, Vol. 15 (September/October 1973); and (e) *Annual Defense Department Report, FY 1975*, Report of the Secretary of Defense James R. Schlesinger to the Congress on the FY 1975 Defense Budget and FY 1975–1979 Defense Program (March 4, 1974).

a. The United States utilizes helicopters for mine sweeping. These can be embarked on any of the twenty-six carriers listed in the first and second rows above, and on some surface warships.

30-ship Soviet advantage will be roughly compensated by a U.S. lead of nearly 35 percent in aggregate tonnage.

• In number of submarines, the Soviets will have a major advantage, boasting 209 attack submarines in 1980, of which 76 will be diesel-powered units. About one-third of the Soviet submarine fleet will be equipped with cruise missiles—a particularly potent weapon against surface warships. The United States will have a completely nuclear-powered force of 86 units. None of the U.S. submarines are likely to have cruise missiles; but they are distinctly superior to their Soviet counterparts in other important qualitative aspects, such as quietness, which makes them less susceptible to detection.

• Overall, the two navies are very different entities and are designed for different purposes. Lacking a rival sea power of any magnitude for most of the postwar period, the United States fashioned its Navy primarily as a vehicle for projecting U.S. air power and manpower ashore in distant regions of the globe. This orientation partly explains U.S.

emphasis on sea-based air power, on the Marines and amphibious assault shipping, and on forces to support warships while they are deployed in distant regions. During the same period, the Soviet Union built its fleet primarily for strategic defensive purposes: to deter and if necessary to defend against attacks on the Soviet homeland from the sea, and to limit the role of the United States and other Western powers in regions close to Soviet shores, notably the Middle East. This explains Soviet emphasis on submarines, on land-based strike aircraft, and on cruise missiles.

The two navies now seem to be converging somewhat in the relative priorities they each accord to the different functions of seapower—witness the new U.S. emphasis on controlling the seas and increasing Soviet deployments to distant regions. Moreover, regardless of their design criteria, naval forces are potentially useful in multiple roles. Soviet submarines built in order to counter Western aircraft carriers, for example, can also be used to sink merchant ships conveying supplies to U.S. forces in Europe. And, similarly, U.S. antisubmarine warfare forces built to defend shipping to Europe against submarine attacks could potentially be used against Soviet strategic submarines.

But organizations as large and as old as the two navies change, in a fundamental sense, only very slowly. Thus the U.S. and Soviet fleets for some time are likely to remain very different and very difficult to compare. There is no simple way to add up ships and determine the quantitative balance. Neither can a force level comparison take into account the striking qualitative differences between the two fleets: the vast differences in the performance characteristics of ships, weapons, aircraft, and electronic equipment. While there might be a consensus of expert opinion as to whether the United States or the USSR has supremacy in one area of naval capability or another, any assessment of the degree of difference, or the implications of such differences for aggregate capabilities should be treated cautiously. And even the most elaborate comparative methodology cannot fully account for the relative utility of the two navies in peacetime situations; within some limits, a navy's political value is likely to result more from the way in which it is used and described than from the technical capabilities of its hardware.

These difficulties in force comparisions are of more than academic significance. The political consequences presumed to flow from global or regional comparisons of the U.S.–Soviet naval balance have played a major role in recent decisions concerning U.S. naval force levels and modernization rates. For example, this year the decision to maintain larger U.S. naval forces in the Indian Ocean has been justified almost exclusively on the grounds that a growing Soviet naval presence in the region requires additional U.S. naval deployments.[10] This decision could have an important effect on future U.S. Navy force levels and, consequently, on future Navy budgets.

In the fiscal 1975 defense proposal, the decision to maintain an augmented U.S. naval presence in the Indian Ocean meant a request for $32 million to improve the runway and harbor and to expand other U.S. support facilities on the British island of Diego Garcia. The total cost of this project will be $82 million. More important, requirements stemming from augmented Indian Ocean deployments led to the decision to postpone the previously scheduled retirement of two aircraft carriers. This decision will cost about $150 million in direct operating expenses each year the retirements are delayed.

Future budgetary implications are much greater, resulting mainly from the way a decision to increase U.S. forces in the Indian Ocean could affect decisions on U.S. aircraft carrier force levels and building rates. In turn, the number of aircraft carriers in the U.S. inventory strongly affects the number of escort vessels, support ships, and air wings maintained in the active Navy.

If all other carrier deployments remain unchanged, a decision to keep a carrier task group continuously in the Indian Ocean would imply the addition of three carriers to U.S. force levels. The rule of thumb generally applied in such calculations assumes that so long as the ships are not based within the deployment region, necessary maintenance and overhaul schedules, training needs, and the time delays required to outfit and transit between the ship's home port and its overseas operating region, require three carriers in the inventory

---

10. For the past two years, the USSR typically has maintained about 16 ships in the Indian ocean; 4 warships, 1 submarine, and the rest support vessels of various sorts. At times, the Soviet force has been increased to as many as 31 vessels including 9 warships and submarines. The United States maintains a permanent force of two destroyers and a command ship. The United States also dispatches task forces into the region on an intermittent basis. These task forces usually consist of an aircraft carrier, 4 to 6 escort ships, and some support vessels. Until the 1973 Middle East war, such intermittent deployments were infrequent. Now, however, they are the rule rather than the exception. Between October 1973 and April 1974, 3 U.S. carrier task forces and a smaller force centered on a nuclear-powered frigate were deployed to the Indian Ocean. In total, the U.S. maintained an augumented force for 84 percent of this six-month period.

for every one kept on station. Escort ship, support ship, and airwing force levels would have to be adjusted accordingly. Such additions to U.S. Navy force levels would involve acquisition costs of about $4.8 billion.[11] Once these forces joined the fleet, the Navy's annual direct and indirect operating outlays would rise by another $800 million.

Thus the requirement to maintain a carrier task force in the Indian Ocean could prove to be a major budgetary issue. In addition, it could create expectations in the Soviet Union regarding new U.S. commitments that could lead to a further step-up of the USSR's own deployments to the region.

The decision to deploy large U.S. naval forces to the Indian Ocean therefore raises these questions:

- In the absence of additional U.S. deployments, how would U.S. interests be jeopardized if Soviet naval deployments in the Indian Ocean were to exceed our own?

- How would an increase in the U.S. naval presence counteract such negative political consequences?

- Are the political costs of a naval imbalance in the region sufficient to justify the potentially large expenditures likely to result from additional U.S. deployments in the region?

- Are alternative methods of preventing the development of a naval imbalance in the region—such as negotiating mutual restraints on deployments with the Soviet Union—feasible at this time?

Of course, decisions on aircraft carrier force levels depend on a number of factors, some of which will be of far greater consequence than new requirements for Indian Ocean deployments. Of particular importance are assessments of the potential vulnerability of aircraft carriers and judgments as to the political consequences of scaling down standing deployments of aircraft carriers in the Mediterranean Sea and Western Pacific Ocean. Nonetheless, imposition of a requirement to maintain a carrier task force in the Indian Ocean for most of the year, if added to existing requirements for carrier deploy-

---

11. This calculation assumes that the minimum number of additional units justified by the new deployment would be added to existing forces (3 carriers, 10 escorts, 2 support ships, and 2 airwings of 80 aircraft each). Additionally, it is assumed that—as described in Chapter 4—less expensive individual units would be procured whenever possible. A less optimistic appraisal of such decisions would result in estimated acquisition costs close to $8 billion.

ments, could have a significant influence on future decisions concerning the Navy's shipbuilding program and force levels.[12]

The Military Balance in Europe

The prospective balance of forces in central Europe between the member countries of the North Atlantic Treaty Organization and the Warsaw Pact is probably the single most important consideration involved in decisions about the size, structure, and readiness of U.S. general purpose forces. Assessments of the military balance in Europe are of particular importance for decisions pertaining to the size and characteristics of ground combat and tactical air forces; the design of Navy antisubmarine warfare forces; and the role, characteristics, and levels of tactical nuclear weapons.[13]

There are now 4⅓ U.S. divisions and 22 U.S. tactical air force squadrons deployed in Europe. The equipment for another 2⅔ divisions is stockpiled on the continent. In the event of a crisis, the latter divisions would be airlifted from their bases in the United States, take up their predeployed equipment, and move expeditiously to the front lines. According to Secretary Schlesinger, at least 5 more active divisions, a number of reserve brigades, and 38 active and reserve tactical air force squadrons round out the force that the United States is prepared to commit to NATO's central front. Moreover, the United States stockpiles sufficient war reserves so that these 12 divisions and 60 tactical air force squadrons could fight for "longer than we believe that the Pact could sustain its attack."[14]

Since, in the event of a crisis, both the United States and the Soviet Union could significantly bolster the forces that they usually maintain in the region during peacetime, projections of the military balance in Europe must assess the situation at several points in time: at the onset of a crisis—mobilization (M) day—and at various points following a

12. The general issues of carrier force levels are discussed in Charles L. Schultze and others, *Setting National Priorities: The 1973 Budget* (Brookings Institution, 1972), pp. 121–27; and Arnold M. Kuzmack, *Naval Force Levels and Modernization: An Analysis of Shipbuilding Requirements* (Brookings Institution, 1971).

13. The military balance in Europe was discussed in *Setting National Priorities: The 1974 Budget*, pp. 353–59. A more complete account of the balance and its implications for U.S. forces can be found in Richard D. Lawrence and Jeffrey Record, *U.S. Force Structure in NATO: An Alternative* (Brookings Institution, 1974).

14. *Annual Defense Department Report, FY 1975*, Report of the Secretary of Defense James R. Schlesinger to the Congress on the FY 1975 Defense Budget and FY 1975–1979 Defense Program (March 4, 1974), p. 91.

decision to mobilize: M + 30 days, M + 60 days, M + 90 days. Often, choices must be made between capabilities that would be pertinent early in a crisis and those that would not be available in the combat theater until later on. For example, for a given cost, one could maintain either a number of troops on active duty in Europe, and therefore almost immediately available for combat, or a much larger number of reserve forces in the United States, which would not become available for some time. As mentioned in Chapter 4, changes in the U.S. posture for Europe envisioned in the fiscal 1975 budget proposal point to a greater emphasis in U.S. military planning on requirements to fight a short war with the Soviet Union in Europe (with some hedges against the possibility that protracted conflict might develop). This is being done partly at the expense of preparations for longer wars, but it is also adding to the cost of U.S. general purpose forces.

This new emphasis helps explain the measures proposed to improve the readiness of those U.S. combat forces already in or destined for Europe. The readiness of a military organization can be thought of as its potential to deploy and operate combat units in accordance with their designed objectives. This depends on both the quantity of men, equipment, and supplies available, and on such qualitative considerations as how well the men are trained and the condition in which the equipment is maintained. In brief, readiness specifies the amount and competence of available combat power.

For several years now, a series of reports from the General Accounting Office (GAO) and other indicators have pointed to deficiencies in the readiness of U.S. forces planned to be used in European contingencies. The GAO found particularly serious problems in the combat readiness of Air Force squadrons, in the quantity and condition of equipment prepositioned for use by the two and two-thirds quick reinforcement divisions, and in the condition of equipment of Army divisions in the United States.[15] Specific measures suggested by the administration to improve the readiness of U.S. general purpose forces were described in Chapter 4. It should be noted that these proposals will require expansion of some support forces. Increasing inventory levels, improving logistics networks, and reducing mainte-

15. Comptroller General's Report to the Congress, "Readiness of the Air Force in Europe," B-146896 (April 25, 1973; processed); ibid., "Problems with U.S. Military Equipment Prepositioned in Europe" (March 9, 1973; processed); and ibid., "Need for Improvement in Readiness of Strategic Army Forces" (May 8, 1972; processed).

nance backlogs all demand more manpower in support units (19,000 civilians alone). Thus, unless overall manpower levels are expanded, these measures will limit the degree to which the Defense Department can attain its objective of shifting manpower from support to combat categories.

The administration's decisions to increase the number of active-duty Army divisions (perhaps by as many as three), to cut back on reserve components, and to augment airlift capacity also seem to be founded on the judgment that the key to maintenance of a favorable military balance in Europe lies primarily with the magnitude of ground combat power which the United States could deploy to the continent within the first thirty days of a decision to mobilize. The decision to add more Army divisions is the most important one in terms both of future capabilities and future defense budgets.

Adding divisions will provide more of a margin for error in the very uncertain calculations of what is required to meet the threat to Europe's central front. Although the twelve-division–sixty-squadron commitment to NATO appears adequate, in combination with allied forces, to provide a balance of combat capabilities in central Europe sufficient to deter a Warsaw Pact attack, should deterrence fail, for whatever reason, and conflict erupt in central Europe, the outcome of the fighting would be hard to predict. NATO's position, in fact, can be made to appear more precarious simply by evaluating certain key assumptions more pessimistically—particularly those concerning the speed or covertness with which the opposition could mobilize and deploy its forces.

The Soviet Union's continuing programs to modernize its ground forces provide another reason for uncertainty about the military balance in Europe. Interest centers on a new Soviet tank, the T-70, which is now entering production and which is thought to be of a radically new design and therefore possibly of markedly improved capabilities. NATO never has attempted to match opposing forces in Europe quantitatively on a one-for-one basis, relying instead on its technological edge and on the qualitative superiority of its weapons. Continuing advances in Soviet weapon technology mean that the United States may find it more difficult to assure continuance of this qualitative edge, which implies that greater significance might be ascribed to any quantitative imbalances in the future.

Concern about U.S. commitments other than those to NATO strengthens the argument for adding divisions to the U.S. force structure. If twelve Army divisions were deployed to NATO's central front, under present force levels the United States would be left with one Army division in Korea, three Marine divisions, and nine reserve divisions. At least one of the Marine divisions would probably be used on NATO's flanks (for example, in the Mediterranean). The reserve divisions are of limited utility; most experts doubt that a reserve division could be deployed in less than six months. Thus, should a conflict—say in Korea—erupt simultaneously with one in Europe, the United States would have available at most two Marine and one Army divisions, and would therefore be hard pressed to meet its commitments without resorting to the use of nuclear weapons. This concern reflects, of course, second thoughts about the adminstration's decision in 1970 to discard the previous planning requirement that U.S. conventional forces should be sufficient to fight simultaneously in two major conflicts.

The decision that the United States should add Army divisions to its force structure also depended on factors other than evaluations of the military balance in Europe, and possible simultaneous needs for combat forces elsewhere in the eventuality of such a conflict. One such consideration is whether the Army could have been induced to move toward greater manpower efficiencies without the incentive of more combat units. Past experience does not provide grounds for great optimism on this score. A second consideration is how the announced policy of creating more divisions may affect negotiations with the USSR for mutual and balanced force reductions (MBFR) in Europe. Clearly, the least expensive way to ensure a stable balance in Europe is to induce the Soviets to control the size and character of their own forces. The administration's proposals to create more U.S. ground combat forces may well have been at least partly designed to bring about such an outcome in the talks now under way in Vienna.

Nonetheless, the decision to add Army divisions to the force structure implies substantial expenditures in the future. Annual direct and indirect operating costs will come to about $1 billion for every division added to the force. Also, new divisions must be equipped; for an armored division, these one-time expenses would total about $450 million. Finally, either the new units must be stationed in Europe or their equipment predeployed there—both unlikely eventualities—or additional airlift capacity must be purchased if the new divisions are to be useful in a short war. Incremental expenditures necessary for these purposes are difficult to estimate but would not be negligible.

The magnitude of these costs alone is sufficient reason to expect careful review of the decision to expand the Army's force structure in the future, as trends in the military balance in Europe become more clear, as the negotiations toward mutual force reductions in Europe progress, and as the scope of potential savings in manpower assigned to support elements is defined.

The Range of Choice in Defense Spending

A broad consensus now seems to exist in the United States about the objectives of U.S. foreign policy and about those foreign interests that are most important for national security. In a general sense, there also is agreement on the roles which U.S. military forces play in protecting those interests. However, even within this framework of common assumptions, contrary views on the specific relationship between alternative military postures and the achievement of foreign policy objectives, and alternative interpretations of the direction, extent, and meaning of recent trends in the military balances described above allow widely differing conclusions with regard to the proper size and composition of the defense budget.

It is generally agreed that the United States has an interest in ensuring that *Western Europe* does not again succumb to war, political extremism, or economic isolation and depression. This objective has now been met for more than twenty-five years, and deployment of U.S. forces in Europe plays an important role in its continuance. U.S. troops contribute to the presently perceived balance between the Warsaw Pact countries and NATO power in central Europe, and between German and non-German military power in Western Europe. They also help to maintain the close association between Western Europe and the United States. All of these are important underpinnings of the peace and prosperity that have characterized Western Europe for the past quarter of a century. There are some grounds for doubt, however, as to whether this deployment of U.S. forces will be needed on the same scale in the 1980s as it is now. A smaller number of U.S. forces might well achieve the same effect as the current presence of 300,000 troops in Europe and the backup forces in the United States committed to NATO—particularly if there is an MBFR agreement or significant progress toward closer integration of Western Europe's military forces.

The likelihood of overt aggression against *Japan*, as against Europe, is remote. The dangers lie elsewhere: in Japan's possible reliance once more on national military—and perhaps nuclear—power to assure its security and economic welfare. Large-scale Japanese rearmament would be profoundly destabilizing in Asia. Japan is most likely to remain a lightly armed nonnuclear power in the context of a close U.S.–Japanese association which convinces Japan's leaders and public that U.S. policies will safeguard Japanese concerns. Many Japanese see the deployment of U.S. forces to Japan itself, to Korea, and to the seas about Japan as a necessary guarantee that this will be the case. If tensions in the area continue to decline, the level of local U.S. force deployments needed to make this guarantee credible may also decline. As in Europe, however, if pressures for a larger and potentially destabilizing Japanese national military effort are not to grow, some deployment of U.S. forces in the region will remain prudent.

In the *Third World,* U.S. security interests are generally seen as limited to a few areas. The United States continues to have a special interest in excluding hostile external bases and forces from the Caribbean. The defense of Korea, as we noted, is viewed by many Japanese as important to their country's security; they may make the same calculation, albeit on a lesser scale, about Taiwan. The commitment to Israel is likely to remain one of the constants in U.S. foreign policy. But none of these interests suggest the need for as sizable U.S. forces as in the case of Western Europe and Japan. The Middle East is potentially the most explosive area; but even here, U.S. forces that might be required are subsumed within the U.S. forces committed to NATO. If significant progress is made toward an effective settlement in the Middle East, the need for U.S. naval deployments to the eastern Mediterranean could decline along with the need for U.S. land forces deployed in Europe. Outside these specific areas, the United States' principal interest in the third world is perceived to be to help attain a reasonable degree of economic progress; over the longer term, a developing world that succumbed to poverty and bitterness could be expected to threaten global peace and prosperity in ways that are none the less real for being hard to predict.

U.S. relations with the *communist countries* are, for the most part, a function of U.S. interests in the developed and developing countries. Confrontations between the United States and the Soviet Union or China have focused on third nations, not on bilateral issues. Hence, perceived requirements for U.S. military forces to balance communist power proceed largely from U.S. interests in the noncommunist areas noted above. There is one exception, however; the competition in strategic nuclear power seems to have a life of its own. Whatever happens elsewhere, U.S. strategic forces are viewed as necessary to balance and to deter Soviet strategic power. While U.S. strategic power is now sufficient from a military standpoint, and while it is difficult to foresee trends that would change this situation, the question remains as to whether such power will continue to be politically adequate. One test of political sufficiency is whether U.S. strategic forces continue to deter Soviet leaders from any attempt to exploit their military power in ways that might endanger peace. There is little evidence on which to base a judgment, but it seems reasonable to assume that Soviet views will hinge to a considerable degree on how confidently the U.S. government views its own capabilities.

Much the same might be said of the views of other nations toward the strategic balance, and of Soviet and third nation views toward the other military balances discussed in this chapter. A good deal more attention is likely to be paid to political attitudes toward defense in the United States than to the details of the U.S. defense posture— assuming, of course, that a radical decline in U.S. military capabilities relative to those of its adversaries is avoided. Moderate reductions in forces, based on rational appraisals of military and political needs, are less likely to jeopardize important U.S. interests than are reductions based on a broad evaluation that discounts the role of force in international affairs. This is a very imprecise guide to defense policy, but defense is an area in which prudence enjoins policymakers to be as aware of the uncertainty as of the importance that must attend many decisions.

It is perhaps because of these two factors—the high cost of being wrong and the uncertainties attending judgments—that Congress has been loathe to tamper with the defense budgets proposed to it by the executive branch in the past.

Most congressmen feel that they have neither the personal expertise nor the staff resources to challenge the administration's judgments in the field of national security. Of course, there are exceptions, and particular issues—such as the Safeguard ABM System or U.S. troops in Europe—sometimes have galvanized congressional initiatives to change administration policies. On the whole, however, congressmen have been content to exhort the administration to be as efficient as possible in the management of resources allocated to defense, to protect the interests of their home districts with regard to decisions on military bases or defense contracts, and to cut the proposed defense budget each year, by no more than 4 or 5 percent. The indications are that reception of the fiscal 1975 defense proposal will be no different. If anything, the political atmosphere in Congress is more receptive than usual to the administration's defense program.

Nonetheless, this is a year in which the congressional debate about the defense budget will be of more than ordinary significance. The Nixon administration has reached two fundamental judgments about the nation's defense requirements. First, it recognized that there is indeed room for greater efficiency in the management of defense resources, as critics have long maintained. Reductions in support forces, cuts in headquarters personnel, pruning of strategic air defenses, slowdowns in some weapon modernization programs, initiatives to develop less expensive weapon systems, elimination of some kinds of reserve forces, closer association of reserve and active duty units, and other initiatives contained in the fiscal 1975 defense proposal have all been urged for several years from both within and outside the Pentagon. In accepting these suggestions, however, the administration reached the second judgment that the savings which result from these measures to improve the efficiency of the nation's defense structure should be turned into greater combat power. As a result, it is proposed that in the future, spending for defense increase at roughly the same rate as the nation's economy, which means that there would be no room for a shift in federal spending from military to civilian purposes.

Alternative views may be suggested, without challenging the common set of foreign policy assumptions described above.

Defense expenditures could decline as a share of gross national product if military forces were planned on the basis of either or both of the following assumptions: (1) a more optimistic appraisal than that expressed by the Department of Defense of trends in the military balances described in this chapter, or (2) that achievement of the political purposes believed to be served by increased U.S. military capabilities—reassurance of allies, deterrence of risky initiatives by adversaries, leverage in arms control negotiations—depend to a greater extent upon the generalized image of the United States power held by foreign nations. In turn, this image, within some limits, is likely to depend more on factors such as the strength of the U.S. economy, the U.S. willingness to participate actively in world affairs, and the strength of the U.S. political leadership than on the specific details of the nation's military posture.

One stance on the proper size of the defense budget based on such evaluations would suggest that efficiencies proposed in the 1975 budget be enacted, but that combat capabilities remain at the levels outlined in the original fiscal 1974 request. The adoption of this strategy might result in a fiscal 1980 defense budget some $10 billion less than that projected for the administration's program.

A second stance, based on less pessimistic views of the military balance or more narrow judgments as to the utility of military force in the present international system, would argue for actual reductions in combat capabilities in addition to the cuts justified solely on the basis of efficiency. The size of such reductions would vary of course with the specifics of the forces proposed to be cut, but defense budgets some $20 to $25 billion less than the fiscal 1980 projection of the administration's position would more or less define the lower limit of serious proposals in this regard.[17]

On the other hand, events during the past year, particularly the Soviet role in the Middle East and other setbacks in East-West détente, could be taken to demonstrate the need for defense budgets larger than that proposed by the administration. Such a view would be based mainly on a more pessimistic appraisal of trends in the military balance, on a greater suspicion of Soviet motives and long-term intentions, and on the accordance of greater importance to military force in determining the future course of international political and economic relations. While comprehensive and detailed proposals for defense programs larger than the one suggested by the administration have not been made public in recent years, one could easily sketch a program for accelerated weapon modernization and augmented force levels that might cost $5 billion to $10 billion more than the administration's program in fiscal 1980.

IN SUM, judgments about the relationship between alternative military postures and the achievement of foreign policy objectives, much more than technical military considerations, are the major determinants of the size of the investment in national security. All the more reason, therefore, to encourage thorough public discussion of the defense budget.

17. See, *Setting National Priorities: The 1974 Budget*, pp. 394–402, for details of such proposals.

6. Federal Energy Policies

IN 1973 AMERICA AWOKE to an energy crisis. After years of seemingly unlimited supplies of energy products at low prices, it suddenly appeared that the oil wells had run dry. Gas stations were closed on Sundays and often early on other days, absurdly long lines formed at their pumps, heating oil was rationed, plane flights were canceled for lack of fuel, farmers had no fuel to plow their fields or to dry their crops, and truckers, angry at high fuel prices and delays, went out on strike.

Even though the dollar amounts involved are relatively small, the Budget Message accords special attention to the energy question. The President announced Project Independence, which allocates $10 billion for an accelerated program of energy research and development over the next five years. He has also proposed a Unified Transportation Assistance Program, which was partly justified as an energy measure. Tax proposals include a new windfall profits tax on oil producers and the tightening of certain tax advantages that favor U.S. producers operating in foreign countries. Congress has been considering further provisions in various energy bills ranging from a rollback of prices to the removal of such long-standing tax provisions as percentage depletion. These measures—the choices each involves in terms of overall policy objectives and strategy—are the subject of this chaper.

First, we briefly describe the nature of the energy problem, the underlying objectives of government energy policies, and certain

133

broad strategies for achieving these objectives. We then examine the administration's budgetary proposals to see how they relate to these objectives. And we conclude with a specific discussion of each proposal—its advantages and disadvantages—together with some alternatives that merit consideration.

The Nature of the Energy Crisis

The facts of the energy situation are by now fairly well known. U.S. energy demands, in part stimulated by prices which have been low by world standards, have grown rapidly in the past fifteen years— at an average rate of almost 5 percent since 1960. Today the United States, with 6.5 percent of the world's population, consumes about 35 percent of the world's energy, or roughly twice as much per capita as the other developed countries.[1]

Traditionally these energy needs have been supplied domestically. The United States has always produced its own coal (about 18 percent of current consumption of energy), natural gas (33 percent), hydroelectric power (4 percent), and nuclear power (1 percent). It is only in petroleum (amounting to 44 percent of domestic consumption) that the United States has had to draw on foreign supplies, and even this is a relatively recent development. The mandatory oil import quota held petroleum imports at roughly 20 percent of domestic consumption throughout the 1960s. But as demand continued to grow rapidly, and domestic production leveled off due to the gradual exhaustion of the best domestic reserves, the need for imported petroleum products accelerated. The oil import quota was selectively relaxed in the late 1960s and early 1970s, and it had to be abandoned altogether in April 1973 when a gasoline shortage threatened. As a result, projections made before the Arab countries' selective embargo on oil exports indicated that imports would grow rapidly, particularly those from the Middle East. Whereas in 1973 imports amounted to 35 percent of domestic petroleum consumption, with 30 percent of these imports coming from the Middle East, pre-embargo projections had these proportions rising sharply for the rest of the decade.[2]

1. W. N. Peach, *The Energy Outlook for the 1980's*, A Study Prepared for the Use of the Subcommittee on Economic Progress of the Joint Economic Committee, 93 Cong. 1 sess. (1973), p. 8.
2. Energy Policy Project of the Ford Foundation, *Exploring Energy Choices: A Preliminary Report* (Washington, D.C.: The Energy Policy Project, 1974), p. 6.

The events in the Middle East therefore hit the United States at a time when its demand for petroleum imports was growing rapidly and domestic supplies were more or less constant at 1970 levels. The selective embargo by Saudi Arabia, Kuwait, Libya, and other Arab countries was accompanied by a production cutback amounting to 12 percent of world demand and, later, by an enormous price increase by all petroleum-exporting countries, which raised international prices for petroleum to more than three times their early 1973 levels. The price increase changed the nature of the energy crisis; it meant that even if the selective embargo were lifted the United States and other consumer nations would have great difficulty in paying the going world prices.

The problems caused by this energy shortage are as pervasive as they are serious. Internationally, the production cutbacks and higher petroleum prices are expected to increase the earnings of petroleum-exporting countries by over $60 billion between 1973 and 1974, about $10 billion of which is from the developing countries. The payments from developed countries are causing serious inflationary problems. The increased payments from developing countries—almost 20 percent more than their annual foreign aid receipts—threaten the ability of many of these countries to maintain even their current modest development efforts. If such payments continue, they may reduce essential imports of food and fertilizer to dangerous levels in many nations.

The United States has fared relatively well by international standards, but there have of course been grave difficulties here as well. Government policymakers have had to face several different types of problems. The most immediate, for the newly formed Federal Energy Office, was simply to survive the short-run pinch without acute shortages of any of the essential petroleum products. This goal now seems to have been achieved. There have been dislocations, but for the most part no major disasters. The second type of problem (discussed in Chapter 3) is how to deal with the macroeconomic implications of the energy shortage, which in 1974 is likely to cause a simultaneous rise in the unemployment rate and the rate of inflation. The third type of problem—the one on which we focus here—concerns long-run government energy objectives and strategy. What, after all, is the government trying to achieve, and how should budgetary policies be adapted to reach these goals?

Federal Energy Policy Objectives

For the most part energy is produced and consumed in the private sector in the United States. The appropriate role for budgetary policy can then be most easily described in terms of how private market prices fail to reflect the true desires of society: where, and in what way, should the government use its budgetary instruments to improve on the price structure and patterns of production and consumption established by the free market?

It is generally agreed that there are four important grounds for government intervention:

• *Short-run protection of consumers and business firms against international trade disruptions.* Energy is essential in so many areas that the government has to take measures to ensure that households and firms are insulated against the effects of short-term trade disruptions of the sort experienced in 1973.

• *Long-run protection against resource exhaustion.* Most energy sources are finite; thus the U.S. government may have to protect future generations from the effects of excessive present-day depletion and consumption of these exhaustible supplies.

• *Protection of the environment.* Similarly, the government should, through its taxing and regulatory powers, ensure that any environmental costs are reflected in the price structure which guides the production and consumption of energy resources.

• *Assurance of a proper distribution of income between producers and consumers.* Since oil prices and profits have increased so greatly there has been a massive shift of purchasing power away from households and toward oil companies. The government might, therefore, want to take certain actions to modify this shift.

Protection against International Trade Disruptions

Certainly, the most important of these objectives at the present time is to minimize the disruptions caused by either reductions in the supply of foreign oil or increases in its price. Petroleum is an indispensable commodity in the United States because it is so widely used and so difficult to replace. Consequently, the nation will be dependent on imports of Middle Eastern petroleum until the year 1980 at the earliest, and probably beyond that date. This gives petroleum-exporting countries very great economic power, which some of them may be tempted to use to influence U.S. foreign policy. Although at this stage of national and worldwide economic development it is inconceivable that the United States would be able to protect itself against foreign trade disruptions in all, or even many, essential commodities, petroleum is one commodity for which it might be both feasible and worthwhile to make the effort. If such a policy were followed, the United States and the rest of the world might have much greater leverage in dealing with petroleum-exporting countries, and the United States might be in a much better position to conduct its foreign policy and to limit world prices for petroleum.

There are two ways to reduce dependence on imports. One is to become self-sufficient, the goal of the administration's announced Project Independence. The other is to adopt what might be called an import disruption insurance policy. A policy of self-sufficiency at least in its strictest sense implies that the United States would not import any of its energy products, while an insurance strategy encourages such imports so long as they are cheaper than domestically produced supplies and so long as certain measures are taken to protect the economy against import embargoes or price increases. In this sense, the insurance strategy, while it may only be feasible within certain limits, would be much better geared to maintain low-cost domestic consumption than self-sufficiency. It can take advantage of any future glut in the world market that might force petroleum prices down to lower levels, whereas self-sufficiency cannot.

The disruption insurance strategy features two key elements: stockpiling or establishing standby reserves that could quickly expand domestic supplies should foreign imports be restricted; and measures, such as coupon rationing schemes or even the support of alternative modes of urban transportation, that would quickly reduce demand. The latter is one of the justifications for subsidizing mass transit, as proposed in the 1975 budget. The insurance strategy also implies that government-owned energy resources—the large oil shale deposits in Wyoming, Colorado, and Utah, Alaskan oil, offshore oil on all three coasts—might be used like temporary stockpiles. Supplies would only be released to the market if foreign trade or other disruptions drove prices to very high levels. On the negative side, such a strategy argues strongly against high import tariffs or quotas to keep prices high throughout the entire domestic market. The government might guarantee high prices in some instances to assist infant industries that might eventually produce substitutes for petroleum, but this should only be done on a temporary and restricted basis.

The main problem with the insurance strategy is that it may be limited in scope. It may become very costly to stockpile enough petroleum to provide real protection, to keep government-owned reserves in a state of sufficient readiness, or to maintain spare urban transit capacity. In this case there would be no choice but to try to achieve full or partial self-sufficiency in energy. Again, this could be accomplished by measures either to increase supply or to reduce demand. The government could support a vigorous research and development program to develop substitutes for imported petroleum—oil shale, coal gasification or liquefaction, nuclear power. Or the government could support activities such as urban mass transit that would reduce the demand for energy. Finally, whatever the underlying strategy, the government should eliminate any tax advantages that encourage foreign rather than domestic petroleum investment, and thus run counter to the objective of protecting against trade disruptions.

Protection against Resource Exhaustion

The second objective concerns the fact that fossil fuels, which now account for 95 percent of U.S. energy consumption, are in finite supply. In other industries when demand increases producers simply produce more, but there are natural limits to the production of fossil fuel resources. These limits can easily be overrated—current estimates indicate that the United States has between 50 and 100 years' supply of natural gas and conventional petroleum, over 100 years' supply of oil shale, almost 800 years' supply of coal, and nearly inexhaustible supplies of uranium for nuclear fission and hydrogen for nuclear fusion. Nevertheless, the federal government might be prepared to take conservation measures to preserve exhaustible fuel supplies.[3] In this sense, conservation policy is intended to protect the low-cost consumption of

3. Estimates of the amount of oil, coal, and natural gas that ultimately can be recovered from deposits in and offshore from the United States vary greatly. These relatively conservative estimates of ultimate recovery from potential resources (expressed in years' supply at 1972 rates of domestic consumption) come from the following sources: oil and natural gas resource estimates and recovery rates: O. N. Miller and others, *Future Petroleum Provinces of the United States* (Washington: National Petroleum Council, 1970), pp. 1–2; shale resource and recovery estimate: P. K. Theobald, S. P. Schweinfurth, and D. C. Duncan, *Energy Resources of the United States*, Circular 650 (Washington: U.S. Geological Survey, 1972), pp. 25–26; coal resource and recovery estimate: ibid., pp. 3–4; Consumption rates, 1972: *Fiscal Policy and the Energy Crisis*, Briefing Material Prepared by the Staff of the U.S. Senate Committee on Finance, 93 Cong. 1 sess. (1973), p. 3.

future generations just as the strategy of import independence protects that of the current generation.

But what the appropriate policy should be is not entirely clear. Economic theory suggests that if investors have realistic long-run expectations, the free market will set appropriate prices for reserves of finite mineral resources. If prices become too low, encouraging rapid consumption and depletion of resources, impending scarcities and higher prices will be perceived by investors who will then bid up prices and discourage use. If prices become too high, as may be the case in the current world market, investors will eagerly invest in new supplies and bring down prices. Since the private market does have these equilibrating properties, the case for explicit government conservation policies hinges on whether private expectations are generally appropriate from a social point of view—whether, in fact, the private market places the appropriate premium on present, as opposed to future, production and consumption.

Although it is possible to make a case for government intervention to conserve resources as a policy to be followed most of the time—on the grounds that the private market will, if anything, encourage too much current instead of future consumption—that argument may not be relevant to today's needs. It seems strange to advise a nation struggling under the immediate effects of the Arab embargo and price increases to worry about the low-price consumption of future generations. Prices have already risen to such levels that it is hard to describe them as being too low; supplies have been temporarily cut so drastically that it is absurd to limit the rapid expansion of domestic production. Therefore, if the short-run problem is to be solved, the United States must allow maximum short-run expansion of domestic output even if it depletes the supplies available for future generations.

In the longer run, however, maximum domestic output may eventually lead to difficulties, and conservation could become a more important priority. This suggests that the federal government should, at a minimum, eliminate current tax advantages such as percentage depletion and the provision that producers may "expense" their intangible costs of drilling, which actually encourage depletion of exhaustible fossil fuel resources relative to other substitute forms of energy whose supplies are inexhaustible.[4] The conservation objective also implies a vigorous energy research and development program in areas

4. See page 159 below.

such as nuclear fusion, geothermal, and solar energy to find long-run inexhaustible substitutes for fossil fuels.

Protection of the Environment

A third objective is to protect the environment. Many types of environmental pollution are directly related to production and consumption of energy fuels—offshore oil drilling may risk spillage and cause water pollution, stripmining of coal defaces the landscape and creates undesirable waste matter, burning high-sulfur coal and oil leads to heavy concentrations of sulfur oxides and particulate matter in the air, and burning automobile gasoline to heavy concentrations of carbon monoxide and smog-producing oxidants. The true social cost of consuming these energy resources is therefore higher than that set by the free market, because the production and consumption of these commodities by some worsens the environment for everyone else. This calls for federal action to see that environmental costs are included in the prices that motivate producers and consumers.

The two broad strategies proposed to alleviate pollution side effects are, first, to prohibit certain activities; and, second, to use various kinds of taxes and other charges so that the social costs are included in the relevant prices. There are cases where highly toxic substances make outright prohibitions mandatory, but in general this strategy tends to emphasize the incompatibility of the two goals of increasing energy production and preserving the environment. The alternative approach of forcing producers and consumers to pay the true social cost of their actions may largely eliminate this incompatibility. Such a quasi-price system can resolve environmental conflicts just as the true price system resolves conflicts between domestic and foreign producers, present and future consumers, and so forth. If, for example, coal-mining companies were allowed to stripmine but were forced to pay for their own waste disposal and to repair the landscape, they would treat this payment as a cost just like any other cost, the price of coal would rise by some appropriate amount, and consumption demand would be appropriately reduced. Coal producers would then have an incentive to restore the landscape, just as the market today stimulates them to find cheap ways of mining coal.[5]

5. See Allen V. Kneese and Charles L. Schultze, tentatively titled *Controlling Air and Water Pollution: Economic Incentives versus Regulation*, a joint project by Resources for the Future and the Brookings Institution (Brookings; forthcoming, 1974), for an argument of this position.

Although conflicts between the goal of protecting the environment and that of expanding domestic energy supplies have risen often during the past year, the most significant budgetary question in this area concerns subsidies for urban mass transit, where the two goals are in harmony. The private automobile has always been one of the prime sources of air pollution in urban areas. In addition, it imposes other social costs, such as those for road construction and maintenance. Thus there are grounds either for taxing urban automobile commuting, possibly through a parking tax, or for subsidizing mass transit to reflect these social costs. This may be a particularly opportune time for mass transit subsidies because the current high prices and recent lack of gasoline in many large urban areas have dramatized the need for alternative forms of transportation.

An Equitable Distribution of Income

Most people would agree that the federal government has an interest in using its tax and transfer system to bring about a more equitable distribution of income than that generated by the free market. Although this issue is usually not relevant to a discussion of any one industry, the size and pervasiveness of the market for fuels is so enormous that short-run disruptive events such as the energy shortage can create tremendous windfall profits for large petroleum and natural gas firms, larger even than could be involved in important new federal programs for tax or welfare reform. There are correspondingly large losses for consumers in all income classes. These massive shifts in purchasing power are all the more painful when they occur at a time when households and businesses are suffering the chaos and dislocations of an energy crisis. An argument can be made that these windfall profits should be diverted either to the federal treasury or back to consumers, provided that measures can be devised to accomplish this without adversely affecting incentives to expand production or restrict consumption.

There are two alternatives. Either the federal government can let energy prices rise and tax away profits or it can prevent prices from rising in the first place. The latter approach is more direct and seems to be more popular—it was followed for many years by the Federal Power Commission in regard to natural gas, and a petroleum price rollback was also a part of the Energy Emergency Act which the President vetoed in March 1974. There is doubt, however, that such measures do more than transmit misleading market signals. If it really costs more than $0.22 per thousand cubic feet (the regulated price throughout the 1960s) to produce enough natural gas to satisfy demand, no particular social purpose is served when producers have no profit incentive to exploit natural gas costing more than $0.22 and when consumers consume as if the price were only $0.22. Such a policy to limit prices only creates unsatisfied demand now and real scarcities and very high prices later. At the same time, on certain occasions it could be desirable to limit the rapid price increases resulting from the economy's difficulty in adjusting to short-run disruptions —both to maintain household purchasing power and to prevent these temporary increases from developing into a more permanent inflation —as long as there are sufficient inducements for households to restrict consumption and producers to expand production.

How These Objectives Can Be Achieved through the Budget

We have already mentioned some ways in which budgetary instruments such as research and development expenditures, urban mass transit subsidies, and special tax measures can be used to achieve the four objectives discussed above.

They are summarized in Table 6-1. Except for elimination of percentage depletion and "expensing" of intangible drilling costs, all have recently been proposed by the administration.

The budgetary implications of these items are given in Table 6-2. Besides showing the two expenditure initiatives—energy research and development and urban mass transit support—the table also lists four major tax subsidy proposals. The administration's windfall profits tax is unique to energy producers and clearly belongs in this category, together with the special tax provisions that subsidize domestic and foreign operations of oil and gas firms. Table 6-2 does not include a host of other energy-related items in the budget—revenues from leasing offshore oil deposits, expenditures of the Tennessee Valley Authority and the Federal Power Commission, and so forth—because they involve no important policy changes.

Explicit budgetary totals are given for fiscal 1975 and very tentative estimates for 1980. The administration plan for energy research and development, for example, entails expenditures of $10 billion for five years, of which the first installment is $1.5 billion for fiscal 1975. We have therefore estimated that by 1980 expenditures will be running

Table 6-1. Relation between the Objectives of Energy Policy and Major Budgetary Instruments

	Energy policy objective			
Budget instrument	*Protection against trade disruption*	*Exhaustion of energy resources*	*Protection of the environment*	*Redistribution of income*
Research and development, near-term technologies	X	...	X	...
Research and development, inexhaustible resource technologies	...	X	...	...
Urban mass transit support	X	...	X	...
Windfall profits tax	...	...	...	X
Elimination of percentage depletion or of expensing intangible drilling costs[a]	...	X	...	X
Elimination of foreign tax advantages	X	...	...	...

a. Not proposed by the administration, but recommended by the House Ways and Means Committee.

at the annual rate of $2.0 billion. The Unified Transportation Assistance Program is allocated $2.5 billion in 1975 and $2.7 billion in 1980. The windfall profits tax is estimated to bring in $3 billion of net revenues in fiscal 1975. The revenue loss implied in continuation of depletion allowances and intangible drilling costs is estimated at $3.1 billion for 1975 and very tentatively at $3.7 billion in 1980, though the latter figure could be higher or lower depending on the 1980 price of oil and the amount being produced. It is similarly difficult to estimate the revenue gain achieved by the administration's proposed elimination of foreign tax advantages, but it is not a very large amount.

Expenditures for Research and Development in Energy*

Whereas the administration proposed spending $10 billion on energy research and development over a five-year period, the Senate passed a bill that goes even further, allotting $20 billion to this purpose over a ten-year period.

Although the $1.5 billion total outlay for fiscal 1975 is small in relation to that for defense and space research, it is nonetheless more

* Prepared with the assistance of Carl R. Gerber.

Table 6-2. Budget Items Relevant to Energy Objectives, Fiscal Years 1975 and 1980
Billions of dollars

Budget item	1975	1980
Research and development	**1.5**	**2.0**
Nuclear breeder reactor	0.4	
Nuclear fission	0.2	
Nuclear fusion	0.1	
Coal	0.3	
Solar and geothermal energy	0.1	
Environment	0.1	
Conservation	0.1	
Other	0.2	
Urban mass transit	**2.5**	**2.7**
Construction of transit facilities, mainly rail	0.7	0.7
Highway construction and improvement[a]	1.1	⎫ 2.0
Mass transit, optional use	0.7	⎭
Tax subsidies for energy producers	**−0.1**	**3.5**
Windfall profits tax	−3.0	
Continuation of percentage depletion	2.7	3.2
Continuation of expensing, intangible drilling costs	0.4	0.5
Elimination of foreign tax advantages	−0.2	−0.2

Sources: Tabulations prepared by the U.S. Office of Management and Budget; "Unified Transportation Assistance Program," Fact Sheet released by the Office of the White House Press Secretary, February 13, 1974; Gerard M. Brannon, "The Revenue Costs for Energy Tax Incentives: Underlying Assumptions," Tax Analysts and Advocates, *Tax Notes*, Vol. 2 (Feb. 4, 1974), pp. 5–10; testimony of Secretary of the Treasury George P. Shultz before the House Committee on Ways and Means, in "Department of the Treasury News," S-357, Feb. 4, 1974.

a. In fiscal 1975, $0.2 billion of this money *can* be spent on mass transit; if not, it is available for highways. In fiscal 1980, the entire amount can be spent on either mass transit or highways.

than twice the amount spent in 1973. In earlier years these expenditures were heavily concentrated on nuclear research—specifically on the development of the fast breeder reactor—but the 1975 requests show sharp increases for research and development of coal, solar, and geothermal technologies and for various other environmental and conservation programs.

There is an important difference between energy research and energy development programs. In research on, say, power from nuclear fusion or geothermal energy, the payoff is likely to be distant and uncertain. Although some projects of this nature are being conducted in the private sector, it is generally not profitable enough for private industry to carry out the type of basic research needed to develop new energy sources. Hence the government might be required to support these activities in line with its long-run conservation objectives.

The more immediate aspect concerns the development of technologies for replacing imported petroleum. Here the objective is not so much discovering basic scientific principles as it is promoting the development of certain industries. There is a whole series of strategic decisions that must be made to determine the character of government support. What is the rationale for public support? Would the process be developed anyway in the private sector? Can the process be carried out on a large enough scale? Will foreign competition inhibit development investment? Is some sort of price guarantee warranted? Should there be joint public-private partnerships, or even public corporations? These activities also raise important questions of industrial organization, such as whether it makes sense for the government to plow large sums into research on substitutes for oil without at the same time limiting the degree to which oil companies can buy up oil shale, coal, and natural gas resources, and thereby limit the competition from these potential substitutes. The government is just beginning to confront these questions.

A final question is whether government-supported research should concentrate on expanding supplies or on reducing demands for energy. The administration's proposal includes a small amount of funding for demand reduction research, mainly to improve the efficiency of processes for generating, transmitting, and storing electrical power. This type of research seems eligible for public support because the profit rates of private power companies are regulated and they may not have sufficient incentive to do their own research. Whether the government should go beyond this in supporting demand-reduction research depends on whether there are promising research activities of general applicability that would not be undertaken by the private sector. These activities might be much less costly than projects that expand supply, or they might simply duplicate the efforts of private producers to find ways to reduce their own energy demands or the energy required to use their products.

Each of the proposed techniques to increase domestic output of energy and thereby increase protection against short-run trade disruptions and long-run resource exhaustion raises somewhat different issues in science, engineering, and economics. We briefly consider them in turn and suggest guidelines for public policy.

Conventional Petroleum

An important way to expand domestic energy output in the relatively near term is to produce more oil and natural gas from existing wells.

If the natural energy in a reservoir is used to extract the oil, an average of only 25 percent of the petroleum will be recovered. Secondary and tertiary techniques, such as gas or water injection, flooding, and explosive fracturing, can raise this percentage to about 40 percent, and new techniques may increase the ultimate recovery rate to as high as 60 percent. But there will still remain a large volume of discovered, but economically unrecoverable, oil in the ground. There are also supplies of oil and natural gas in wells previously abandoned or considered uneconomic, and in reservoirs deeper than existing ones or located on the outer continental shelves. Further engineering research might lead to new ways of capturing more oil and gas from each of these sources.

Yet it is doubtful that this research should be supported by the government. World and relevant domestic prices for petroleum have more than tripled in three years and there has been a similar increase in the supply price for natural gas; both provide enormous price incentives for existing private producers to expand drilling operations. There are no extraordinary capital costs for this type of drilling, it is not significantly more risky than present-day drilling operations, and, as we suggest below, the current cash resources of existing producers are more than adequate to undertake ambitious new investment programs. All this would argue against large federal investment in this form of research, though it would suggest also that the natural incentive of higher prices in encouraging supplies should not be impeded.

Oil Shale

Although the United States still has plenty of conventional undrilled petroleum, an even greater potential source of oil is a laminated marl rock (shale) containing a tarlike material called kerogen, or oil shale. When heated to 450 to 600 degrees centigrade, kerogen releases a number of liquid and gaseous petroleum products along with pure carbon. These products can then be refined to produce the petroleum products in use today. Most observers consider oil shale to be the next most economic source of petroleum, or "backstop" technology.

While some oil shale technology has been laboratory-tested, a pilot plant operated, and the first of extensive government-owned lands in the West put up for bid, the technology is still in a relatively unsophisticated early stage. Present estimates of the cost of producing petroleum from oil shale are on the order of $6 a barrel, well below the current supply price of from $8 to $10 for new domestic oil. But there are several drawbacks to the development of oil shale as an alternative fuel source. Significant environmental costs involved in producing oil from shale—the process requires much water and presents a massive waste disposal problem—imply that the true social cost of oil shale might run higher than $6 a barrel. Moreover, the production process requires large capital investment and, hence, reasonable assurance to private entrepreneurs that the price will remain near its present level for a period of time. Were this not the case, mischievous foreign exporters could continually frustrate prospective oil shale producers by reducing prices just as the industry was getting on its feet. Research could be helpful in eliminating these drawbacks by developing in situ techniques (techniques for removing oil from shale without removing the shale from the ground, thus eliminating the waste disposal problem), in reducing the required amount of water, and in improving the methods for recovering oil from poorer quality deposits.

The question of whether the development of the oil shale industry should be supported by the government is a difficult one for policymakers. In favor of government support are the potentially significant increase in domestic petroleum output, the large capital costs and concomitant risk to be incurred by private investors, and the concern for possible environmental dangers. An argument against such support is the fact that private companies now are bidding for leases on government-owned shale lands and apparently think they can earn profits without government aid because they consider it likely that prices will remain high. It would be unfortunate for the government to support private industry when there is no need—this type of support soon becomes the next generation's "tired old government program." It could be just as unfortunate, however, to pass up an opportunity for possible commercial exploitation of the large U.S. shale resources for lack of the relatively small government outlay which might be required.

This question leads to a quandary about how to proceed with the development of the oil shale industry. Shale programs are not a significant feature of the administration's research and development plan. Instead, it prefers to rely on the high current prices for petroleum to stimulate the needed expansion of output, although it is offering publicly owned shale lands for lease at an accelerated rate. One way to introduce explicit governmental support would be through a publicly owned corporation to develop and produce energy from sources such as shale. This idea has the advantage of creating a special corporation that could serve as a yardstick for measuring oil company prices and profits; but it does rest on the possibly questionable supposition that the government can somehow produce oil at lower prices than private industry. An intermediate possibility, suggested by Hendrik Houthakker, which is more consistent with the basically private nature of the petroleum industry, would be a limited-duration government price guarantee program.[6] The federal government could lease its shale land as it does now, and agree beforehand to purchase a certain quantity of petroleum for a price of, say, $7 per barrel for a period of, say, five years. If the price for petroleum remained above this level, private producers could sell their output on the market without government intervention. If prices fell, the government could buy up the oil and either sell it on the market at a loss or stockpile it. The government could also hold these plants on a standby basis as part of a disruption insurance strategy. Government expenditures would thus not be unduly large even if petroleum prices fell, and in any case would end after the five-year period. But even though the government cost in these circumstances would be minimal, private producers would have price assurances for a reasonable length of time and presumably would be able to develop the industry. The adoption of this program would also eliminate pressures for import tariffs or other measures to maintain *all* domestic petroleum prices if world prices fell—the only supported price would be that for the infant shale industry.[7]

Coal

If the United States has abundant supplies of undrilled petroleum and shale, it has astronomical amounts of coal—enough to last almost 800 years at present rates of production or to supply the world's energy needs for nearly a century at vastly increased rates of production. Thus sometime in the future coal seems destined to resume the prominent role it played in the past. Accelerated programs for coal

6. See the testimony of Hendrik Houthakker before the U.S. Senate Committee on Interior and Insular Affairs, July 11, 1973.

7. We should also mention that such a price guarantee could even be given to individual plants, producing from oil shale or any other source, which install innovative technologies.

research also constitute the biggest new initiative in the administration's research proposal. Programs for research on the mining, usage, and pollution control aspects of coal represent one-fifth of the administration's budget for energy research and development for fiscal 1975, almost triple the amount spent in previous years.

There are four major grades of U.S. coal: anthracite, bituminous, subbituminous, and lignite. These classifications indicate the amounts of fixed carbon compounds, volatile organic compounds, water, sulfur, and ash in each grade. Anthracite coal, the most desirable coal in terms of both energy content and cleanliness, is in relatively short supply, constituting less than 2 percent of U.S. reserves. Most present use is of bituminous coal, the next most desirable form, but in the future it will be necessary to turn to the other two lower grades, which constitute somewhat more than half of the remaining reserves.

Coal causes serious environmental difficulties both when it is mined and when it is burned. The cheapest form of mining is strip mining, which has resulted in highly publicized problems of land reclamation. Deep mining has also been responsible for a long string of environmental problems including acid mine drainage, erosion, silting of streams, and fires, as well as very hazardous and unhealthful conditions for miners. Finally, the burning of coal produces harmful sulfur oxides and other particulate matter. Although the government-sponsored research proposed by the administration could presumably attack each one of these problems, it is important to remember that the simple device of taxing coal to reflect the true social costs of production and consumption, such as through a tax on sulfur emissions, would also generate strong incentives for private research in these areas.

Assuming the environmental problems of mining can eventually be solved, the most promising long-run way to use coal in the United States may be to convert it to either synthetic natural gas or synthetic petroleum, removing the undesirable sulfuric components in the process. The processes for gasifying coal are the furthest along—in fact, one process, the Lurgi method, has been used in Germany for over thirty years and is used in a commercial plant that began operation in New Mexico in 1974. The fact that private industry seems ready to take this step is encouraging, and raises considerable doubt that public subsidies would be required. Several other processes for developing gas from coal have also been laboratory-tested, each with advantages and disadvantages for different types of consumption, but more research is needed in every instance to determine economic feasibility. This could be the way for technology to provide near-term help in increasing the domestic output of energy resources—natural gas is a very clean and versatile fuel, and processes for coal gasification are almost commercially viable, costing roughly $1.50 per thousand cubic feet. (The present price for domestic natural gas is $0.52 per thousand cubic feet but rising; for imported liquified gas from Algeria it is about $1.20.)

It is also possible to synthesize petroleum from coal, though present estimates put the cost of petroleum from this source somewhat above that for oil from shale. The first government-funded pilot plant is under construction, however, and it will undoubtedly lead to future cost reductions, which could make such synthetic petroleum commercially feasible.

Nuclear Fission

The only new source of energy which the government has subsidized significantly in the past is nuclear power. The Atomic Energy Commission was established at the close of World War II and in recent years has been spending at the rate of about $0.5 billion per year on civilian energy research and development. Despite these expenditures, nuclear power has been something of a disappointment. Although it was introduced commercially in 1957, nuclear power accounted for only 4 percent of U.S. electricity generating capacity and 1 percent of total energy consumption in 1973.[8] These proportions are likely to increase, however, with the recent increases in fossil fuel prices. The administration has proposed a 20 percent increase in research and development expenditures on nuclear power, to a total of $0.7 billion in fiscal 1975, and it is trying to reduce the very long delays in approving and licensing nuclear power plants.

All present nuclear generation of electricity is based on the fission of uranium 235, an isotope which makes up less than 1 percent of natural uranium ore. Neutrons split this isotope into two parts, in the process releasing tremendous amounts of energy and neutrons that trigger additional fissioning. The energy released is then used to heat water or gas, which in turn generates electricity. Although a number of questions still remain unanswered as to the economic feasibility,

8. Peach, *The Energy Outlook for the 1980's*, pp. 4, 21.

safety, and environmental hazards, various systems are now in use throughout the world. In the United States the principal systems incorporate water-cooled reactors, though a commercial high temperature gas-cooled reactor is also under construction.

There are basically two problems with these processes. First, uranium 235 is relatively rare, a fact which has led to a separate technology designed to enrich natural uranium. Various enrichment processes are becoming commercially acceptable, but they also require tremendous amounts of energy. Second, water-cooled reactors are not very efficient—they use only about 1 percent of the fission energy of natural uranium (fuel efficiency) and can make use of only 32 percent of the energy they produce (operating efficiency). The gas-cooled reactors will do better, having a fuel efficiency of nearly 20 percent and an operating efficiency of 39 percent. But in the long run the best solution to this problem could be to use the fission-created neutrons to breed new fissionable material and hence add to energy supplies. This is the basis for the breeder reactor. In addition to having a fuel efficiency of from 50 to 70 percent and an operating efficiency of 40 percent, the breeder also effectively eliminates the need to conserve energy resources—it has been estimated that this process will extend present uranium supplies for about a million years. In the words of Robert Solow, "If this is not a backstop technology, it is at least a catcher who will not let by too many passed balls."[9]

But there are many serious problems with the breeder. The most difficult involve the present high cost of the process, currently about 20 percent above that of nonbreeding reactors, which is itself somewhat above the price of generating electricity from petroleum and natural gas.[10] The breeder is unlikely to become competitive unless the price of uranium oxide rises well above today's levels, hence making less efficient use of uranium 235 unprofitable. It also has rather questionable environmental aspects, particularly the disposal of long-lived radioactive wastes (unavoidable in any fission process). As these wastes accumulate, there would be an ever-increasing risk of environmental contamination. There is also a potentially serious problem of prevent-

9. This remark is taken from Robert Solow, "The Economics of Resources, or, the Resources of Economics," in American Economic Association, *Papers and Proceedings of the Eighty-sixth Annual Meeting, 1973* (*American Economic Review*, Vol. 64, May 1974).

10. See William D. Nordhaus, "The Allocation of Energy Resources," in *Brookings Papers on Economic Activity* (3:1973), p. 544.

ing nuclear theft. Consequently, most observers do not believe the breeder will be used until at least the 1990s, and some question whether it ever will.

Historically, U.S. energy research has supported nuclear power at the expense of nonnuclear power, and the breeder reactor at the expense of more immediately relevant forms of nuclear power. In fiscal 1973, for example, the total budget for energy research and development was $0.7 billion, of which the breeder alone received $0.3 billion and other nuclear power $0.2 billion. Although spending on both the breeder and other nuclear power have been stepped up in fiscal 1975, the most interesting feature of the administration's current proposal for energy research is the shift in emphasis toward coal and other nonnuclear forms of energy such as solar and geothermal power. Given the immediacy of today's needs and the potential safety and environmental dangers of nuclear power, this shift in emphasis appears long overdue. In fact, one could question why a strategy such as Project Independence should feature any increases at all in spending on the breeder reactor, since long-run conservation needs to which the breeder is addressed have not changed much in the past year.

Other Energy Sources

There are several other promising, but more speculative, sources of energy. Probably the most immediately relevant is solar energy. This can be used directly, in either heating and cooling buildings, or indirectly by collection through a large centralized system used to generate electricity. It is obviously inexhaustible (if it is not, there will be more to worry about than energy). Although there has been little research on solar energy until very recently, at least the heating and cooling process could be commercially competitive in some regions within a very short time. Demonstration houses and plants using solar heating are now being built; in 1973 the House of Representatives passed a bill authorizing $50 million over five years to subsidize the development of solar-powered heating and cooling systems.[11]

Another process features geothermal energy, or heat from the inner earth. The most widely used form of this energy source is a system in which water percolated into a region of fractured hot rock is used to heat houses or generate electricity. Although geothermal energy

11. H.R. 11864, 93 Cong. 1 sess.

is used in other countries and there are usable geothermal resources on federal lands in this country, there has been little systematic exploration to date of the potential for geothermal power.

A third source of energy, which has been supported to some degree by past research, is nuclear fusion. Whereas nuclear fission involves the splitting of heavy nuclei, fusion involves merging light nuclei such as the hydrogen isotopes deuterium and tritium to form a new element, thereby releasing tremendous amounts of energy. Deuterium is found in water and tritium may be bred from lithium, which is abundantly available. Thus nuclear fusion is also based on an inexhaustible resource supply. However, its main problem and the reason it may be only a long-run alternative is that the fusion reaction takes place at temperatures of millions of degrees, which makes it difficult to contain.

One of the enduring benefits of the energy crisis of 1973–74 is that it may stimulate research on these and other promising technologies. Each could well substitute for exhaustible supplies of fossil fuels, and for this reason alone should be a good investment for government-supported research, even at the cost of abortive efforts in one or another direction. With the breeder reactor, which has benefited from high expenditures for many years, there is no good reason to accelerate research efforts in response to the international trade needs of the 1970s. But such a speedup in other areas that have not benefited from high past expenditures redresses a serious imbalance in U.S. policies for long-run energy research and development.

Transportation Policies*

The second important new budgetary expenditure is in urban transportation. The administration has proposed the creation of a six-year, $16 billion Unified Transportation Assistance Program (UTAP) to help large cities improve their own highways and mass transit facilities. Although much of this is a consolidation of previous grant programs, the administration's bill increases spending by about $400 million in fiscal 1975 (to a level of $2.5 billion) and by slightly more for each of the next five years.

Subsidizing urban mass transit is related to the underlying objectives of energy policy in two ways. First, it is an element in a strategy

* Prepared with the assistance of Wilfred Owen.

to protect gasoline consumers against world trade embargoes. If large cities had mass transit systems with some excess capacity, many people who normally drive to work could switch to alternative, energy-conserving modes of transportation when the need arose. Standby transportation capacity of this sort could then serve the same purpose as standby reserves of petroleum. Even if it proved infeasible to maintain standby capacity, urban mass transit systems could also prove valuable in reducing vulnerability to international trade disturbances simply by reducing demand for petroleum.

A second rationale for subsidizing urban mass transit is the environmental issue. Automobiles are among the worst causes of air pollution, noise, and congestion in large cities; and the straightforward device of inducing commuters to switch from private autos to mass transit is an important part of any real effort to improve the urban environment. Previous intermittent efforts along these lines have focused on general encouragement of bus use and banning of automobile traffic in certain areas of the city. These measures have not appeared successful—the number of automobile users continues to grow and the proportion of commuters using mass transit continues to fall. In 1974, however, the sharp increase in gasoline prices may do what years of more half-hearted efforts could not do to encourage people to use mass transit. This price increase, in a sense reflecting shortcomings in previous government policies to protect gasoline consumers, may have for urban automobile commuters a somewhat different meaning because they have probably never paid prices high enough to cover the environmental costs of their commuting.

The administration's UTAP proposal is a special revenue sharing measure. Like other such proposals in education, manpower, and law enforcement, the administration plan consolidates existing grant programs. It combines $1.1 billion of urban highway grants with $1.4 billion of Urban Mass Transportation Administration grants into a single program of $2.5 billion for fiscal 1975.

Thirty percent of the UTAP authority ($700 million) is to be retained in a discretionary fund for mass transit (mainly rail) capital improvements on a project application basis. The remainder ($1.8 billion in 1975) is to be distributed according to size among cities with populations of 50,000 or more (there is a separate, smaller, authority for rural areas). In 1975, $0.7 billion of this money is available for rail or bus transit—for either capital improvements or operating assistance (with limited amounts available for the latter)—and the rest for highways. In 1976 and 1977, the authorization for mass transit increases to $0.8 billion and $0.9 billion, while the authorization for highway construction and improvement remains at its 1975 level of $1.1 billion. In 1978, when the Highway Trust Fund expires, the mass transit and highway grant programs are consolidated, with the entire amount available for whatever uses the local government wants to make of it, though no more than 50 percent can be used for mass transit operating expenses. After 1978, the program will be funded out of general revenues. The matching rate for grants is made uniform at 80 percent for the federal share and 20 percent for the local government. Finally, there is a "maintenance of effort" provision which attempts to prevent localities from reducing transit expenditures out of their own funds.

This plan has two desirable features. First, the program provides for some increase in the ability of city governments to aid mass transit. In 1975, this is reflected in the more rapid growth of the transit portion than the highway portion, in the later years by letting city governments spend highway and nonhighway funds as they please. Second, the plan allows urban governments to subsidize the operating deficits of transit companies, and hence keep fares low relative to the cost of automobile commuting, instead of having the aid restricted as at present to purchasing transit equipment.

The one drawback is common to all special revenue sharing proposals. The administration's plan to give city governments the freedom to spend what formerly were highway monies on mass transit and what formerly were capital grants on current operating deficits is a step in the right direction. But it would have been possible to go even further and require that all money be directed toward mass transit through a categorical grant. Leaving matters up to city governments is undoubtedly better than forcing continued subsidization of the private automobile; it may not be better than forcing subsidization of mass transit.

Specific Issues in Energy Tax Policy

The most prominent issue is whether to tax or otherwise limit the enormous windfall profits of oil companies in 1974 and later years. According to the Department of the Treasury, profits of twenty-two of the largest U.S. oil comapnies increased over 50 percent in 1973, to a level of $9.1 billion. Depending on the price of petroleum, they are expected to rise to possibly twice this level in 1974. This would raise after-tax profit rates (on equity) of large oil companies to almost 30 percent, roughly triple those for other sectors and triple the 1972 rates for these same companies.[12] Although, as the firms themselves argue, 1972 profits were somewhat depressed, the current rates of return are enormous by any historical standards. Moreover, they were derived largely from the foreign operations of these companies. In this sense, the firms have benefited from the same actions of international exporters which have put the rest of the country in such great difficulty. Hence, there may be reason to tax oil companies and possibly rebate some of the revenue to consumers. Several measures have been proposed to limit the profits, or to increase the profits taxes, of oil companies. In December 1973 President Nixon recommended a windfall profits tax; a rollback of petroleum prices was included in the Energy Emergency Act which the President vetoed in March 1974; the House Committee on Ways and Means has proposed a gradual phase-out of oil depletion allowances; and the administration has also recommended tightening the tax treatment of U.S. oil companies operating in foreign countries.

Limitation of Profits

The idea of limiting windfall profits to restore some notion of distributive equity raises one of the oldest and most difficult questions of public policy analysis. On one side, it is argued that profits resulting from price increases serve a useful function because they indicate to firms where to invest resources, and to shareholders and lending institutions where to invest their capital. These windfall profits arise all the time in the normal course of economic activity, as do windfall losses, and a dangerous precedent would be established if the government began taxing or regulating away such profits every time they occurred. This would distort the proper functioning of the free market price system by both limiting supplies and, for price controls, eliminating incentives to reduce consumption. The problem may be especially critical for temporary measures in the natural resources industries, because if these regulations are too oppressive, resource owners

12. Data are from the testimony of Treasury Secretary George P. Shultz before the House Committee on Ways and Means, in "Department of the Treasury News," S-357, Feb. 4, 1974.

may simply postpone production—leading to even greater scarcities—until these regulations are lifted.

Yet in this case there are certain problems with such a line of reasoning. For one thing, the Treasury estimates that a large part of the increase in profits results from the foreign operations of oil companies, not from domestic operations where it is desirable to encourage increased production. For another, the presumption of free entry of firms into the petroleum industry in response to profit incentives is not a very realistic one. The oligopolistic concentration of the oil industry, the enormous capital costs of refining, the high degree of vertical integration of most petroleum companies, the fact that large companies control the most productive petroleum sources and even supplies of competing resources, the increasingly high price which must be paid to secure drilling rights on new fields being put up for bid by the federal government—all these factors make this presumption dubious. If entry into the petroleum industry is effectively limited or even foreclosed by such forces, this argument against limiting windfall profits is weakened.

Even without free entry, however, there are still strong reasons for preserving the price and profit incentives of the market, both to discourage consumption temporarily and to encourage increases in supplies from existing firms. Fortunately there are ways in which this can be done, while at the same time eliminating some of the windfall profits. The underlying principle of such techniques is to permit high prices and profits on increases in current output but not profits earned solely by price increases on present output levels. The Cost of Living Council devised one such scheme when in August 1973, it limited the ceiling price on the base-month output of a barrel of crude petroleum (called "old" oil) to $4.25 (since raised to $5.25), while allowing an unlimited price on output in excess of this base-month output ("new" oil). Although this measure has led to complications such as different consumer prices for products according to their blend of old, new, and imported (which sold at still other prices) petroleum, it did limit current profits to some degree without destroying the incentives to increase the production of petroleum.

WINDFALL PROFITS TAX

There are similar possibilities for achieving reasonable compromises between the goals of resource allocation and income redistribution through taxation. The administration's windfall profits tax, which is really an excise tax, imposes no tax at all on the first $4.75 per barrel of oil (for a standard grade of petroleum), a 10 percent excise tax on the price of petroleum between $4.75 and $5 per barrel, a 20 percent excise tax on the price between $5 and $5.35, and so on up to 85 percent on the price above $6.75 a barrel. This rate structure would be raised gradually, so that after three years there would be no tax at all on petroleum selling for less than $7 a barrel, the administration's current estimate of the price at that time; after five years the tax would be phased out completely. The administration estimates that the tax would increase government revenues by $3 billion in fiscal 1975: a $5 billion increase in excise tax revenues offset by a $2 billion reduction in corporate profits taxes. The tax would enable the Treasury to absorb a portion of the increased profits without reducing short-run incentives for increasing production as long as prices stay below $6.75 a barrel. Because the tax is temporary, longer-run petroleum investment should not be affected.

EXCESS PROFITS TAX

An alternative tax, included in an early version of the Energy Emergency Act, is an excess profits tax. Instead of being based on a price per unit of output as is the administration's tax, a pure excess profits tax of the type adopted during World War I, World War II, and the Korean war would tax only profits in excess of some "normal" base-year amount. But this normal base-year amount is very difficult—indeed impossible—to define, raising serious equity problems for firms which had abnormally depressed or inflated profits in the base period, and serious administrative problems when these equity problems are confronted. Moreover, it becomes particularly difficult to assess excess profits taxes of oil companies which have diversified into a variety of different product lines. Further, any tax based on profits could encourage firms to make wasteful expenditures simply for the sake of lowering reported profits, and to exercise less vigilance in watching over production costs. Experience with previous excess profits taxes demonstrates that petroleum firms can easily spend enough to eliminate any excess profits tax liability. Finally, the excess profits tax would not treat increases in profits resulting from expanded production any more favorably than increases in profits due to higher prices, which would make it inferior to the price control technique of the Cost of Living Council.

ROLLBACK OF PETROLEUM PRICES

A third measure, which was eventually included in the vetoed version of the Energy Emergency Act, is a straight rollback of petroleum prices. This provision limited the price of old oil to $5.25 per barrel and new oil to $7.09 for a fourteen-month period. It would have had supply incentives more or less similar to those in the administration's own windfall profits tax proposal—that is, in the very short run the price that induces expansion of supply is limited to $7.09, while after fourteen months it could go higher. Unlike the administration's proposal, it would not have allowed price increases to induce temporary demand reductions, but neither would it have allowed these price increases to generate inflation. As long as prices are allowed to rise gradually toward their medium-term levels, it may be sensible to prevent them from rising above these levels in the short run.

INCENTIVES TO EXPAND SUPPLY

Any temporary tax measure could encourage energy producers to withhold production until the tax is abolished if output prices are generally expected to remain high beyond the duration of the temporary tax. In order to counter this effect, there could be an additional provision that gives a credit against this tax for production of new oil in excess of some base-period amount. Were this credit in effect, it would be possible to tax profits at higher rates (at prices below $6.75) in the administration's measure, and to bring in more revenue, but still provide for a strong incentive to expand current production. An alternative suggestion would credit against the windfall tax any energy-producing investments. This alternative seems less desirable than the credit for new production, however, because it would not directly subsidize current production, only investment, and may be quite wasteful if firms drill for the sake of drilling. Further, as discussed below, energy-producing investments by the oil industry are already quite heavily subsidized by the regular income tax system.

Special Subsidies for Domestic Energy Producers

Whatever is done in the way of limiting after-tax profits, there are also some long-lived features of the U.S. tax system which deserve careful examination in light of the objectives of energy policy outlined above. The most prominent example concerns two special subsidies for domestic producers of petroleum, natural gas, and coal: percentage depletion allowances and deductions from profits of the intangible costs of drilling and exploration. These long-standing features of the income tax system stimulate domestic production from exhaustible resources at the expense of other forms of production, and thus seem to be at variance with the government's long-run conservation objective.

PERCENTAGE DEPLETION

A basic principle of the United States income tax on all manufacturing producers is that only those profits remaining after all costs attributable to earning the income have been deducted should be taxed. Thus, if capital depreciates during the process of production, these capital costs should be subtracted from gross revenues before computing taxable profits; whereas if firms purchase new equipment, these costs should not be deducted.[13] For minerals producers, however, it has always been difficult to define these tax concepts because there is no generally agreed-on value of the stock of minerals being depleted. After early attempts at approximating depletion costs on the basis of the estimated "discovery value" of the mineral resources, Congress in 1926 amended the tax code to replace discovery value depletion with an optional provision for percentage depletion, which allowed producers to deduct a certain percentage (now 22 percent for oil and gas, 15 percent for oil from shale, and 10 percent for coal) of their gross receipts from taxable profits. Although this depletion deduction cannot exceed 50 percent of the taxable income of the property during the tax period, the total tax deductions that result over the lifetime of the property are not limited to the initial cost or value of the depletable asset, as would be the case for depreciation of capital in manufacturing.

EXPENSING INTANGIBLE DRILLING COSTS

A second provision, evolving not from the legislative process but from administrative regulation, also allows minerals producers to deduct from taxable income the intangible (noncapital) costs of drilling wells and preparing them for production. This "expensing" provision,

13. Apart from the 7 percent investment credit intended to stimulate all forms of private investment.

apparently originally intended to refer mainly to dry-hole drilling costs and adopted before percentage depletion, has been extended through the years and now includes costs that clearly represent investment in productive mineral resource deposits, being tantamount to completely accelerated or immediate depreciation of most of the costs of drilling.

WHILE THERE MAY be grounds for either measure as a substitute for conventional depreciation, there appears to be no reason to confer *both* benefits on producers of mineral resources. Expensing intangible drilling costs gives a greater benefit than the corresponding accelerated depreciation for manufacturing producers because the cost write-off is immediate; percentage depletion gives potentially an even greater benefit because the cost write-off is limited only by the productive ability of the property. The combination of the two is then very powerful indeed. It has been estimated that these benefits are equivalent to an investment tax credit in oil and gas of about 50 percent, as opposed to a 7 percent credit for other plant and equipment investment. Similarly, the effective profits tax rate after all credits is currently about 15 percent for domestic petroleum and natural gas production, as against 46 percent for all U.S. firms.[14]

This double deduction of capital costs for minerals producers results in a large revenue loss (possibly $2.7 billion in fiscal 1975 for percentage depletion and $0.4 billion for expensing, depending on the price of petroleum), and its elimination would by itself partly satisfy redistributional objectives. While it may appear inconsistent to be reducing subsidies for fossil fuel investment now, with an energy shortage, there are, as we mention above, important long-run conservation drawbacks to this particular form of subsidy. It also encourages vertical integration, and hence reduces competitive incentives for increasing supplies, by inducing producers to increase the prices at which they sell oil to themselves and others just to raise their depletion allowance. Because of the lower allowable rate and lower capital intensity for coal mining, it subsidizes investment in relatively scarce gas

14. See Susan R. Agria, "Special Tax Treatment of Mineral Industries," in Arnold C. Harberger and Martin J. Bailey (eds.), *The Taxation of Income from Capital* (Brookings Institution, 1969); Gerard M. Brannon, "The Role of Taxes and Subsidies in United States Energy Policy" (Ford Foundation, Energy Policy Project, manuscript in preparation); *An Analysis of the Federal Tax Treatment of Oil and Gas and Some Policy Alternatives*," Prepared for the Senate Committee on Interior and Insular Affairs, 93 Cong. 2 sess. (1974).

and oil as opposed to relatively plentiful coal. Thus 1974, when oil and gas prices are already high enough to induce expanded supplies, might present a good opportunity for making this long-needed change in tax policy.

In more specific terms, the tax treatment of firms which deplete resources relative to firms which do not could be standardized by eliminating either percentage depletion or the expensing of intangible drilling costs. The argument presented above suggests that in terms of short-run incentives it would be better to eliminate depletion allowances, which raise after-tax profits on old investment, than the expensing provision, which is a generous inducement to new investment. The Treasury's revenue gain is also much larger with the elimination of depletion allowances. But whatever the case, if percentage depletion is eliminated, it might also be desirable to limit the expensing of intangible drilling costs to bring them more into conformity with other rates of depreciation; while if expensing is eliminated, it might also be desirable to limit total lifetime depletion allowances on a property to the initial investment. Because it still might be desirable to encourage the finding of new resources in line with the government's conservation objectives, certain subsidies might be retained for investment in new energy sources such as oil from shale, gasification or liquefaction of coal, or geothermal power. There could also be an investment credit for exploratory, as opposed to developmental, drilling, as the administration proposed in April 1973.

These distinctive tax provisions for domestic oil and gas producers have been in effect for a long time, and there have been many arguments in their behalf. There are valid grounds for supporting the development of a strong domestic oil and gas industry to protect against the vicissitudes of international trade. But it is debatable whether this should be done by subsidizing the depletion of domestic supplies, as the tax law now does, or by the research and development and stockpiling strategy discussed above. It has also been argued that drilling for petroleum is very risky but, again, whether the risks for large firms like those in the oil industry, making thousands of drills per year, are really greater than for firms in other forms of business is debatable. Certainly, their long-run profit rates or interest costs do not indicate that investors should be unusually fearful of investing in petroleum industries. A further argument is that these distinctive provisions may prevent profits taxes from discriminating against capital-intensive oil companies, yet the Treasury does not provide similar subsidies to other capital-intensive industries. Finally, one could argue that past investments were made on the basis of these provisions and that the rules of the game should not be changed in midstream. Although such changes are by no means unusual in the petroleum industry, this consideration might justify a change which phased these benefits out over a period of time, as the Ways and Means Committee bill in fact does.

Foreign Tax Provisions for Energy Producers

Another problem concerns the tax treatment of income from the foreign branches of domestic oil firms. Just as there is a question as to whether the United States tax code should be subsidizing depletion of existing resources, there is an even greater question as to whether it should be subsidizing investment in foreign sources of supply. Certain provisions in the tax code appear to do this, and these provisions bear reexamination now that the difficulties of relying on petroleum imports have been illustrated so dramatically.

The tax treatment of income earned by United States firms from their foreign investments is determined by two basic and well-accepted principles. The first is that the United States follows standard international conventions in allowing host countries to assess the first tax on the foreign profits of U.S. branches and subsidiaries; the second is that the United States tries to.standardize the tax treatment of its own firms between foreign and domestic investment so as not to encourage or penalize either one. This leads to the imposition of the normal 48 percent corporate tax rate on income earned here and abroad, but with a dollar-for-dollar tax credit for all income taxes already paid to foreign countries on earnings abroad. But it does not allow a dollar-for-dollar tax credit for operating costs such as rents, royalties, and excise taxes. These items are deducted before computing taxable profits, but not credited against tax liabilities, both here and abroad.

The combination of these well-accepted principles can lead to a rather bizarre tax situation for the large U.S.-based international oil companies. In the first place, because of percentage depletion and expensing of intangible drilling expenses, the U.S. tax liabilities on foreign petroleum operations are already low without any credits, on the order of 30 percent of gross profits. Then, because in petroleum-exporting countries the rights to land are typically held by the government, it becomes difficult to distinguish creditable income tax payments to these governments from deductible royalties. In fact, most payments are currently considered by the Treasury as income taxes and are thus credited against the U.S. tax liability of the foreign operation. This is true even though many of these countries do not have general income taxes and this tax is quite specific to petroleum—indeed, it is quoted in dollars per barrel just as royalties or excise taxes would be. There are, in other words, strong grounds for believing that payments to the host country should be treated either as a royalty or an excise tax, both of which are only deductible, and not as a creditable income tax. Because the high creditable taxes, about 90 percent of profits, generally exceed the low U.S. tax liabilities, U.S. oil companies have accumulated large amounts of unused credits. Through another provision, they have been allowed to apply these unused credits to mineral-related operations in low-tax third countries to reduce U.S. tax liabilities there. The relationship of these provisions then seems calculated to inspire investment in oil-related operations in low-tax third countries—Caribbean refineries and tankers registered in Liberia, Honduras, and Panama—rather than domestic investment.

At present, therefore, the large U.S. oil companies typically pay no U.S. tax at all on their foreign operations, and worse, they usually have excess credits which they can use to make tax-free investments in low-tax third countries. This is a clear subsidy of foreign investment in these third countries at the expense of domestic investment—contrary to the goal of encouraging independence from foreign trade—and encourages the growth of large, vertically integrated multinational companies, which conflicts with antitrust objectives.

Certain steps could be taken to redress these shortcomings. President Nixon proposed in his January 1974 energy message that depletion allowances be eliminated for the computation of taxes on the operations of foreign branches of U.S. oil companies. Whatever the merits of domestic depletion allowances, this seems a step in the right direction. The President also asked the Treasury to review its regulations that treat payments to foreign governments as income taxes and not as royalties or excise taxes, the intention being that only about half these payments would be creditable. The Treasury estimates that these provisions together would increase U.S. government revenues by only a small amount, say by $0.1 to $0.2 billion, but they would substantially eliminate the excess foreign credits and limit the inducement to tax free investment in third countries. Further steps, which might also be desirable to limit this inducement and increase revenues even more, would be to consider the entire payment to foreign governments deductible and to introduce a per-country limitation which would not allow excess credits from one foreign operation to reduce the tax liability from operations in other countries.

THE ENERGY CRISIS has generated some extremely difficult choices for public policymakers, between the different and partially conflicting objectives and between the various strategies by which these objectives can be achieved. However, even though difficult decisions lie ahead, there may be some enduring value in America's brush with an energy shortage simply in forcing these choices to be confronted. Many of the likely policy changes resulting from the energy crisis—upgrading the research efforts, improving mass transit grants, and eliminating distinctive tax preferences for energy producers—should have been made long ago, but might never have been made without an energy crisis to illuminate the weaknesses of current policies.

7. Federal Responsibilities for Income Support

NINETEEN SEVENTY-FOUR is the tenth anniversary of the government's declaration of war against poverty. The war is by no means over, but the decade has seen a rapid growth in federal antipoverty programs. Cash income maintenance programs will account for about 32 percent of federal outlays in fiscal 1975, and programs to help people buy essentials for another 11 percent. These income support measures have become the main government weapon against poverty in recent years, particularly with the declining impact of aid for social programs. Although more income support for the needy has alleviated poverty, it has also compounded the difficulties of reforming and simplifying the nation's welfare system.

In this chapter we review trends in poverty and federal income support programs, and we consider various ways in which the federal government could improve the status of those millions of Americans who still have very low incomes.

The Poverty Population: 1959–72

Between 1959 and 1972 (the latest year for which full data are available), the number of people of all ages in the United States living in

Table 7-1. Persons below the Poverty Level, by Age and Sex of Head of Family, Selected Calendar Years, 1959–72[a]

Age and sex of family head	1959	1966	1968	1972	1972 incidence of poverty[b] (percent)
Number of poor persons (thousands)					
65 years and over	5,679	5,111	4,633	3,734	18.6
Under 65 years					
Family with female head	8,115	7,841	7,970	9,385	37.9
Family with male head	25,695	15,558	12,786	11,341	7.1
Total	39,490	28,510	25,389	24,460	11.9
Percentage of poor persons					
65 years and over	14.4	17.9	18.2	15.3	...
Under 65 years					
Family with female head	20.5	27.5	31.4	38.4	...
Family with male head	65.1	54.6	50.4	46.4	...
Total	100.0	100.0	100.0	100.0	...

Source: U.S. Bureau of the Census, *Current Population Reports*, Series P-60, No. 91, "Characteristics of the Low-Income Population, 1972" (1973), pp. 15–17. Detail may not add to totals because of rounding.

a. "Families" include unrelated individuals. The poverty level is based on an index developed by a Federal Interagency Committee in 1969. The index is based on the Department of Agriculture's 1961 economy food plan, adjusted annually for changes in the consumer price index. The poverty level for a nonfarm family of four was $2,973 in 1959 and $4,275 in 1972; adjustments are made for consumption requirements of families of different sizes, sex and age of head, and farm-nonfarm residence.

b. Incidence of povery refers to the percentage of persons in each age and family status category below the poverty level.

poverty[1] fell by 15 million people, or 38 percent (Table 7-1). This decline masks different trends for different demographic groups. The incidence of poverty among the elderly was cut in half during these thirteen years, as the number of people over sixty-five rose and the number of *poor* old people declined. The most dramatic improvement in income status occurred among people living in family units headed by a man under retirement age. By 1972 only 7 percent of these people were poor. The number of poor in family units headed by a woman, however, decreased very little between 1959 and 1968. After 1968 the number actually increased. By 1972, 38 percent of these people were poor.

It should be remembered that real incomes were rising gradually during this period, so that a family at the poverty line was becoming worse off in relation to the rest of the population.

1. Those who had cash incomes below the poverty line as defined by the federal government. This measure of poverty represents the level of income required to purchase a fixed market basket of goods and services. Thus the poverty standard is adjusted for rising prices, but not for growing average real incomes.

Table 7-2. Federal Outlays on Programs for Cash Income Maintenance and Helping People Buy Essentials, Selected Fiscal Years, 1960–75

Millions of dollars

Program	1960	1970	1973	1975
Cash income maintenance				
Social security	11,018	29,685	48,288	64,351
Public assistance to aged, blind, and disabled	1,449	1,979	2,000	25
Supplemental security income	...	...	41	4,770
Veterans' compensation and pensions	3,312	5,229	6,401	6,548
Federal civilian retirement	1,821	4,192	6,954	10,229
Benefits for disabled miners	...	10	952	879
Aid to families with dependent children	612	2,163	3,922	4,322
Unemployment compensation	2,375	3,369	5,362	7,065
Total	**20,587**	**46,927**	**73,920**	**98,189**
Helping people buy essentials				
Medicare	...	7,149	9,479	14,191
Medicaid	...	2,727	4,600	6,508
Food stamps	...	577	2,208	3,926
Other food	324	833	1,433	1,744
Housing	279	1,279	1,420	2,292
Higher education student aid	498	1,625	3,880	4,556
Total	**1,101**	**14,190**	**23,020**	**33,217**

Sources: *The Budget of the United States Government*, together with *Appendix* and *Special Analyses*, for relevant years.

Federal Outlays for Income Support

Most federal income support programs are geared to one or another of the demographic groups. There are, for example, six cash income maintenance programs designed primarily to help the aged and disabled population. These programs, the first six listed in Table 7-2, will account for over $85 billion of the $98 billion in federal outlays for cash income maintenance. Aid to families with dependent children (AFDC), primarily for poor families headed by a woman, is a far smaller program but it has grown sevenfold in the fifteen years since 1960. Except for a small portion of the AFDC program, families headed by a man receive cash assistance only from unemployment compensation, which of course is not focused on the poor and is restricted to those with a work history in covered occupations.

The programs to help people buy essentials, which provide aid in kind, are also directed toward different groups. The largest is Medicare, which helps all the elderly and many disabled persons to meet most of their medical expenses. Recipients of public assistance and some near-poor families as well receive aid under Medicaid, the other medical assistance program. The food stamp program is unique in the broadness of its potential coverage: any family falling below certain prescribed income and asset limits is eligible to participate. As Table 7-2 indicates, this is the fastest-growing program of the 1970s. Other food, housing, and higher education student aid programs provide assistance to a limited number of families, not all of whom are poor.

Federal income support programs for the aged and disabled, giving cash and in-kind assistance, are large and growing rapidly. Families with a head of working age get much less. Fatherless poor families receive both cash assistance and several forms of in-kind aid to which they become entitled because of their welfare status. Poor families with a father, on the other hand, have no special cash assistance program and are clearly eligible for only one form of in-kind assistance—food stamps.

Poverty in the Aged and Disabled Population

About 19 percent of the elderly were poor in 1972, despite their income from social security and other assistance programs. The impact of public programs on this group can only be understood, however, if one knows (1) how many elderly people would have been poor without the transfer of public funds and (2) how much in-kind assistance has contributed to their welfare.

Effect of Income Support Programs in the Early Seventies

In 1971 over half of the aged and disabled families would have been poor had it not been for public transfer programs (see Table 7-3).[2] But nearly all these "pre-transfer" poor families received some form of public transfer payment. Social insurance programs are the most important poverty-reducing transfers for the aged (and for the population in general). Over half of the elderly pre-transfer poor were moved out of poverty by social security. Other programs had comparatively little effect. The principal public assistance program specifically for the aged in 1971 was the old-age assistance program

2. Different data sources classify the population in different ways and no single source is available for all time periods. Statistics used in this chapter, therefore, cannot be presented in a uniform manner with respect to demographic characteristics. In each instance, we state whether the data apply to family units or individuals, and whether or not the elderly are included.

Table 7-3. Poverty Status of All Families and of Families with Heads Aged 65 or over, or Disabled, before and after Receiving Transfers, 1971[a,b]

Type of family	Total number of families (thousands)	Families poor before transfers		Families poor after receiving social insurance		Families poor after receiving social insurance and public assistance		Percent of families poor before transfers that received transfers
		Number (thousands)	Percent of total	Number (thousands)	Percent of total	Number (thousands)	Percent of total	
All families[c]	72,046	15,059	20.9	10,290	14.3	8,627	12.0	80
Families with a head 65 years or over	12,974	6,977	53.8	3,348	25.8	2,971	22.9	97
Families with a head who is disabled	3,567	2,041	57.2	1,640	46.0	1,296	36.3	89

Source: Michael C. Barth, George J. Carcagno, and John L. Palmer, *Toward an Effective Income Support System: Problems, Prospects, and Choices* (University of Wisconsin, Institute for Research on Poverty, 1974).

a. Families include unrelated individuals. Social insurance includes old-age, survivors, and disability insurance, and unemployment compensation. Public assistance includes cash assistance from federal, state, and local sources, and the bonus value of food stamps. Transfers include social insurance and public assistance.

b. Other family groups are listed in Table 7-6.

c. All families include the two groups in this table and the three groups in Table 7-6. (Detail may not add to totals because of rounding.)

(OAA); fewer than half of the elderly poor were recipients and the average monthly benefit per recipient was only $78. Moreover, OAA was a state-administered program and benefits in many states were therefore a good deal lower than the national average. In South Carolina, for example, benefits were under $50 a month.

Unlike the aged, only about one-third of the pre-transfer poor families with a disabled head were raised above the poverty level by public aid in 1971. Half of this was attributable to the social insurance programs and half to other forms of public assistance. The major public assistance programs available to the disabled in 1971 were aid to the blind (AB) and aid to the permanently and totally disabled (APTD). As with the aged, the effectiveness of these programs in reducing the number living in poverty was affected by the wide variation in payments among the various state programs. Under AB, for example, average monthly payments ranged from $66 in South Carolina to $165 in New Hampshire.

Recent Changes in Cash Income Maintenance Programs

Since the early 1970s, social security has enormously expanded assistance to poor families headed by an aged or disabled person and therefore has probably considerably reduced the number of poor. The number of beneficiaries has grown 10 percent a year under the dis-

Table 7-4. Number of Beneficiaries and Annual Benefit to Retired and Disabled Families under Social Security, Selected Fiscal Years, 1972–75

Description	1972	1973	1975	Average annual increase, 1972–75 (percent)
Number of beneficiaries (thousands)[a]				
Retired workers and dependents	17,700	18,300	20,200	4.5
Disabled workers and dependents	2,900	3,300	3,900	10.4
Average annual benefit (dollars)[a]				
Retired workers	1,575	1,853	2,229	12.3
Disabled workers	2,043	2,333	2,652	9.1

Sources: *The Budget of the United States Government—Appendix, Fiscal Year 1975*, pp. 456–58, and *Fiscal Year 1974*, pp. 456–58.
a. Excludes survivors receiving benefits.

ability insurance program since fiscal 1972 (see Table 7-4), suggesting that a larger portion of the disabled population will be receiving social insurance benefits by 1975. Average disability benefits have grown 9 percent a year between 1972 and 1975, whereas the rise in the consumer price index is estimated at about 6 percent. Benefits for retired workers and their dependents have also gone up. The average increase in benefits per retired worker (excluding payments for dependents) has risen about 40 percent in the three-year period.[3] Moreover, the 1972 and 1973 social security amendments provide for automatic across-the-board benefit increases in the future. Beginning in 1975, benefits will be raised each June by the same percentage as the consumer price index rose in the previous year. This guarantees that social security recipients will also keep pace with future inflation.

The most important change for these two groups in recent years is the introduction of a new federal program, supplemental security income (SSI). Beginning in January 1974, programs for "adult categories" (OAA, AB, APTD) that were run by the states with partial federal funding are being replaced by a federally financed SSI program. SSI guarantees a uniform minimum income to all people who

3. Since payments are based on a retired worker's wage history, part of this increase can be attributed to the higher past wages of newly retired workers. But even a retired worker who was on the social security rolls in 1972 would have received increases of 20 percent in September 1972, 7 percent in March 1974, and 4 percent in June 1974, cumulating to a 34 percent increase over the three-year period.

qualify on the basis of age, disability, and income status. A single person who qualifies and who has no income at all will receive $146 per month in federal benefits; a couple with no income will receive $219 per month. Beneficiaries with income will not lose any benefits for the first $20 of monthly income from any source (including social security benefits), or from an additional $65 in monthly earnings. Beyond that SSI benefits are reduced (a) by fifty cents for each dollar of *earnings* and (b) by one dollar for each dollar of unearned income—including social security benefits.[4] Thus a couple receiving less than $239 per month in social security or as much as $523 per month in earnings would be eligible for SSI. Since the poverty line for an aged couple in 1974 is about $240 per month, SSI will provide benefits to most of the elderly and disabled poor and to many who are above the poverty level as well.

The Social Security Administration estimates that SSI will provide benefits to over 5 million people in fiscal 1975,[5] compared to 3.2 million who received aid under the state programs in 1972. The elderly will account for most of this increased number of beneficiaries. Many people whose social security benefits disqualified them for OAA will be eligible for SSI because the SSI maximum payments exceed the former OAA maximum in about half of the states.

The growth in recipients and benefit levels under the social security and public assistance programs over the past three years significantly reduced poverty among the aged and the disabled.[6] By 1971, almost all elderly poor people were covered by some form of public aid; since then, rising benefits under social insurance and the introduction of SSI must have appreciably lowered the incidence of poverty, especially in states that had had weak public assistance programs. Many more elderly people will be receiving both social insurance and public assistance in 1975 than in 1972. The rapid growth in the number of disabled recipients under social security probably indicates that all are now covered, and increases in benefit levels since 1971 should have reduced the very high poverty rate among such individuals.

4. For example, an elderly couple who received $150 per month in social security would be eligible for $89 per month in SSI. The maximum SSI benefit of $219 would be reduced dollar for dollar by all social security benefits in excess of the first $20 per month.

5. This figure includes recipients who will qualify for state supplemental payments under SSI as well as those receiving federal assistance.

6. As noted earlier, official poverty statistics are not available for years after 1972.

Table 7-5. Federal In-Kind Benefits for the Aged and Disabled, Fiscal Years 1973 and 1975

Description	1973	1975	Annual percentage change
Number of beneficiaries (thousands)			
Medicare	10,600	12,277	8
Medicaid	6,137	7,714	12
Food	1,590	1,623	1
Housing	814	1,023	12
Federal benefits (millions of dollars)[a]			
Medicare	9,039	13,417	22
Medicaid	2,556	3,739	21
Food	247	402	28
Housing	252	346	17
Federal benefits per beneficiary (dollars)[a]			
Medicare	853	1,093	13
Medicaid	416	485	8
Food	155	248	26
Housing	310	338	4

Source: *Special Analyses, Budget of the United States Government, Fiscal Year 1975*, Special Analysis K.
a. Substantial amounts of state and local government aid are also available to beneficiaries, but are not included here. In the Medicaid program, federal benefits account for only slightly more than half of the total benefit payments.

Recent Changes in In-Kind Assistance

The growth of cash assistance programs understates the progress made in helping low-income households headed by the aged and disabled because of the availability of in-kind benefits provided through programs to help people buy essentials. These benefits are also growing rapidly, and although not counted as income in official poverty statistics (such as those in Table 7-1), they do improve the standard of living of the beneficiaries.

The most important programs of this nature open to elderly and disabled people are Medicare and Medicaid (see Table 7-5). Food stamps and housing assistance also reach many people in these two groups.

In-kind benefits vary widely. Although Medicare is a national program, its benefits vary by state and by racial group. Medicaid benefits also differ from state to state; in 1970 they ranged from zero in Arizona (which had no program) to $1,942 per elderly recipient in New Jersey.[7] Relatively few older people have housing assistance; those

7. These figures include state as well as federal funds. See Chapter 8.

Table 7-6 Poverty Status of Families with a Working-Age Head, before and after Receiving Transfers, 1971[a,b]

Type of family	Total number of families (thousands)	Families poor before transfers		Families poor after social insurance		Families poor after social insurance and public assistance		Percent of families poor before transfers that received transfers
		Number (thousands)	Percent of total	Number (thousands)	Percent of total	Number (thousands)	Percent of total	
Families with children and female head	4,706	2,027	43.1	1,811	38.5	1,237	26.3	83
Families with children and male head	26,671	1.659	6.2	1,522	5.7	1,304	4.9	51
Families without children	24,129	2,356	9.8	1,940	8.0	1,820	7.5	43

Source: Same as Table 7-3.

a. Excludes the elderly (aged sixty-five and over) and the disabled whose family groups are listed in Table 7-3.

b. Families include unrelated individuals. Social insurance includes old-age, survivors, and disability insurance and unemployment compensation. Public assistance includes cash assistance from federal, state, and local sources, and the bonus value of food stamps. Transfers include social insurance and public assistance.

who receive aid get an average of $30 a month as a rent subsidy. Thus the effect of in-kind programs on the standard of living of the aged and disabled poor is quite uneven.

Poverty in Families with Heads of Working Age

The effect of public transfer programs on poor families whose head is of working age and not disabled differs vastly from the effect on families whose head is elderly or disabled. Table 7-6 shows what social insurance and public assistance programs have done to reduce poverty in 1971 for three demographic groups: childless households and families with male or female heads who are of working age.

Three points are worth noting. First, in 1971 families with children and a woman at the head were not moved out of poverty by public programs in the same proportions as the families of the aged. Transfers helped about 40 percent of the poor mothers and dependents cross the poverty threshold compared to nearly 60 percent of the aged.

Second, public assistance played a much larger role in reducing poverty among these fatherless families than it did for the aged and disabled.

Third, neither social insurance nor public assistance had much impact on the poverty status of families with children headed by a man or on childless households. The major reason is that only about half of the pre-transfer poor families in these categories received any public aid in contrast to over 80 percent of those with female heads and 89–97 percent of the aged and disabled (Tables 7-6 and 7-3).

Families with a Female Head and Dependent Children

By 1971 the income status of poor families with a female head was being significantly improved by transfers, especially public assistance (Table 7-6). However, a major reason for the relatively higher incidence of poverty among families with children and a female head than among the aged was incomplete coverage—17 percent of all the families in this category were not receiving any public aid at all.[8]

Mothers and children may be eligible for social security if they survive workers who were covered; presumably almost all those eligible for these benefits receive them. Families could also get help from AFDC provided that they met the eligibility requirements, which vary from state to state. It is mainly because of these varying AFDC eligibility requirements that some poor families with children and a female head received no public aid in 1971.[9] For example, in 1970 when the poverty standard for a family of four was about $4,000, a mother with three children earning as little as $2,500 a year had income too high to be eligible for AFDC in five states.[10]

RECENT CHANGES IN CASH INCOME MAINTENANCE PROGRAMS

There are indications that AFDC coverage of the poor population has improved since 1970. Table 7-7 shows the number of beneficiary

8. If 97 percent of pre-transfer poor families with a female head had received transfers (the percentage for the elderly) and if they were removed from poverty at the same rate as that shown in Table 7-6, they would have had the same incidence of poverty as the aged in 1971.

9. In the 1960s many families who were eligible for AFDC under their state's rules did not receive benefits. By 1970, however, by one estimate, over 90 percent of the female-headed families that were eligible for AFDC under their own state's rules were receiving benefits. Thus by 1971, other causes of AFDC's failure to cover the poor must have been dominant. See Barbara Boland, "Participation in the Aid to Families with Dependent Children Program (AFDC)," in *Studies in Public Welfare*, Paper No. 12, Pt. 1, Prepared for the Use of the Subcommittee on Fiscal Policy of the Joint Economic Committee, 93 Cong. 1 sess. (1973), p. 153.

10. The states are shown in Table 7-7 as states with low income cutoff lines.

Table 7-7. Number of AFDC[a] Beneficiaries and Income Cutoff Lines, States with Five Lowest and Highest Income Cutoff Lines and U.S. Total, July 1970 and July 1973

	Number of beneficiary families		Change, 1970–73		Income cutoff line[b] Amount (dollars per month)		
State	July 1970	July 1973	Number	Percent	July 1970	July 1973	Percent change
Lowest income cutoff lines							
Arkansas	14,100	24,810	10,710	76.0	176	275	56
Georgia	65,400	103,202	37,802	57.8	208	227	9
New Mexico	15,300	17,508	2,208	14.4	203	203	0
North Carolina	36,000	45,924	9,924	27.6	184	184	0
South Carolina	16,100	31,275	15,175	94.3	198	217	10
Five states, total	146,900	222,719	75,819	51.6	194[c]	221[c]	14
Highest income cutoff lines[d]							
California	383,000	415,206	32,206	8.4	432	322[e]	−25.5
Connecticut	24,500	34,502	10,002	40.8	330	311[e]	−5.8
Maine	12,600	20,054	7,454	59.2	349	349	0.0
New Jersey	91,000	117,423	26,423	29.0	347	324[e]	−6.6
New York	302,000	346,934	44,934	14.9	336	380	13.1
Five states, total	813,100	934,119	121,019	14.9	359[c]	337[c]	−6.0[c]
United States, total	2,269,000	3,127,653	858,653	37.8	n.a.	n.a.	n.a.

Sources: U.S. Department of Health, Education, and Welfare, National Center for Social Statistics, "OAA and AFDC: Standards for Basic Needs for Specified Types of Assistance Groups, July 1970," NCSS D-2 (July 1970; processed); HEW, NCSS, "Public Assistance Programs: Standards for Basic Needs, July 1973," DHEW (SRS) 74-03200, NCSS D-2 (7/73) (1974; processed); *Social Security Bulletin*, Vol. 36 (December 1973), Table M-26, and Vol. 34 (January 1971), Table M-26.

n.a. Not available.

a. AFDC, aid to families with dependent children.

b. The income cutoff line is the full monthly standard amount required for basic needs, as reported by each state. It is the amount with which income is compared to determine whether or not financial eligibility exists.

c. Unweighted average.

d. Excludes Alaska.

e. Between 1970 and 1973, California, Connecticut and New Jersey began using flat allowances. In 1970 these states used an itemized list of expenditures to determine eligibility and the amount of the grant. Thus, if a family was living in a relative's house, no allowance would have been made for rent. Under a flat allowance system, income is compared to a fixed amount for basic needs regardless of the family's actual expenditures.

families (caseload) and the income cutoff line (the level of income above which families would not qualify for AFDC aid) for the five states with the lowest and the five with the highest cutoff lines in the country in 1970. In those with the lowest 1970 cutoff point (a family income of less than $208 a month), the caseload rose over 52 percent in the 1970–73 period, compared to 38 percent for the country as a whole. In these states, many poor female-headed families that were formerly ineligible for public assistance are now likely to be covered.

By contrast, in the five states with highest income cutoff points in 1970 (a family income of more than $330 a month) caseloads have not risen as sharply, in part because most of these states reduced their income cutoff levels. Many people who left the AFDC program in the latter states were probably not poor in the first place. Hence, even the projected slowdown in overall AFDC caseload growth—the administration expects the number of beneficiaries to grow only 3.5 percent between fiscal 1973 and 1975—is not likely to reduce AFDC coverage of the poor.[11]

While coverage has improved, monthly payments under AFDC have not. The administration estimates that between 1972 and 1975, average monthly benefits per recipient will increase only 14 percent, well under the rate of inflation for that period. Families with children and a female head receiving social insurance benefits, on the other hand, have been given increases comparable to those given to the aged beneficiaries, well in excess of the rate of inflation in recent years (see Table 7-4).

RECENT CHANGES IN IN-KIND ASSISTANCE

Growth in programs to help people buy essentials has undoubtedly eased the low-income status of mothers with dependent children. Although comprehensive data are not available, those we use here reveal two interesting developments.

First, by as early as 1971 virtually all AFDC families were eligible for Medicaid, 59 percent participated in the school lunch programs, 13 percent received public housing benefits, and 68 percent had either food stamps or surplus food benefits.[12] Since federal outlays under these programs have more than doubled in the last five years (Table 7-2), it seems likely that the above percentages have risen for the entire AFDC population.

Second, food stamp benefits have grown so rapidly that they have had a fundamental impact on the income status of these poor mothers with dependent children. Although all AFDC families are eligible for food stamps under current law, many have not participated because the program was not available in their area. By mid-1974, however, all counties will have a food stamp program and participation should increase.

11. Between October 1972 and October 1973, the number of AFDC recipients in the United States fell by 1.7 percent. But in four of the five states with tight eligibility standards listed in Table 7-7, the number of recipients grew. California and New York, two of the states with the easiest eligibility requirements, accounted for by far the largest caseload decrease. See Social Security Administration, *Social Security Bulletin*, Vol. 36 (March 1973) and Vol. 37 (April 1974), Table M-27.

12. See James R. Storey, "Public Income Transfer Programs: The Incidence of Multiple Benefits and the Issues Raised by Their Receipt," in *Studies in Public Welfare*, Paper No. 1, p. 28.

The food stamp program provides a recipient with a monthly coupon allotment, the size of which is based on the cost of feeding a family of a given size. For example, from January to June 1974, the monthly coupon allotment is $78 for a family with two members and $142 for a four-person household.[13] Participants buy these coupons from the welfare agency that administers the program, paying an amount that depends on monthly net income. The latter includes most usual sources of incomes and also public assistance; it allows deductions for income and payroll taxes, child care expenses for working parents, and shelter costs in excess of 30 percent of income after taxes. In addition, 10 percent of wages up to a limit of $30 per month is excluded. For every dollar of monthly net income, food stamp recipients must pay about 30 cents for their coupons (after the first $25 in monthly net income, for which the coupons are free). An AFDC family of four, receiving $200 in public assistance and paying $80 a month in shelter costs ($180 in monthly net income) would have to pay $47 to receive food stamps worth $142 at the store. The bonus value of the coupons—the excess of the value of the coupons over the purchase price—would thus be $95 a month. Hence, food stamps can boost an AFDC family's income considerably.

The inverse relation between food stamp bonus values and AFDC payments greatly reduces the interstate differentials among welfare families. Table 7-8 shows the maximum AFDC payments for a family of four in the five highest- and five lowest-paying states. These sums, which are available to a family with no other resources, show a sixfold difference: from $60 a month in Mississippi to $364 a month in Michigan. But when the bonus value of food stamps is computed for families receiving maximum AFDC payments and is added to cash assistance, total resources for the family in Michigan are only about twice as great as those for the Mississippi family.

There is reason to question whether each dollar in food stamp bonus value can be counted as the same as a dollar in cash assistance because food stamps are tied to a specific use. If a family would not normally spend its monthly coupon allotment on food, bonuses would not be worth as much as cash assistance. So far the evidence seems to be that food stamp recipients do place a high value on their bonuses. Even though such a recipient may choose a lower monthly coupon value than the maximum permitted by his family's size (and pay less

13. In July, these allotments will increase by 5.6 percent as a result of food price inflation.

Table 7-8. Monthly Value of AFDC Payments, 1973, and Food Stamp Bonus Values, 1974, Four-Person Family with No Earned Income, Selected States

Dollars

State	Maximum AFDC payment[a]	Food stamp bonus value[b]	Total family resources
Five states with lowest maximum payment for basic needs			
Alabama	104	117	221
Arkansas	130	111	241
Louisiana	110	114	224
Mississippi	60	142	202
South Carolina	108	120	228
Average[c]	**102**	**121**	**223**
Five states with highest maximum payment for basic needs[d]			
Massachusetts	358	47	405
Michigan	364	53	417
Minnesota	339	53	392
New York	354	47	401
Vermont	335	47	382
Average[c]	**350**	**49**	**399**

Sources: U.S. Department of Health, Education, and Welfare, "Public Assistance Programs: Standards for Basic Needs, July 1973"; U.S. Department of Agriculture, News Release, "Food Stamp Program Expanded" (October 30, 1973).

a. AFDC, aid to families with dependent children. Based on basic needs budget.

b. Assumes that the AFDC family pays rent at the monthly amount for basic needs under the state's payment standard.

c. Unweighted average.

d. Excludes Alaska and Hawaii.

for it), only 5.6 percent chose to do so in 1972.[14] However, with recent rises in food stamp coupon allotments, the picture may change.

By narrowing state-to-state differences in the resources of AFDC families, the food stamp program has reduced the need to nationalize the AFDC system. However, even when food stamp bonuses are counted as regular income, mothers with children who receive aid only from AFDC and food stamps remain well below the poverty line, especially in low-paying states.

The Working Poor

About half of the nation's poor people live in families that are not headed by an aged or disabled person or in a family with dependent children and a female head. Only a small proportion of these families—childless couples, single people, and male-headed families with

14. See testimony of Edward J. Hekman, in *Agriculture—Environmental and Consumer Protection Appropriations for 1974*, Hearings before a Subcommittee of the House Committee on Appropriations, 93 Cong. 1 sess. (1973), p. 645.

children—were below the poverty threshold in 1971 (see Table 7-6). But since there are so many of these families in the total population, they bulk large among the poor. The proportion of pre-transfer poor families in these groups that receive transfers is much lower than in other groups. Table 7-6 indicates that in 1971 only about half of them received any form of public aid.

However, even though these families do not benefit significantly from public aid, their poverty incidence is declining rapidly (Table 7-1). This is because the head of the family is generally working and receiving rising wages that reflect productivity advances.[15]

CASH INCOME MAINTENANCE

The "working poor" concept has governed the nature of public support programs for this demographic group. Since it is assumed that the heads will be (and should be) working, the only cash assistance programs available are related to work.

The first of these is a small program under AFDC (AFDC-UF for the unemployed father), undertaken at each state's option, which provides cash assistance to families with dependent children and a male head if the father is "unemployed." If the father works more than 100 hours a month, he loses eligibility even if he remains poor. Although AFDC-UF was operating in about half of the states in 1971, only 136,000 families received benefits—less than 10 percent of the pre-transfer poor families headed by males at that time. The program only accounts for about 6 percent of the AFDC caseload and program costs.

Second is the unemployment insurance system, which is described more fully in Chapter 3. Although this program covers some working-poor family heads, it is not of major importance in reducing poverty. It does not cover at all the large number of poor family heads who work full time at low wages, or those who are unemployed for lengthy periods. Finally, those who are poor because they have short, but frequent, spells of joblessness are ineligible for unemployment compensation.

In any event, cash assistance for poor families with a male head is not a very significant source of income. Less than one-sixth of such

15. In 1972 in about 90 percent of the poor families headed by a male who was not ill, disabled, or retired, the man worked at some time during the year. In fact, over 45 percent of these males worked full time for fifty or more weeks in the year.

families reported that public assistance payments accounted for more than a quarter of total income in 1972. Similarly, only 15 percent of poor unrelated individuals (people not living with relatives) received as much as 25 percent of their income from public assistance in 1972. By contrast, public assistance accounted for over one-quarter of income for more than one-half of all poor families with a female head.

RECENT CHANGES IN IN-KIND ASSISTANCE

The most significant recent change in public aid that has affected the working poor is the growth of the food stamp program. This is available to all families who meet the income requirements and thus is the only major federal program open throughout the country to poor families headed by a man. In 1971 about 10.5 million persons used the food stamp program, and about one-third of them were not on public assistance.[16] For fiscal 1975, it is estimated that 16 million persons will use food stamps, and that as many as 6 million may be in families not on public assistance, many of whom are among the working poor. Coverage of this group is roughly estimated to double between 1971 and 1975.

If, in 1972, food stamps had been available at the early 1974 level of payments, poverty would have been far less widespread among families with children and a male head, provided that all families eligible for food stamps had participated. Table 7-9 shows that about two-thirds of the income deficit (the difference between the poverty level and actual family income) for these families would have been wiped out by the bonus value of food stamps. Since the aggregated income deficit of these families was $3 billion in 1972 (out of a U.S. total deficit of $12 billion), the effect of food stamps on this group alone is impressive.

Even with food stamps, however, working-poor families are worse off than other poor family groups. Few get any significant cash public assistance. Few qualify for Medicaid, although many more will get medical assistance if national health insurance is enacted (see Chapter 8). Thus the recent expansion of the food stamp program has narrowed—but not eliminated—the differences in treatment of various categories of poor families.

16. Since Table 7-6 counts the food stamp program as public assistance, a significant fraction of the 51 percent of the pre-transfer poor families with children and headed by a man that received transfers were probably getting food stamps.

Table 7-9. Income Deficit and Food Stamp Bonuses for Poor Families with a Male Head, by Size of Family, 1972[a]

Size of family	Number of families (thousands)	Average income deficit (dollars)	Food stamp bonus (dollars)	Total income deficit before food stamps (millions of dollars)	Total income deficit after food stamps (millions of dollars)
One child	394	1,417	864	558.3	217.9
Two children	399	1,528	996	609.7	212.3
Three children	313	1,765	1,080	552.4	214.4
Four children	265	1,867	1,236	494.8	167.2
Five children	177	2,043	1,224	361.6	145.0
Six children or more	146	2,362	1,608	344.9	110.1
All families	1,694	...	...	2,921.7	1,066.9

Sources: U.S. Bureau of the Census, "Characteristics of the Low-Income Population, 1972," pp. 132–33; U.S. Department of Agriculture, "Food Stamp Program Expanded."

a. Food stamp bonuses are computed under rules established January 1, 1974. All computations are made at the mean of the class. Food stamp recipients were assumed to have no deductions or exclusions from income, which implies that bonus values are understated in the table. All poor families were assumed to qualify for food stamps.

Do Income Support Programs Need Reform?

The growth of income support programs in recent years has made the case for welfare reform less compelling than it was five years ago. In 1969, when President Nixon proposed the Family Assistance Plan, the principal arguments in favor of the proposed reforms were:

• The absence of cash assistance—or any other form of substantial aid—to the working poor was claimed to make the whole welfare system unfair. Families whose earner worked hard, but at low wages, got nothing from the transfer system, and were often worse off than some AFDC families which had no working members.

• AFDC caseloads were expanding dramatically. Many attributed this growth to family dissolution induced by AFDC's failure to provide assistance to husband-wife families. As a political matter, the "runaway" growth in AFDC greatly increased interest in doing something about the "welfare crisis."

• The great disparity among states in both AFDC and benefits for adults was considered inequitable and in need of remedy.

• It was alleged that AFDC discouraged work and was driving mothers out of the labor market.

• Paying their share of welfare costs was believed to be draining the coffers of many state and a few local governments.

All of these arguments for reform of the welfare system are much weaker today.

How the Situation Has Changed

Since 1969, a uniform national system of public transfers for the aged and disabled has been created, providing a minimum income and increasing the coverage. Social security benefits have expanded and coverage of the disabled has been extended. SSI has put a national floor under public assistance benefits to adults. Medicare now covers many disabled people. Food stamps are available to supplement the incomes of aged or disabled people whose incomes remain low despite the growth in all of the aforementioned programs.[17]

The food stamp program, which in 1969 served only 4 million people, now serves four times as many. It closes many of the gaps in the welfare system so apparent in 1969. As noted earlier, it appreciably narrows interstate differentials in AFDC payments. Moreover, it is a form of assistance to the working poor that is nationwide and uniform.

There are two significant changes in the AFDC program that have weakened the case for replacing it. First, the AFDC caseload is no longer growing at the previous rapid pace. The sharp increase in AFDC recipients up to the early 1970s was probably because people who were eligible under their state's regulations were applying for and receiving benefits for the first time. In the last few years, however, caseload growth has slowed markedly, and it now seems to depend mainly on state discretionary action to change AFDC eligibility requirements.

The other major change in AFDC came about as a result of an amendment to the AFDC law enacted in the late 1960s. Prior to 1969, an AFDC recipient who worked had her public assistance check reduced for each dollar earned (apart from some work-related expenses). Thus, recipients faced a very high "tax" on earnings, and this feature accounted for much of the sentiment that AFDC discouraged work. The "tax" is now much lower. Under current law, states must allow AFDC recipients to keep the first $30 of monthly earnings; thereafter the AFDC payment is reduced by 67 cents for

17. In the original legislation, persons eligible for SSI were to be made ineligible for food stamps. However, by the time the SSI program took effect in January 1974, the law had been changed so that recipients who could meet the income requirements for food stamps would be eligible for that program until July 1974.

every dollar earned. Union dues, payroll and income taxes, and all work expenses related to earnings are then added back into the AFDC payment. An AFDC mother who earns $120 a month but who incurs work-related expenses of $25 would lose only $35 in AFDC benefits.[18] Thus the $120 earnings makes her family $85 better off (earnings up $120; AFDC payment down $35). In practice, then, the implicit tax rate in the AFDC program is probably around 50 percent and, taken in isolation, the AFDC program does not seem structured to cause massive work disincentives.[19]

Finally, state and local governments do not seem to be under such financial duress as they were five years ago. The SSI program relieved states and localities of paying about $1 billion in welfare costs. Food stamps, which are fully federally funded, have taken some pressure off states to raise cash payment levels in the AFDC program. And general revenue sharing, economic growth, and other factors that have improved the fiscal position of state and local governments have made fiscal relief a good deal less compelling an argument for welfare reform than it used to be.

The New Rationale for Reform

And yet, in 1974, after all the growth in income support over the past five years, reform of the transfer system still ranks high on the agenda of the administration and many other people. There are now three major reasons for believing that a thorough reform of the income support system is needed.

A first reason for changing the income support system is simply that, after a decade of sharp increases in outlays for transfers under federal and state auspices, poverty has not been eliminated. Furthermore, the overall distribution of income has not changed substantially. In 1963, there were 36 million people with incomes of less than half the median income in the nation; by 1971, even though the poverty count dropped, 36 million people still had incomes below half

18. The grant is reduced by two-thirds of $90 in earnings (after the $30 exclusion) but $25 in work-related expenses is then added back to the grant.

19. In the example, the average tax on earnings is 29 percent ($35 divided by $120), but the tax on an additional dollar (marginal tax) would be higher. No single number can characterize the implicit tax in the AFDC program because each welfare office has wide discretion, especially in deciding which work-related expenses to reimburse. See Robert I. Lerman, "Incentive Effects in Public Income Transfer Programs," in *Studies in Public Welfare*, Paper No. 4, pp. 1–78.

the median.[20] Since transfer programs are a major public instrument for bringing about a narrowing in income differences, many have concluded that these programs have to be radically revised if they are to perform the function of redistributing income.

Second, the income support system has become so complex, uncoordinated, and costly that many problems of inefficiency and inequity have arisen. Poorly educated people are thrown up against a system that requires filling out multiple—and often unintelligible—forms to qualify for aid under the various programs. This complexity makes it inevitable, on the one hand, that a costly bureaucracy be maintained to administer the programs and, on the other, that people in similar circumstances are treated differently. The introduction and growth of the many programs of aid now available has increased federal outlays considerably and not all of the extra costs have benefited the poor. Reformers believe that all these outlays are not necessary to achieve the programs' objectives.

Several inequities have already been cited as reasons for reform. Although food stamps have narrowed the gap between different groups of poor people, poor mothers with dependent children can still qualify for substantial cash assistance, while poor families of the same size and income status but with employed male heads cannot. The growth of in-kind programs that do not provide uniform benefits has created other unfair situations. A welfare family living in public housing in a state with a generous Medicaid program and having a child in college on a federal scholarship may be made much better off than a similar welfare family not receiving housing assistance in a state with barebones medical assistance whose child has dropped out of school and is trying to learn a trade.

The uncoordinated growth of income support programs may also create disincentives to work, arising out of the combined impact of several programs on a recipient family. As noted previously, AFDC rules may have reduced the marginal tax on a recipient's earnings to about 50 percent. But if an AFDC family is also receiving in-kind assistance, an earnings increase will reduce food stamp benefits, pub-

20. See *Setting National Priorities: The 1974 Budget*, p. 42. It should be noted, however, that with the growth of in-kind assistance programs, the benefits of which are not counted in these statistics, the well-being of the low-income portion of the population has improved. In addition, the fraction of all people with incomes below half the median did fall from 20 percent to 18 percent between 1963 and 1971. Finally, a growing number of family units are headed by "low-income" students and others whose decision to form a separate unit may be more a sign of affluence than of inequality.

lic housing rent subsidies, federal student aid assistance, and so on. Thus a given family, depending on how many programs it participates in, may face much higher charges against earnings than are apparent from looking at the effects of any one program in isolation. Moreover, the combined benefits of the many programs potentially make not working at all a tempting alternative.[21] Thus reformers seek to eliminate some in-kind programs or to greatly lower the implicit tax rate in cash assistance.

Third, recent research has made the prospect of moving to a universal cash assistance program seem less risky than in the past. As we discuss later in this chapter, most major overhauls of the income support system involve a plan in which the federal government guarantees a minimum level of income to people with no other earnings at all and then reduces the grant by a fraction of each dollar earned. A major stumbling block to the introduction of such a plan has been the fear that many people would simply withdraw from the labor force or greatly reduce work effort if they were guaranteed a minimum level of income.

A recent field study raises serious doubts about such a conclusion. The New Jersey graduated work incentive experiment was a test of the effects of a negative income tax on labor supply in families with a male head—the major group not now covered under cash assistance programs. Families cooperating in the experiment were guaranteed a minimum income (guarantee level) ranging from 50 percent to 125 percent of the poverty level; tax rates on earnings varied from 30 percent to 70 percent. After three years of experimentation, analysis of data showed that there was virtually no difference in the labor force participation between the experimental and the control-group families. White husbands in the experiment worked, on average, only two hours less per week than husbands in the control group, while black husbands did not reduce their work effort at all. Although there was a reduction in the labor force participation of wives in the experimental group, its impact on family income was negligible.

Moreover, analyses of the New Jersey data do not indicate any

21. Vee Burke and Alair Townsend, "Public Welfare and Work Incentives: Theory and Practice," in *Studies in Public Welfare*, Paper No. 14; Robert Lampman, "The Role of Income-Conditioning in the American System of Transfers" (paper presented at the Annual Meeting of the American Economic Association, 1973), forthcoming in American Economic Association, *Papers and Proceedings of the Eighty-sixth Annual Meeting, 1973* (*American Economic Review*, Vol. 64, May 1974); Henry J. Aaron, *Why Is Welfare So Hard to Reform?* (Brookings Institution, 1973).

relation between changes in labor supply and the various tax rates and guarantee levels. Hence, the evidence seems to indicate that for husband-wife families—which supply most of the labor force of the nation—no substantial withdrawal from work would accompany a negative income tax program. At worst, some secondary workers might shorten their hours or stay at home instead.[22] Thus in designing a universal negative income tax plan, guarantee levels and tax rates can be determined mainly by social and broad economic considerations; fear of inducing a permanent welfare class by the design of the program seems much less germane.

Strategies for Change

The rapid growth of cash and in-kind assistance has elicited several strategies for the future of the income support system. First, those who point to the improvements made in recent years are willing to leave the system alone, to "do nothing." At the other pole are those who believe that the problems created by recent growth make "major overhaul" a desirable approach. In between are those who accept the present income support programs but see the need for "tuning up the system."

Do Nothing

Advocates of the "do nothing" strategy maintain that the programs are already remedying many of the problems that plagued the income support system in the past. They also believe that any feasible major change in the system will inevitably make some current recipients of support worse off. It is impossible to design a universal negative income tax system, for example, that maintains the benefits of current recipients of SSI, AFDC, food stamps, and other in-kind programs without imposing punitive taxes on recipients or vastly increasing federal costs. It is argued, therefore, that any attempt to design a major overhaul of the income support system will hurt at least some current beneficiaries.

A reduction of aid to present recipients of assistance may have un-

22. All the results reported in this and the previous paragraph are derived from initial analyses of the data from the New Jersey experiment. Many qualifications will undoubtedly arise as the data are reanalyzed. For further reports on the experiment, see U.S. Department of Health, Education, and Welfare, "Summary Report: New Jersey Graduated Work Incentive Experiment" (1973; processed); Albert Rees, "An Overview of the Labor-Supply Results," and Harold W. Watts and others, "The Labor-Supply Response of Husbands," both in *Journal of Human Resources*, Vol. 9 (Spring 1974), pp. 158–80 and pp. 181–200, respectively.

intended effects. From a political point of view, it is hard to convince legislators that causing losses to some relatively low-income people is a bona fide "reform." Thus attempts to "reform" the system may open a Pandora's box of legislative attempts to "grandfather" recipients, or to compel states to maintain the benefits of those who would lose, or to simply sweeten the pot—possibly in the wrong programs.

Moreover, even if a bill that would cause small losses to only a few people could be enacted, such a policy might have adverse social and economic consequences. A working family receiving a small food stamp bonus for several years may well believe that such a subsidy is its right and it will have adjusted its spending patterns to the aid.[23] To take away this right could cause hardship and might even lead to a loss of public confidence in government. Although economic hardships are caused every day by government policies (for example, when unemployment is caused by fiscal or tariff policy) and rights are often canceled (for example, when a long-standing contract is not renewed), such actions are rarely undertaken under the banner of social progress.

Under these premises, "doing worse" is seen as the principal alternative to "doing nothing" and advocates of the latter are therefore willing to live with an admittedly complex, uncoordinated system that does not solve all of the problems of poverty or income redistribution.

The strategy of doing nothing by no means implies that the federal income support budget will be frozen at current levels. Table 7-10 shows projections of current income support programs based on existing laws. The 1975 outlay base is expanded in future years by two factors. Benefits under all existing programs are assumed to expand both with relevant price indexes and with projected growth in the relevant beneficiary population. It is assumed that real benefits under existing programs remain constant[24] and that no new programs are undertaken (see Chapter 9 for further details on these projections).

Even under these circumstances, income support expenditures will increase by $60 billion, or nearly 50 percent, between 1975 and 1980. When projections of outlays for income support programs are com-

23. The most optimistic forecast for the earliest date a major overhaul of welfare could be implemented is fiscal 1978, so current programs will be in operation for several more years in any event.

24. The exception is in programs where real benefit improvements are automatic. This is the case in social security, unemployment compensation, and federal employee retirement programs where benefits rise with wages as well as with the price level.

Table 7-10. Projections of Federal Outlays for Income Support Programs, Fiscal Years 1975, 1977, and 1980[a]

Outlays in billions of dollars

Program	1975	1977	1980
Cash income maintenance, total	**97**	**115**	**144**
Social security	64	77	98
Supplemental security income	5	6	7
Aid to families with dependent children	4	5	6
All other	23	27	34
Helping people buy essentials, total	**33**	**39**	**47**
Medicare	14	16	20
Medicaid	7	7	9
Food stamps	4	6	7
All other	9	10	11
Income support, total	**130**	**154**	**191**
Total as percent of all federal outlays[b]	43	45	47

Source: Authors' estimates. Detail may not add to totals because of rounding.

a. Full employment is assumed for all years. The rate of inflation of the private GNP deflator is assumed to be 7.5 percent in calendar year 1974 and 3 percent a year thereafter (see Chapter 9).

b. See Chapter 9, Table 9-3.

pared to projections of total federal outlays (using the same assumptions), the cash income maintenance share rises from 32 percent of the total in 1975 to 35 percent in 1980, while outlays to help people buy essentials rise from 11 percent to 12 percent of total outlays during the period (see Table 9-3).

From the point of view of budgetary planning, therefore, a policy of doing nothing in income support will result in an increasing share of projected federal outlays for these programs, largely reflecting built-in growth in the number of beneficiaries.

Tuning Up the System

The uncoordinated growth of income support programs in recent years has created a myriad of apparent inequities in the assistance available to different people with equally low incomes. In addition, it has provided new possibilities for improving the incomes of the poor without undertaking a costly overhaul of the whole income support system. In this section, we discuss several possible reforms that illustrate both the problems and opportunities under existing programs. The reforms we describe attempt to improve the existing system by:

- Improving the coordination of social security and SSI programs.

- Providing more aid to working poor families.
- Reducing differences in AFDC payments in various states.

SSI AND SOCIAL SECURITY

The SSI program covers those ineligible for social security and those whose social security benefits are low. By the middle of 1974, SSI benefits will reach a minimum of $1,752 a year for an individual and $2,628 for a couple, or approximately 75 and 90 percent, respectively, of the estimated poverty line at that time. Many states will supplement SSI payments.

Nearly one-fifth of all elderly social security recipients, or 3.7 million people, will receive SSI as well. Thus improving the integration of these programs becomes important. One problem is that social security benefits will in the future be automatically adjusted for inflation while, under present laws, SSI will not. The effect of this asymmetry is that when prices rise and social security checks go up, elderly and disabled people living on SSI alone receive no benefit increases. Moreover, even those who receive both SSI and social security will not get any increase in monthly payments as inflation proceeds.

This happens because SSI grants are reduced dollar-for-dollar by social security receipts (after the first $20 per month). This arrangement is both inequitable—only wealthier social security recipients are protected against inflation—and has unfortunate tax consequences. SSI is financed out of general revenues while social security benefits are paid out of receipts from the payroll tax. Thus, in inflationary times, the effect of having a cost-of-living escalator only in social security is to impose an increasing share of the support provided to the elderly and disabled poor on the regressive payroll tax.

The administration's proposed solution to this anomalous situation is to provide an automatic cost-of-living escalator in the SSI program. Such a provision would guarantee an SSI recipient the same protection against inflation that social security recipients receive, and maintain the relative balance of the burden of financing old age assistance between general revenue and payroll taxes. If enacted, the proposal will increase federal outlays for the SSI program because current recipients will receive larger payments as the price level rises and because, as the SSI maximum grant is raised, more people will become eligible. We estimate that the outlay implications of a cost-of-living escalator in SSI will amount to somewhat more than $1 billion by fiscal 1980, and have incorporated these increases in the budget projections in Table 7-10.

Another problem in integrating the SSI and the social security programs is the very small advantage given to people who have worked for many years and qualify for minimum social security benefits. For example, a person retiring in July 1974 who worked long enough to qualify for minimum social security payments would receive about $95 a month. If he or she had no other income, the SSI program would pay about $71 a month, bringing total income to $166. Another person who never paid any social security taxes and who became eligible at the same time would qualify for $146 per month in SSI if there were no other source of income. Many people would question whether it is fair that only a $20 per month advantage accrues to the person who paid payroll taxes for many years.

There are several possible solutions to this apparently inequitable treatment of aged people. One is to reduce SSI by only a fraction of each dollar of social security received. If social security benefits were "taxed" at less than a 100 percent rate in SSI, joint SSI–social security beneficiaries would be better off than other SSI recipients. As long as social security minimum benefits are fairly high, such an advantage might be seen as justifying the past payments of social security taxes. Reducing the tax on social security to 67 percent (while continuing the present exclusion from taxation of the first $20 per month) would raise outlays under SSI by $1 billion to $2 billion in 1975, and $2 billion to $3 billion by 1980, as more people became eligible for somewhat larger SSI payments. Alternatively, recipients of both SSI and social security could be allowed to keep a flat sum—say, the first $30 rather than $20—of monthly social security payments without losing any part of their SSI grant. This procedure would reward all combined program recipients equally, while the reduced tax rate on social security would relate gains to social security benefits received.

Ultimately, full coordination of SSI and social security will require recognition that the function of the social security system is vastly different when an income support program like SSI exists. Traditionally, under the old-age insurance program, workers with a history of low wages have been awarded social security benefits that are a larger percentage of their earnings than those with high wages. Before SSI, it was necessary to maintain these high minimum payments under old-age insurance since it was the only national income support program for the aged. Now that the SSI program exists, it should be possible to remove the income support element from social security and base its benefits simply on the average wage earned by workers. Low-wage earners would receive very little in social security benefits upon retirement but they would be covered by SSI. High-wage retirees might receive even more benefits than at present. With this dual system, old-age insurance benefits would be "taxed" at a low rate under the SSI program, thereby aiding the integration of the programs for recipients eligible for benefits under both. The upshot would be a considerably larger SSI income support program, whose benefits would replace the now inflated social security minimums, and a smaller, payroll-tax-financed, "pure" wage-related retirement system.[25]

RAISING FOOD STAMP BENEFITS

The food stamp program, as noted above, is the principal form of federal aid to families that do not qualify under one of the categories for cash assistance. Most of these families are headed by men and include children; some are childless, nonaged, nondisabled individuals and couples. The food stamp program covers near-poor and poor as well. For example, a working father with three dependents who earns as much as $7,200 is eligible for the food stamp program. A large family, with six members, can qualify with earnings up to about $9,800.[26] Moreover, both coupon allotments and income cutoff lines for eligibility in the food stamp program are adjusted twice a year to reflect higher prices of food; thus relatively low-income families will not lose eligibility because of inflation. In this section, we consider the case for an increase in food stamp benefits over and above the automatic inflation adjustment.

According to one estimate as many as 50 million persons will be

---

25. For an extended discussion of these and other proposals for revision of SSI, see James R. Storey and Irene Cox, "The New Supplemental Security Income Program—Impact on Current Benefits and Unresolved Issues," in *Studies in Public Welfare*, Paper No. 10; Michael K. Taussig, "The Social Security Retirement Program and Welfare Reform," in ibid., Paper No. 7, and Joseph A. Pechman, Henry J. Aaron, and Michael K. Taussig, *Social Security: Perspectives for Reform* (Brookings Institution, 1968).

26. This assumes that a married couple files a joint income tax return without itemizing; that all earnings are subject to social security tax; and that there are no deductions for state and local taxes, union dues, child care, rent and so on. These assumptions tend to underestimate the maximum incomes that qualify for food stamps. The estimates are based on July 1974 food stamp rules.

eligible for food stamps at some time during 1974, and by fiscal 1977 the total could rise to 60 million.[27] However, the administration estimates that about 16 million people will participate in the last months of fiscal 1975; many potentially eligible people do not apply, especially if their eligibility will last only a few months or if the bonus value of their stamps is very small. As noted previously, by mid-1974 food stamps will be available throughout the nation, and participation levels should eventually increase.

The universal nature of the food stamp program and its broad coverage make it a promising vehicle for equalizing aid among different categories of poor families. Indeed, short of a major overhaul of the welfare system, the only alternative way to raise the real incomes of poor and near-poor working families is to lower their taxes. But the food stamp program is better designed to direct aid to relatively low-income families than most feasible tax changes.

To illustrate this point, in Table 3-2 of Chapter 3 we presented the distribution of benefits for four tax cut plans focused on low-income people. The plan which conferred the most benefits to low-income families was a measure that introduced a low-income allowance and personal exemption into the social security tax. But even in this plan, 60 percent of the tax benefits would go to families with incomes above $10,000. In contrast, a simple 10 percent increase in the bonus value of food stamps to current recipients would concentrate virtually all of the federal outlays on families with incomes below $10,000. Thus as a means of aiding poor and even near-poor families, food stamp benefit increases have much better leverage than even the most focused of tax cuts. They can bring assistance to the poor without spreading benefits throughout the income distribution.

There are two principal difficulties to surmount when raising food stamp bonuses. The first is that under the existing rules every time monthly coupon allowances (the value of the stamps at the store) are increased, the income eligibility level is increased by a multiple of the allowance increase.[28] Expanding income eligibility may make sense

27. Many of these people would be eligible for only a few months; thus, the number of participants in any given month would necessarily be less. See Burke and Townsend, "Public Welfare and Work Incentives."

28. For example, if coupon allowances were raised by $10 a month for all family sizes, families with gross earnings of about $40 a month over the previous eligibility limit would become eligible for food stamps.

for food stamp increases that take place automatically as food prices rise. But there is no particular reason to extend eligibility limits in the kind of liberalization of benefits under discussion here. To extend eligibility limits would be very costly because eligibility now extends to the densest portion of the income distribution. Even a small change in the income levels eligible for the program could vastly expand the number of participants. The expansion of beneficiaries can be avoided by a simple expedient. When a food stamp beneficiary pays for his or her monthly coupons, the food stamp office could rebate (in food stamp coupons) 10 percent of the difference between the regular monthly coupon allotment and the purchase price.[29] Very low-income families would get a full 10 percent increase in the value of their food stamp coupons while higher-income recipients would receive a smaller increase. Thus federal costs of a food stamp increase can be limited by restricting eligibility for the program to those already eligible and, in addition, bonus value increases can be concentrated on those with the fewest resources.

Another objection to a food stamp benefit increase is that it may distort consumers' choices. If current monthly coupon allotments are just about what a family needs to spend on food, increased food stamp coupons, it can be argued, would lead the family to waste its money on unneeded food, to sell the coupons (which is illegal), or to sell the food it purchases with the coupons. However, families can always choose to purchase less than the maximum monthly coupon allotment and pay proportionately less. So, in practice, the objection is valid only for families that receive free, or nearly free, food stamp allotments[30] (it would not make sense for such families to take less than the full allotment). As yet, there is no convincing evidence that food stamp recipients in substantial number are engaging in the practices that would arise if food stamp coupon allotments became excessive. Should that happen, there may be pressures to switch support either

29. For example, a family of four will be eligible for $150 in monthly coupons in July, 1974. If the normal purchase requirement for the family is $115, the food stamp office would dispense $153.50 in coupons to the family. The extra coupon allowance of $3.50 is 10 percent of the bonus value.

30. In 1972, 5 percent of the households receiving food stamps got them free. About 25 percent of the households paid less than $26 a month for food stamps. The average food stamp recipient pays for about half of his coupon allotment. See Loretta Rowe and John Galvin, "Food Stamp Participation: A Profile," *Food and Nutrition*, Vol. 3 (December 1973), pp. 8–11.

to other in-kind programs (housing allowances, for example) or to move to an all-cash support system.[31]

There is then a case to be made for a limited, but not major, increase in food stamp benefits. A small increase would further the goals of providing more aid to working-poor families and at the same time narrow differences among welfare recipients in different states. Federal outlay increases could be limited and most of the benefits would go to the most needy.

RAISING AFDC BENEFITS

While AFDC benefits in some states are so low that they should be raised, a true reform of the program requires a major rethinking of the objectives of federal income support and should probably be undertaken only in the context of a major overhaul of the transfer system. In this section, we discuss the problems of raising AFDC benefits.

In 1973, there was wide variation in maximum benefits payable to a family of four under AFDC in the various states (Table 7-11). With the poverty line for a family of four at about $4,500, it is not clear that any state makes really adequate cash payments, but the states at the bottom certainly do not. Even though food stamps raise total resources disproportionately in the states with low payments (Table 7-8), AFDC families in those states with no other income remain well below the poverty line. It is natural, then, that a component of many reform proposals is the raising of payment levels in the lowest-paying states, by a federal takeover of AFDC.[32]

There are major problems with the federal government raising payment levels in the AFDC program. One is simply where to draw the line. If the federal government were to establish a $2,400 payment minimum for a family of four with no other income, AFDC families in only one-third of the states would be better off; recipients of the AFDC maximum in the remaining states (containing about 70 percent

---

31. Another proposal, reminiscent of the suggestion that gasoline rationing coupons be transferable, is that food stamp recipients be allowed to sell their coupons. Such an arrangement is a cumbersome way of distributing the equivalent of cash.

32. The federal government could raise AFDC payments in low-paying states in other ways as well—by mandating increases, or changing cost-sharing arrangements. Most of these alternatives raise similar problems to the ones discussed in the text.

Table 7-11. Maximum Family AFDC[a] Payment to Four-Person Families, by Number of States, and Distribution of Recipients in These States, July 1973

Level of payment (dollars)	Number of states[b]	Percent of AFDC recipients
Under 1,600	6	11.5
1,600–2,399	12	18.6
2,400–3,199	14	14.0
3,200–3,999	12	34.6
4,000 and over	7	21.3
Total	51	100.0

Source: U.S. Department of Health, Education, and Welfare, "Public Assistance Programs: Standards for Basic Needs, July 1973."
a. AFDC, aid to families with dependent children.
b. Includes District of Columbia. West Virginia payment figure is for July 1971.

of the AFDC population) would be worse off (Table 7-11).[33] Even at a $4,000 payment level, AFDC recipients in seven states, with 21 percent of the AFDC population, are doing better under existing state plans. This means that any nationalization of AFDC must either institute a very high maximum payment or must allow and supply incentives for state supplements, both of which are costly measures.

The role of the states in any federalization of AFDC is a key issue. Given that states will be allowed to supplement a federal minimum AFDC, there are conflicts in the possible federal goals for the states that make design of a policy very difficult. On the one hand, if the federal government is trying to minimize migration of low-income people motivated by differential welfare benefits, state supplements, especially in wealthy states, should be discouraged. On the other hand, it is the wealthy states that now provide high AFDC payments, so that if the federal goal is to prevent AFDC families from being made worse off, incentives to provide state supplements must be generous.[34]

There is no easy way to resolve the conflicts. A similar problem arose over the SSI program when it was introduced. In that case, Congress stipulated that states already paying above the new federal minimum for adult categories could maintain their higher benefits provided that such supplements were extended to all persons eligible

33. The percent of AFDC recipients shown in Table 7-11 refers to all recipients, not just those receiving maximum payments. Unless the mix of recipients varies widely among the states, these percentages are a rough approximation of the percentage of the AFDC population that would benefit or lose from a national plan.
34. For an extended discussion of these and related points, see Irene Lurie, "Current Public Assistance Benefits and an Assessment of State Supplementation under Proposed Federal Alternatives," in *Studies in Public Welfare*, Paper No. 7.

for SSI. If such benefits were to cost the state more money than their adult assistance costs in 1972, the federal government would pick up the difference. However, any future increases in state supplements would have to be borne by the state. In essence, then, the federal government tried to protect all past beneficiaries from loss and to ensure that newly eligible people were treated like existing beneficiaries without any cost to a state. But because the federal government would not participate in any future increases in state supplements, the long-run hope was that as the federal SSI standard was raised state supplements will steadily diminish. Thus the SSI rules on state supplements offer a test of how the federal and state roles might be coordinated in a program to raise AFDC payments. It is too early to tell what the results will be.

Beyond the difficulties in sorting out state and federal roles in a partial reform of AFDC, it is clear that such a policy would conflict with other goals of reforming the income support system. Raising AFDC payments would widen the gap in federal assistance between different poor families with children, with those having an employed male head falling further behind. It would be ironic to expand food stamp payments, at least in part to improve the status of the working poor, and then to raise AFDC payments so as to worsen the relative position of the working poor. The only sensible ways out of the dilemma are:

• To increase benefits under in-kind programs that are available to all poor families regardless of their demographic makeup. We have illustrated such a change in food stamps. Chapter 8 describes several national health insurance proposals that would replace Medicaid with a program covering all poor and near-poor families in a uniform manner.

• Undertake a major overhaul of cash assistance payments so that all poor families are covered under a uniform national plan.

TUNING UP THE INCOME SUPPORT system might involve two partial reforms. Building on existing programs, one reform would allow aged and disabled people who receive both social security and SSI benefits to keep a larger proportion of their social security benefits and to be protected against inflation. Another, a food stamp bonus increase over and above regular cost-of-living increases, could be instituted with the additional subsidies directed toward the most indigent food stamp beneficiaries. This second reform would be a modest step in the direction of expanding aid in the program with the fewest categorical restrictions, thus bringing about a more equal treatment of different groups of low-income people. This illustrative tuning-up package would involve federal expenditures of about $2 billion in fiscal 1976 rising to about $4 billion in 1980, or only a 1 to 2 percent increase in the income support budget in those years.

Major Overhaul

If past history is any guide, retaining the current structure of the public transfer system—the categories of aided and unaided people, the multiple programs, the mixed state and federal system—will not bring about a substantial narrowing of income differences. If redistribution of income is regarded as the major function of the public transfer system, just patching up the existing structure of transfers may not attain that goal. Even if such a strategy did redistribute incomes, the uncoordinated and overlapping programs are surely an inefficient way to do it. This section reviews the attributes, costs, and issues raised by a major reform of public transfer programs.

UNIVERSAL DEMOGRANTS

The simplest and most extreme proposal is for a universal demogrant plan, fully integrated with the income tax system, along the lines suggested by Senator George McGovern in the 1972 presidential campaign. An illustration of the characteristics of such a program is as follows. The government would give every citizen a grant of $1,000 per year (the *guarantee level*). Since the total grants under such a plan would amount to over $200 billion dollars, the federal government would have to broaden the tax base and impose a substantial tax in order to pay for the grants. Suppose a 40 percent *marginal tax rate on all incomes* were introduced to finance the grant. Then the demogrant system for a family of four with no income would provide $4,000; $1,600 to a family with $6,000 income (a grant of $4,000, tax of $2,400); zero to a family with $10,000 income (*break-even level*); and a family with $15,000 income would pay a net tax of $2,000 (a $4,000 grant, tax of $6,000). Thus, in practice, grants would actually be paid only to those families below the break-even level. Much less than $200 billion would actually be transferred.

A universal demogrant system could introduce many variants on this basic scheme. For example, the plan just outlined would create tremendous net income differences for families of different sizes earning the same income. A couple with four children earning $8,000 would receive a net grant of $2,800, while a single person earning $8,000 would pay a net tax of $2,200. For equivalent earnings, after-tax incomes would be nearly twice as large for the family as for the single person. Thus most demogrant plans would offer grants differentiated by age; for example, $1,400 per adult and $600 per child.

Universal demogrants have the advantage of simplicity and are effective as redistributors of income. The demogrant is simply a conversion of existing personal exemptions in the federal income tax into tax credits—at a much higher level, to be sure—with the single added proviso that the taxpayer is allowed to convert tax credits that exceed tax liabilities into cash. The universal demogrant is also a manipulable redistributive measure in that by varying the amount of the demogrant different degrees of redistribution could be achieved for special groups (for example, the aged, blind, and disabled could be given double demogrants).[35]

Simplicity and effectiveness notwithstanding, a universal demogrant plan has not proved politically attractive in the past. Any program that sets reasonable grant levels is quite expensive and can be made to look even more so. Because payments would be extended to so many people, demogrants would require large-scale tax reforms. While such reforms do improve the equity of the tax-transfer system, they also add powerful special interest groups to the opposition. For these reasons, it may be more feasible not to try to reform the positive income tax system along with the welfare system, but to seek less ambitious ways of overhauling income support programs.

UNIVERSAL NEGATIVE INCOME TAX

Another possibility, first suggested by Milton Friedman, is a negative income tax. Like a demogrant, the universal negative income tax covers all categories of people, specifies a guarantee level at zero income that varies with family size, and allows the grant to phase out as income rises. Unlike the universal demogrant, however, a universal negative income tax does not necessarily involve any major revisions in the positive income tax laws and is usually designed to confine cash

35. A thorough discussion of demogrant proposals is given in Benjamin A. Okner, "The Role of Demogrants as an Income Maintenance Alternative," in *Studies in Public Welfare*, Paper No. 9, Pt. 1. Brookings Reprint 272.

allowances to the lower end of the income distribution, thus greatly reducing costs.

The basic advantage of a universal negative income tax over the present system is that it will eliminate the unequal treatment of poor families who fall into different demographic categories. The most important changes are the coverage of families with children and a male head who is neither unemployed nor disabled, and the coverage of childless couples and individuals. Up to now, American social policy has assumed that people in these categories should work for their income and that cash assistance was either unnecessary or a tempting alternative to work. The growth of the food stamp program and the growing acceptance of national health insurance indicate that the public now accepts in-kind assistance to such individuals. But the provision of cash assistance to working families has not yet won public approval.

A universal negative income tax, if it provided generous guarantee levels, could eliminate the need for several existing income support programs, and for state supplements as well. Thus a generous federal plan would narrow interstate differences in income support programs.

By converting the existing welfare system into a uniform federal cash program, the negative tax could bring administrative simplicity to the income support system. An agency such as the Internal Revenue Service could accept relatively simple income declarations, compute the benefits, and send out the payments, just as it does with the regular income tax. (However, recent legislative experience indicates that what looks simple on the drawing board can become very complex in actual law.)

Federal outlays required to support a universal negative income tax program in 1976, and the federal cost of some of the programs it might replace, are given in Table 7-12. A federal guarantee of $4,000 for a family of four, about three-quarters of the poverty standard for this family, would provide a maximum payment for AFDC families equal to or above those currently in force in forty-four states. The $4,000 guarantee level would probably have to be combined with a tax rate of no more than 50 percent in order to maintain coverage of the existing AFDC population and not raise actual tax rates. This program would cost the federal government an estimated $22 billion in 1976. But such a figure overstates the net cost to the federal government because at least some existing programs could be replaced.

Table 7-12. Gross Federal Cost of a Universal Negative Income Tax, Calendar Year 1976, and Cost of Three Existing Income Support Programs, Fiscal Year 1977

Guarantee level for a family of four[a] (dollars)	Marginal tax rate on earned income[b] (percent)	Total cost in 1976 (billions of dollars)
Negative income tax		
3,200	67	11.8
3,200	50	13.9
3,200	33	19.8
4,000	67	17.8
4,000	50	21.9
4,000	33	33.2
4,800	67	24.3
4,800	50	30.9
4,800	33	48.8

. . . .

Existing programs, federal cost only, fiscal year 1977	
Supplemental security income	5.6
Aid to families with dependent children	4.9
Food stamps	5.9

Source: TRIM model, Urban Institute.

a. The $3,200 guarantee level for a family of four provides $1,060 for each of the first two family members; $540 each for the third, fourth, and fifth members and $440 per person above five in the family. The $4,000 guarantee level provides $1,340 for each of the first two family members, $660 each for the third, fourth, and fifth members, and $560 for each member above five. In the $4,800 guarantee plan, $1,600 is provided for the first two family members, $800 for each of the next three, and $500 for each family member thereafter.

b. The marginal tax rate on unearned income is 100 percent.

The prime candidate for replacement is the AFDC program. However, since seven states with 21 percent of the AFDC caseload now set higher maximum payments for a family of four, some provision for state supplements may be necessary, and if the federal government were to share in the cost of such supplements, all of the projected $5 billion (Table 7-12) in federal AFDC costs would not be eliminated.

Many people now eligible for SSI would be covered at somewhat lower benefit levels under this negative income tax plan, suggesting that SSI could not be eliminated entirely either. SSI maximum payments in fiscal 1977 will be about $1,900 for a single person and $2,800 for a couple, slightly above those in this plan, under which single persons would receive a maximum of $1,340 per year and a couple would receive $2,680. Moreover, the negative tax program sets quite tight rules as to the "filing unit." That is, the costs are computed on the assumption that elderly and disabled people who are part of a household headed by a younger person would receive benefits only as a member of that household, receiving the small benefit the program pays for extra individuals in large families. Under SSI, many such people can file individually to their advantage. Thus, the plan under discussion worsens the position of some SSI beneficiaries.

Even if the food stamp program were retained, its cost would fall with a universal negative income tax because the grants received under such a program would count as income to food stamp recipients, thereby reducing the bonus values to which they were entitled. However, eliminating food stamps, which is the intent of most people who advocate a universal negative income tax, raises a number of problems. Many AFDC recipients in high payment states would be made much worse off if both AFDC and food stamps were eliminated by a universal negative tax. AFDC recipients of maximum payments who live in states with maximums over about $3,200 a year would suffer losses if food stamps were replaced by a $4,000 negative tax program with a 50 percent tax on earned income.[36] In 1973, nineteen states paid maximums in excess of $3,200. Of course, AFDC recipients in these states may be receiving aid under many other in-kind programs; thus a loss of food stamp benefits may not be so serious a social loss.

On balance, we estimate that about two-thirds of the projected $16 billion costs of the AFDC, SSI, and food stamp programs could be saved if a negative income tax with a $4,000 guarantee and 50 percent tax were introduced. The remaining third could be used for state supplements under AFDC, federal payments to SSI recipients whose income would be cut severely by the negative tax plan, or continuation of a much smaller food stamp program. Thus, the net federal cost of this $4,000 guarantee level plan would be reduced to about $11 billion, if the potential savings in existing programs are taken into account.

Even a program of this magnitude would lower the income of some beneficiaries. Most of the measures that could be taken to protect such people would significantly increase the costs of a negative tax program.

The negative tax plans shown in Table 7-12 use an annual "accounting period" (the period of time over which income is measured) to

36. AFDC families with earnings would be even worse off than those receiving the maximum payment if food stamps were eliminated because the negative income tax reduces the grant by 50 cents per dollar of earnings while the food stamp bonus only falls 30 cents per dollar of earnings.

determine eligibility and benefits. Under the three existing welfare programs, a very short accounting period is used, usually a month. Since there are many more temporary poor than permanently poor people, a negative tax plan with a strict annual accounting period would fail to aid many people who are now eligible for cash and in-kind benefits.

Thus one change would be to institute a monthly accounting period (with monthly reporting of income) as the determinant of payments in the negative income tax program. Such a change would increase the costs of the negative tax plan by several billion dollars. While such an accounting period might protect some short-term needy persons, it would entitle a large number of farmers, teachers, and other non-poor people with irregular patterns of income to benefits. Other accounting periods, using average income over a period of several months, seem less costly yet able to meet short-term need.[37]

Liberalizing the rules on what constitutes a filing unit under a negative income tax is another program variant to consider. Any program that sets higher guarantees for the first few members of a filing unit than for additional members creates incentives for households to split up. In the estimates presented in Table 7-12, a minimal amount of such splitting was assumed to take place in response to a negative tax program. But, depending on the exact filing rules set under an actual program, the costs presented in the table may understate the true costs. It is impossible to state any one estimate of the cost of the various possible filing rules and household responses, but very liberal filing rules could easily add several billion dollars to federal net costs.

The plans shown in Table 7-12 impose a 100 percent tax on unearned income. Thus, another modification would be to tax unearned income (such as social security, interest, rents, private pensions) at less than 100 percent, if for no other reason than to avoid discouraging private saving. Converting the 100 percent tax on unearned income to a 50 percent tax under the $4,000–50 percent plan is estimated to cost the federal government an additional $5 billion to $7 billion a year. Most of this added cost would be due to the large number of social security recipients who would become eligible for the program under a 50 percent tax on unearned income.

Alternatively, the guarantee level or tax rate could be changed from

37. See Jodie T. Allen, "Designing Income Maintenance Systems: The Income Accounting Problem," in *Studies in Public Welfare*, Paper No. 5, Pt. 3, pp. 47–97.

Table 7-13. Number of Families with and without Children and Number of Persons Eligible to Participate in Universal Negative Income Tax Programs, 1976

Guarantee level for a family of four (dollars)	Marginal tax rate on earned income (percent)	Number of families with children (millions)	Number of families without children (millions)	Number of persons (millions)
3,200	67	4.4	3.8	24
3,200	50	5.1	4.3	32
3,200	33	10.1	5.7	55
4,000	67	5.6	5.1	32
4,000	50	8.0	6.0	45
4,000	33	14.3	8.3	78
4,800	67	6.9	6.5	40
4,800	50	10.4	7.8	58
4,800	33	18.2	10.9	99

Source: TRIM model, Urban Institute.

the program we have been describing. For example, raising the guarantee for a family of four to $4,800 (about 90 percent of the poverty level in 1976) and retaining the 50 percent tax on earned income, would make it possible to eliminate SSI, AFDC, and food stamps—and poverty. The net federal cost of this program would be about $15 billion. As Table 7-13 indicates, a program of this magnitude would provide benefits to an estimated 58 million people, about a quarter of the U.S. population. So many people would be eligible because all families (with four members) with incomes below $9,600 would be eligible for the program.

Another variation is a negative income tax with a lower tax rate. Such a rate may take on added significance if national health insurance is enacted. All the major national health insurance proposals discussed in Chapter 8 contain provisions for a gradual decrease in benefits in the $5,000 to $10,000 income range. These reduced medical benefits that result from higher earnings under health insurance act like a tax on earnings. Thus in order to hold down the overall tax rate on earnings for a negative income tax beneficiary, it may be desirable to reduce the tax rate in the cash assistance program to compensate for the health insurance tax. The 33 percent tax rate plan does just that, but the gain is bought at a high price. About $11 billion is added to the federal cost of a $4,000 guarantee level program in reducing the marginal tax rate. Since so many families have incomes between $8,000 and $12,000 (the respective break-even income levels of the two plans), the number of beneficiaries would rise by nearly 35 million persons under the low tax plan.

Instituting a universal negative income tax program, even at low guarantee levels, would be a costly undertaking. With any feasible plan, some previous recipients of public aid would be worse off. Rules established for filing units and for benefits available to families of different size would cause changes in family composition that are difficult to predict (and difficult to evaluate even if predictable). Net federal costs would be difficult to estimate.

But these issues are not what have dominated the public debate over negative income taxes; that debate has turned on an even more fundamental question: Is the federal government to provide all people with a minimum level of income as a right, as it already does for categories of people adjudged unable to support themselves? Many fear that a substantial number of people will stop working or work less and live off their federal payments. As indicated earlier, the evidence is against any sizable exodus from the labor market by the millions of working families. But the proof will come only when the nation actually undertakes a universal negative income tax.

The resistance of many political leaders to the concept of minimum incomes by right is shown by repeated attempts to combine a "work requirement" of some sort with a negative income tax. The basic idea is to protect the taxpayer against the development of an idle class by insisting that applicants for public aid either demonstrate their incapacity to work or register for work and accept jobs that would be proffered by the public agency administering the program. Several existing public aid programs contain such requirements, and experience with them has been unfavorable. Work requirements can be demeaning when applicants are forced to take jobs with unfair pay or for which they are unsuited. More commonly, work requirements can be perfunctory—jobs are not available or offered, nor are placements made. "Strong" work requirements could also become an administrative nightmare. Does one force a person who works only part time to take a full-time job? What about a person whose personal habits disconcert his fellow workers? What about a Ph.D. who drives a cab—intermittently?

INCOME SUPPORT PROGRAMS are now at a delicate phase in their history. Recent developments in federal policy suggest that the future

may bring a panoply of in-kind programs that are income tested—
food stamps, national health insurance, student aid, housing allowances, fuel coupons—as the means for dealing with problems in the
future. As more of these programs are introduced, problems of duplication and coordination multiply and it becomes more difficult to
travel the principal alternative path of a universal negative income
tax. The provision of such cash aid to all categories of low-income
families will mean facing up to the desirability of guaranteeing minimum incomes as a matter of right. Until that weighty issue is resolved, however, the growth of the income support system in recent
years has made it possible to continue existing programs, perhaps
with a little tuning up, without abandoning the needs of the low-
income segment of the population.

8. National Health Insurance

by Karen Davis

THE UNITED STATES IS UNIQUE among modern industrial countries
in that it does not have a comprehensive national health insurance
system. President Harry S. Truman proposed national health insurance as early as 1945 but it was not until 1966 that the first major
federal health insurance programs—Medicare and Medicaid—were
implemented. These programs help those typically outside the work
force—the poor, the elderly, and the totally disabled—pay for medical
bills. In recent years, rising medical costs and continuing inadequacies
of private and public programs have created renewed interest in a
comprehensive national health insurance system. Over a dozen national health insurance bills have been introduced in Congress. And
in February 1974, the administration introduced a new bill, which, if
enacted by Congress, would add an estimated $6 billion to the federal
budget at 1975 prices, or about $8 billion in fiscal 1977 when the pro-
gram takes full effect.

Progress toward national health insurance has been slow, not because the present system for meeting the cost of medical care is satis-
factory, but because there is no consensus on the appropriate solution
to the problem. In this chapter, we review the need for national health
insurance and examine the basic issues yet to be resolved. Four major
national health insurance bills are analyzed: (1) the new administration bill, which builds on the current mix of private and public programs; (2) the Long-Ribicoff bill, which would replace Medicaid with

a uniform federal program for the poor as well as provide catastrophic expense protection for all persons; (3) the Kennedy-Griffiths bill, which would finance all medical care through a single federal system; and (4) the compromise Kennedy-Mills bill, introduced in April 1974, which would provide a benefit package similar to that of the administration, but with financing and administration by the federal government. We conclude with an examination of the budgetary implications of the administration and Kennedy-Mills plans.

How Great Is the Need for National Health Insurance?

The current mix of private and public health programs provides medical care and limits the financial burden of large medical expenditures for many persons. Almost 80 percent of the population under age sixty-five has some hospitalization and surgical insurance. Nearly all of the elderly and many of the permanently disabled are covered by Medicare. The federal-state Medicaid program in 1973 paid for medical care services received by more than 23 million low-income persons.

An examination of existing public and private health programs, however, reveals many serious gaps, despite extensive enrollment in private plans and sizable public expenditures.

Private Health Insurance

Over 20 percent of the population under the age of sixty-five has no private health insurance. A disproportionate number of the working poor, of blacks, and of people living in the South are among those uninsured. So are people regarded by insurance companies as health risks. Forty percent of all black people and 60 percent of the poor do not have health insurance coverage. Of persons under age sixty-five, 82 percent have insurance coverage in the Northeast compared with only 72 percent in the South.

Full-time workers are far more likely to have some private health insurance coverage than part-time workers or those without jobs. As shown in Table 8-1, 88 percent of full-time workers have insurance compared with 44 percent of part-time workers and only 27 percent of the unemployed. Furthermore, for any given type of worker, private insurance coverage is much more prevalent among higher-income workers.

Table 8-1. Private Health Insurance Enrollment Rates of Persons under Age 65 Not Covered by Medicaid, by Labor Force Status and Selected Income Class, 1970
Percent

Labor force status of family head	All incomes	Annual income class			
		Poor (under $3,000)	Near poor ($3,000– 5,000)	Middle income ($7,000– 10,000)	High income (over $15,000)
Full-time employed	88	41	73	89	98
Part-time employed	44	35	52	62	...
Disabled[a]	38	20	40	...	...
Unemployed	27	4	20	...	...
All statuses	76	38	65	92	95

Source: Charles E. Phelps, "Testimony before U.S. House of Representatives, Subcommittee on Public Health and Environment" (Rand Corporation, December 14, 1973; processed), Table 6.
a. Many disabled counted in these statistics are now covered by Medicare.

Another serious shortcoming is that most existing plans emphasize hospitalization and do not provide full coverage for outpatient and preventive care. Only half of the population under age sixty-five has any insurance for out-of-hospital services.

Private insurance also frequently fails to cover very large medical expenses. Only half of the population has any major medical insurance, and limits are frequently placed on payments by insurance companies. Even high-wage firms frequently have inadequate provisions, with maximum liabilities often restricted to $5,000. In lower-wage industries, insurance benefits are still lower. In one such industry, hospital benefits of only $15 per day for a maximum of thirty-one days are provided, and the most expensive surgical allowance is $250.[1] One-third of all private hospitalization plans are limited in coverage to sixty days or less. Thus even workers with some private health insurance coverage may be bankrupted if they incur long hospitalization or high medical bills.

Finally, the costs of private health insurance are frequently burdensome. Some 30 percent of full-time workers have no group coverage. Among the self-employed, 75 percent do not have access to group rates. The only options available to such workers are to purchase insurance at high individual rates—where, on average, companies pay out only 53 cents in benefits for every dollar of premiums collected— or be without insurance coverage.

1. U.S. Department of Health, Education, and Welfare, Fact Sheet Package, February 1974.

Medicaid

Many poor people were without needed care before the introduction of the federal-state Medicaid program. Medicaid attempted to alleviate this situation—if not for all poor persons, at least for those on welfare. Half the states also provide coverage to "medically needy" persons who might be forced onto the welfare rolls if they attempted to meet their medical bills directly.[2]

Under Medicaid, the federal government shares with the states the costs of providing a wide range of medical services. The federal share of costs ranges from 83 percent in the lowest-income states to 50 percent in states such as New York, California, and Massachusetts. Each state determines eligibility based on income and asset requirements that vary widely. Medicaid tries to encourage uniform benefits among the states by requiring coverage of basic services such as hospital care and physician services. The states have the option of covering such items as drugs, dental services, optometrist services, and private nurses. Some states have added the full range of optional services, but others cover only a few. In addition, states are permitted to place limits on the extent of coverage of basic services; for example, one state (Louisiana) covers only fifteen days of hospital care, and other states place limits on the number of physician visits. Nearly all states purchase Medicare physician insurance for elderly welfare recipients and pay the patient's share of Medicare costs. In fiscal 1975, Medicaid is expected to spend $12 billion on medical services for 29 million poor and needy persons.

Recent evidence indicates that Medicaid has had mixed success in meeting its original objectives.[3] On the positive side, there have been marked improvements in contact with the medical system by the poor. In 1970, 65 percent of the people with incomes below $3,000 saw a physician during the year, contrasted with only 56 percent in 1963. Furthermore, these gains were not shared by the higher-income groups, so that the poor proportionately increased their use of services in relation to others. Poor pregnant women also began to visit physi-

2. Medically needy persons eligible for Medicaid are individuals who are aged, blind, or disabled, or families with dependent children whose income net of medical expenses is within 133 percent of the public assistance support level.
3. For further elaboration and documentation of the impact of Medicaid discussed in this section, see Karen Davis, "Medicaid—Its Impact on the Poor" (Brookings Institution, 1974; processed).

cians much earlier: 71 percent of low-income women received medical attention in the first trimester of pregnancy in 1970, compared with only 58 percent in 1963.

These gains in use of medical services, however, are not shared equally by all of the poor. Welfare recipients who are eligible for Medicaid visited physicians 40 percent more frequently than other persons with family incomes below $5,000. Furthermore, there are wide variations in benefits even among those covered by Medicaid. For example, whites use the program much more than blacks. Payments for whites are 76 percent higher per recipient on the average than for blacks.[4] Moreover, the difference between rural and urban residents is striking. Average Medicaid expenditures per poor child are less than $5 annually in rural areas compared with $76 in central cities.[5]

These lower Medicaid payments reflect in part a shortage of physicians in rural and minority neighborhoods, lower medical prices, and inadequate health services; and in part the larger concentrations of poor blacks and rural residents in states with limited Medicaid programs. As shown in Table 8-2, states vary greatly in average Medicaid payments per recipient and even more substantially in the proportion of poor persons eligible for benefits. Medicaid payments per child recipient averaged $43 in Mississippi compared with $133 in New York. Moreover, only one-tenth of the poor children in Mississippi received Medicaid benefits whereas nearly all the poor and many of the near-poor children in New York received them. As a consequence, the disparity in payments per poor child was even larger.

Medicare

The Medicare program for the elderly differs from Medicaid in that it is a federal program with uniform benefits. All elderly people covered by the social security program are automatically eligible for hospitalization insurance and 97 percent of those with hospitalization insurance also enroll in the voluntary supplementary medical insur-

4. See Karen Davis, "Financing Medical Care: Implications for Access to Primary Care," in Spyros Andreopoulos (ed.), *Primary Medical Care* (John Wiley, forthcoming, 1974).

5. See Ronald Andersen and others, *Expenditures for Personal Health Services: National Trends and Variations, 1953–1970*, DHEW (HRA) 74-3105 (U.S. Public Health Service, Health Resources Administration, 1973), p. 52.

Table 8-2. Medicaid Payments per Recipient and per Poor Person, and Ratios of Recipients to Poor, by Age and State, 1970

Region and state	Children, under age 21			Adults, age 21–64			Adults, age 65 and over		
	Medicaid payments per child recipient	Ratio of recipients to poor children	Medicaid payments per poor child	Medicaid payments per adult recipient	Ratio of recipients to poor adults	Medicaid payments per poor adult	Medicaid payments per aged recipient	Ratio of recipients to poor aged	Medicaid payments per poor aged
United States	$126	0.55	$69	$408	0.61	$250	$527	0.69	$363
Northeast	132	1.24	163	404	1.31	530	999	0.67	667
Maine	109	0.48	52	321	0.46	147	341	0.32	110
New Hampshire	98	0.46	45	471	0.37	174	150	0.52	78
Vermont	201	0.80	160	361	0.60	215	601	0.72	435
Massachusetts	a	a	a	a	a	a	a	a	a
Rhode Island	134	0.72	97	354	1.02	362	633	1.30	825
Connecticut	149	1.04	155	674	0.53	359	1,803	0.51	918
New York	133	1.68	224	450	1.72	773	1,049	1.02	1,075
New Jersey	153	0.70	108	215	0.63	134	1,942	0.22	433
Pennsylvania	117	0.97	113	329	1.28	422	675	0.38	259
North Central	137	0.49	67	525	0.41	216	700	0.40	279
Ohio	103	0.40	41	435	0.36	156	629	0.29	185
Indiana	89	0.26	23	417	0.22	93	376	0.21	78
Illinois	159	0.70	111	558	0.50	279	546	0.34	185
Michigan	122	0.51	62	573	0.62	356	1,260	0.47	593
Wisconsin	237	0.66	155	848	0.47	395	1,054	0.62	656
Minnesota	143	0.72	103	607	0.40	243	1,044	0.55	573
Iowa	103	0.43	44	319	0.32	101	227	0.32	73
Missouri	80	0.33	26	331	0.33	110	296	0.55	161
North Dakota	142	0.20	29	587	0.22	127	928	0.40	367
South Dakota	114	0.14	17	440	0.14	62	690	0.28	196
Nebraska	120	0.31	38	492	0.31	154	382	0.39	150
Kansas	129	0.51	66	498	0.45	226	478	0.36	170
South	108	0.20	21	349	0.23	79	334	0.53	176
Delaware	64	0.81	52	343	0.48	165	151	0.28	42

Maryland	118	0.73	86	376	0.83	313	464	0.68	316
District of Columbia	171	1.10	189	442	0.72	317	431	0.67	291
Virginia	98	0.20	19	374	0.18	69	250	0.28	69
West Virginia	87	0.38	33	183	0.39	71	135	0.19	25
North Carolina	a	a	a	a	a	a	a	a	a
South Carolina	65	0.09	6	325	0.19	60	475	0.38	180
Georgia	87	0.26	23	447	0.31	139	416	0.71	296
Florida	68	0.20	13	192	0.25	48	351	0.43	150
Kentucky	76	0.38	29	262	0.37	96	231	0.68	158
Tennessee	66	0.16	10	222	0.17	37	166	0.32	53
Alabama	97	0.10	10	446	0.11	48	511	0.49	253
Mississippi	43	0.11	5	264	0.07	20	181	0.49	89
Arkansas	56	0.06	4	179	0.10	17	68	0.19	13
Louisiana	112	0.08	9	260	0.18	46	245	0.94	230
Oklahoma	201	0.37	75	402	0.43	174	583	0.64	372
Texas	215	0.08	17	738	0.09	69	326	0.66	213
West	**122**	**0.96**	**117**	**389**	**1.29**	**500**	**350**	**1.97**	**690**
Montana	127	0.28	35	451	0.26	118	669	0.31	207
Idaho	90	0.26	23	436	0.29	126	829	0.26	217
Wyoming	75	0.18	13	308	0.18	56	273	0.24	67
Colorado	91	0.40	36	340	0.55	186	328	1.34	440
New Mexico	97	0.26	25	352	0.29	103	274	0.37	101
Arizona	b	b	b	b	b	b	b	b	b
Utah	190	0.27	52	329	0.73	240	376	0.50	186
Nevada	119	0.47	56	558	0.34	190	794	0.55	440
Washington	99	0.70	69	317	1.13	359	748	0.67	498
Oregon	99	0.35	35	283	0.47	133	298	0.31	92
California	126	1.33	168	389	1.73	672	321	3.17	1,017
Hawaii	100	0.92	92	319	1.01	322	1,162	0.96	1,119
Alaska	b	b	b	b	b	b	b	b	b

Sources: Medicaid payments and recipients: U.S. Department of Health, Education, and Welfare, Social and Rehabilitation Service, "Numbers of Recipients and Amounts of Payments under Medicaid and Other Medical Programs Financed from Public Assistance Funds,"DHEW Publication (SRS) 73-03153 (1972; processed); poverty population: U.S. Bureau of the Census, Census of Population, 1970, Detailed Characteristics, Series PC(1)-D, Tables 207, 215, 216.

a. Data not reported for Massachusetts and North Carolina. Regional and national totals do not include these states.

b. Arizona and Alaska did not have Medicaid programs in 1970. Regional and national totals do not include these states.

ance plan (SMI) that covers physician services and provides certain other benefits. Recent amendments extend Medicare benefits to persons with chronic kidney disease and persons who have been disabled for two years or more.

Beneficiaries must pay a deductible of $84 covering up to sixty days in the hospital; between the sixty-first and ninetieth days they must pay coinsurance of $21 a day; for the next sixty days they must pay $42 a day, after which hospital insurance ceases. Under SMI they must pay each year the first $60 of physician charges and 20 percent of the remainder. They also pay a monthly premium for SMI, in May 1974 set at $6.30. Federal expenditures under Medicare are expected to total $13 billion in fiscal 1975, covering medical care services for 23.5 million elderly, disabled, and chronically ill persons.

Medicare has markedly increased the elderly's access to medical care services, particularly to institutional services such as hospital and nursing-home care. However, the program still has several shortcomings.

Even though the same set of basic benefits are available to all covered persons regardless of income, race, or geographical location, there are wide differences in the use of services and benefits received by these groups. As in Medicaid, those groups with the poorest health receive the lowest benefits from the program—blacks, rural residents, and persons living in the South.

INEQUALITY BY INCOME

Benefits from the physician portion of Medicare are particularly unequally distributed among income classes. Despite better health, elderly persons with family incomes above $15,000 receive twice as much under Medicare's voluntary supplementary medical insurance program as those with incomes below $5,000.[6] Furthermore, these differences are not attributable solely to advantages that most higher-income persons possess—such as more education or living in areas with a greater concentration of specialized medical resources. Instead, the $60 deductible and 20 percent coinsurance provisions of the physician portion of Medicare pose significant deterrents to the use of medical services by the poor. For those poor persons for whom

6. About half of this difference is accounted for by differences in frequency of use while the other half reflects the greater reliance on specialists and more expensive physicians by higher-income persons.

Medicaid pays the premium, deductible, and coinsurance required by Medicare, use of medical services is commensurate with that of middle-income persons with similar health needs.[7] For poor persons not covered by Medicaid, use of medical services lags substantially behind that of other persons with similar health conditions.

INEQUALITY BY RACE

There are also substantial inequalities in Medicare benefits on the basis of race. Medicare has contributed to the reduction of discriminatory barriers to medical care through its insistence that hospitals provide services on a nondiscriminatory basis as a prerequisite for participation in the Medicare program. Despite notable achievements in access to hospital care for minorities, however, the program has not been very successful in ensuring equality in treatment for other types of medical services, particularly physician and nursing-home services. In 1968, Medicare payments for elderly whites were 30 percent more for inpatient hospital care per person enrolled than for blacks, 60 percent more for physician services, and more than twice as much for extended care facility services. In the South, the racial disparity is greater: whites received 55 percent more for inpatient hospital care, 95 percent more for physician services, and almost two-and-one-half times as much for extended care services. Furthermore, the lower utilization of medical services by blacks is attributable not only to their lower average incomes and poorer education, but to discrimination and other factors associated with race. Elderly blacks' unequal access to these services is particularly regrettable in view of their poorer health status and limited supporting services in the home.

If national health insurance is to provide equal access to medical care for blacks and other minorities, nondiscriminatory practices by providers of medical services must be rigorously enforced. In addition, specific supply programs designed to increase minorities' access to medical care are an essential component of a national health policy.

REGIONAL DISPARITIES

Despite the national uniformity of the Medicare program, there are substantial variations in benefits by location. Elderly persons in the

7. For further elaboration and documentation of the impact of Medicare discussed in this section, see Karen Davis, "Equal Treatment and Unequal Benefits: The Medicare Program" (Brookings Institution, 1973; processed).

West, for example, receive 45 percent more Medicare payments per person than elderly persons in the South. About one-third of this difference reflects regional medical price differences while the rest reflects the lower utilization of medical services by the elderly in areas with few physicians per capita. Urban-rural differences are similar. Persons eligible for Medicare benefits in nonmetropolitan counties received $250 in 1969, compared with $360 for persons in central cities of metropolitan counties. Again, if national health insurance is to provide an equitable distribution of benefits, specific programs to improve the delivery of health care services in rural areas and areas with limited medical resources must be developed.

INCOMPLETE COVERAGE

Since Medicare is restricted to persons covered by social security, several hundred thousand elderly persons do not automatically receive benefits. In 1972, Medicare was amended to permit those elderly people not covered by social security to purchase Medicare hospitalization insurance at a premium sufficient to cover the average cost of the program, or about $400 annually. Since some of those excluded from coverage, however, are very poor elderly persons, such as former domestic workers or migrant laborers, this change is of only limited benefit. Furthermore, the $80 premium charged for coverage under the physician portion of Medicare has deterred about half a million elderly persons from receiving that coverage—and, once again, the poor, blacks, and persons in the South are disproportionately represented among the excluded.

INADEQUATE CATASTROPHIC COVERAGE

Although Medicare meets a large portion of medical bills for many of the elderly, it nevertheless subjects all covered persons to the possibility of burdensome out-of-pocket expenditures. Under the hospital insurance plan, once the patient has been in the hospital for 150 days, the program makes no further payments and the patient is forced to pick up all expenses.[8] Even a patient hospitalized for 150 days would be required to pay over $3,000.

The physician part of Medicare, while placing no limits on the amounts covered, pays only 80 percent of "allowable" physician

8. Coverage is limited to 90 days plus a lifetime reserve of 60 days.

charges. The patient must pay the first $60 of bills, the other 20 percent of the "allowable" fee, and any excess of the actual over the allowable amount. Other services such as private-duty nursing and out-of-hospital drugs are not covered at all. If an elderly person is sick for long enough, he or she may incur ruinous out-of-pocket costs.

What Should National Health Insurance Accomplish?

Medical care can be essential to the prolongation of life, reduction of pain and suffering, and the ability to live a healthy, productive life free of debilitating illness. Protection against medical disability is increasingly regarded as a basic right that should not be denied to anyone because he or she cannot afford professional care. This basic right can be translated into three major objectives for a viable national health insurance plan.

To Ensure That All Persons Have Access to Care

The first major goal of national health insurance should be to ensure that all persons have access to adequate, high quality medical care provided in a manner that respects the rights and the personal dignity of the individual.

While Medicaid has helped many poor persons obtain adequate medical care, almost nine million poor persons continue to be excluded from coverage. Only 40 percent of poor workers in the labor force have even limited private health insurance, and fewer than 10 percent have insurance for nonhospital services. Meeting the needs of those poor who are not well served by the current programs must be a top priority of national health insurance.

To Eliminate Financial Hardship

With the rapid rise in medical care costs, the ability to afford adequate medical care is no longer a problem only for the poor. While public programs and private health insurance mitigate the problems many Americans face in meeting the high cost of medical care, they have failed to protect all persons from the consequences of large medical bills. Thus the second major goal of national health insurance should be to ensure that no family is forced to suffer severe financial hardship for needed medical care.

To Limit the Rise in Health Care Costs

National health insurance could also be one means of stemming the rising tide of medical care costs that are, in part, due to the present system, which covers some kinds of expenses but not others. Private insurance currently emphasizes complete coverage for short hospital stays, so that patients may prefer to be hospitalized even when outpatient or nursing-home care would be cheaper. Hospitals have also taken advantage of assured revenues from insurance plans to provide a wide range of expensive services, leading to ever-rising costs. Complete coverage for short hospital stays under most insurance plans has also reduced incentives for patients and physicians to "police" the medical care market, or to insist that services are efficiently produced and worth the resources devoted to them.

National health insurance could reverse many of these adverse effects. A comprehensive benefit plan with cost sharing, for example, might help reduce the tendency of patients to choose hospital care over less expensive alternatives; curb runaway costs; and promote more efficient organization and delivery of medical services. Alternatively, financial controls and incentives for more efficient practices in a centralized health insurance plan could be designed to promote these purposes. The third major goal of national health insurance, therefore, is to use it to curb inflation in the cost of maintaining a healthy population.

The Administration's Approach

The administration's new national health insurance plan attempts to build upon the present mix of public and private insurance to ensure access to medical care, prevent financial hardship, and control costs. Emphasis is upon filling gaps still existing in the current system and eliminating the most serious shortcomings, rather than upon developing an entirely new, comprehensive system for meeting these goals.

The plan contains three basic components: the employee health care insurance program for working families, the assisted health care insurance plan for the poor, and the federal health care insurance program to replace Medicare for the elderly. The administration estimates that the plan would require $6 billion of federal revenues in

1975 dollars in addition to amounts that would be spent under current programs.

Employee Health Care Insurance Plan

An employee health care insurance plan (EHCIP) is to be purchased jointly by employers and employees from private insurance companies at an estimated premium cost averaging $600 at 1975 medical prices.[9] Employers would contribute at least 65 percent of the premium cost during the first three years, and 75 percent thereafter.[10] Employers also would be required to permit any employee to elect a prepaid group health plan and to apply the employer portion of the premium toward it.

The benefit package is quite broad, and is identical in all three components of the administration's plan. These benefits include hospital care (without limits), physician and other medical services, and drugs. Family planning, maternity services, and well-child care for preschool children are available, as well as dental, eye, and ear care for children under thirteen. Limited mental health and posthospital care in nursing homes and from home health agencies is also provided.[11]

Under the insurance plan, the family would be responsible for the first $150 of medical expenses of each family member (for a maximum of three persons per family), the first $50 of drug expenses per person, and 25 percent of all additional expenses. Total family contributions toward medical expenses, however, would be subject to a ceiling of $1,500.[12]

Employers would be required to offer the employee health care

9. Premiums for individuals are set at 40 percent of the family premium, or an estimated $240 in the first year. No other variation in the premium on the basis of family size may be made. Estimates of costs were based on the incorrect assumption that Cost of Living Council controls on health care costs would not be removed. Actual implementation of the plan is not scheduled until January 1976.

10. The federal government would subsidize employers whose payroll costs increase by more than 3 percent as a result of the plan. The excess over 3 percent will be subsidized by 75 percent the first year and reduced 15 percentage points each year thereafter, with no subsidy after the fifth year. The administration estimates the cost of this subsidy at $450 million during the first year.

11. Hospital care for the treatment of mental illness is limited to 30 days per year (or 60 days of partial hospitalization) and mental outpatient services are limited to the average cost of 30 outpatient visits if rendered in a comprehensive community care center (or the average cost of 15 outpatient visits if from a private practitioner). Home health services are limited to 100 visits per year, and posthospital nursing-home care is covered up to 100 days per year.

12. Not including any premium contribution or any charges by physicians in excess of state-established reimbursement levels.

insurance plan to all full-time employees under age sixty-five and their families. Coverage is voluntary at the option of the employee; however, strong incentives are created for the employee to accept the basic plan. As mentioned above, the employer is required to contribute at least 65 percent of the premium. The employer is prohibited from offering an employee any alternative coverage, nor may the employer contribute toward the cost of any alternative insurance plan (the employer may, however, offer and help pay for insurance coverage *supplementary* to the basic plan). Furthermore, the employer may not offer employees any financial inducement to decline the plan, nor may the employer condition employment on rejection of coverage under the plan. Because of the difficulty of enforcing these provisions, however, employers may give preference to secondary workers, part-time workers, or those declining insurance.

Under the administration plan all employees and their dependents must be offered coverage without regard to their health status. An employer may not discriminate against an individual with respect to employment or compensation on the basis of the health status of the employee or his or her dependents. These provisions should guarantee widespread coverage of families with a full-time worker.

While the administration projects that the group premium rate for a family will be $600, actual rates would be set by private insurance companies. It is expected, however, that competition among carriers would keep premiums at a low level in relation to the actual benefits paid for covered services. In order to ensure that group rates are not excessive for small firms, each insurance company is required to offer coverage at the same premium rate to all employees in firms with up to fifty employees. This provision helps reduce the premium cost of small groups with high-medical-risk individuals by pooling the costs among all groups of a given insurance company.

The employee health care insurance plan is designed to alleviate most of the serious shortcomings of the existing system of private health insurance coverage. By setting a limit of $1,500 on family medical care costs (which will only be incurred by the few families with total medical expenses exceeding about $5,000), the exposure to severe financial hardship resulting from large medical bills would be greatly reduced. Requiring insurance companies to cover all workers and their families, regardless of health condition, and setting a uniform premium for all small groups should make insurance coverage widely available at reasonable premium rates. Since coverage is tied to employment, however, workers changing jobs must also change insurance—incurring some inconvenience, cost, and possibly periods with no insurance protection.

Assisted Health Care Insurance Plan

The second part of the administration's health insurance proposal, the assisted health care insurance plan (AHCIP), would replace most of the existing Medicaid program.[13] This plan would cover people not covered by EHCIP and those low-wage workers who would find out-of-pocket costs to be excessive under ECHIP. AHCIP would contain the same benefit package provided in EHCIP, but would differ in four essential ways. First, cost sharing—premiums, deductible amounts, and coinsurance rates—would be related to income, with the very lowest-income persons excused from premiums and deductible amounts subject only to low coinsurance rates. Second, physicians and other providers of medical services under the plan would be required to accept state-established reimbursement levels and could not assess persons covered by AHCIP any additional charges. Third, the plan would be administered by the states which would contract with private insurance carriers to process claims for AHCIP coverage. Finally, carriers would not underwrite AHCIP business, but would simply be reimbursed for administrative costs.

Since EHCIP does not eliminate possibly excessive medical outlays for lower-income working families, such families might do without essential care even though they had insurance coverage. The administration plan therefore gives all working families with incomes below $7,500 the option of electing coverage under AHCIP with reduced cost-sharing amounts.[14]

Families without a full-time worker would also be eligible for coverage under AHCIP, regardless of income. Realizing that the ability of such families to participate in the cost of their medical care depends crucially upon income, AHCIP relates all cost-sharing amounts to income. The premium, deductible amounts, and coinsurance rates for

13. Medicaid would be retained with the current federal-state matching formula for certain services not covered by AHCIP including: (1) services in a skilled nursing facility or intermediate care facility; (2) care in mental institutions for persons under age twenty-one or over sixty-five; and (3) home health services.

14. Employers are required to contribute to AHCIP the premiums they would have paid if the employees had been covered under EHCIP.

Table 8-3. Cost Sharing under the Assisted Health Care Insurance Plan, by Annual Family Income Class

Family income class[a] (dollars)	Premium[b] (dollars)	Amount deductible per person (dollars)		Coinsurance rate (percent)	Maximum liability (percent of income)
		Drug	Other[c]		
Under 2,500	0	0	0	10	6
2,500–4,999	0	25	50	15	9
5,000–7,499	300	50	100	20	12
7,500–9,999	600	50	150	25	15
10,000 and over	900	50	150	25	$1,500[d]

Source: H.R. 12684, 93 Cong. 2 sess., introduced February 6, 1974.
a. Income groups for single persons are set at 70 percent of the family income levels.
b. For full-time workers, employers also contribute the premiums they would have paid under EHCIP, or about $390 in the first year.
c. Deductible on nondrug services limited to three persons per family.
d. The maximum liability is $1,500 for a family and $1,050 for a single person.

each family income class—whether the family has a full-time worker or not—are shown in Table 8-3.

Since no premium is charged for families with incomes below $5,000, most lower-income families, even if eligible for EHCIP, will probably elect to receive coverage under AHCIP with its reduced cost-sharing provisions.[15] Only those working families that did not understand their obligations under the two plans, that were apprehensive that the quality or amount of care which physicians would be willing to provide would be lower under AHCIP than under EHCIP, or that for reasons of pride preferred to be covered under the "regular" employee plan would elect coverage under EHCIP.

Although premiums are charged for all persons with family incomes above $5,000, some families with high anticipated medical expenses may purchase AHCIP coverage rather than face exorbitant premiums from individual health insurance plans. Even working families with incomes between $5,000 and $7,500 may prefer coverage under AHCIP to EHCIP if their expected medical expenses are quite high.

There are also important differences in administration and total reimbursement of medical care providers. AHCIP is a state-administered plan, with each state contracting with private insurance companies for coverage of eligible persons. Private carriers do not underwrite AHCIP coverage. States simply compensate the carriers for any

15. For example, under AHCIP a working family with an annual income of $4,000 would be required to pay at most $360, or 9 percent of income, on medical bills, rather than as much as 40 percent of income under the employee plan.

expenses in processing benefit claims in excess of premium income plus administrative costs.[16]

Costs of AHCIP are to be borne jointly by states and the federal government—with states paying an average of 25 percent of the cost depending on current levels of state expenditures for Medicaid, ability to pay, and expenditures under AHCIP. States are given the responsibility of setting reimbursement levels for all types of medical care providers and all types of patients. Financial participation by the states in the cost of the plan would help assure that these reimbursement levels would not be set at excessively high rates.

While the assisted health care insurance plan meets most of the serious inequities in the current Medicaid program, some persons now covered by Medicaid would be worse off under the new plan, either because their own payments are increased slightly or because AHCIP does not cover such services as dental care for adults, private-duty nursing, and transportation services, which are covered in a few states with generous Medicaid programs.[17]

Federal Health Care Insurance Plan

The third part of the administration's national health insurance plan would substitute the same broad benefit package provided under EHCIP and AHCIP for the existing Medicare program for the elderly. Like AHCIP, patient payments would be related to income. Unlike either EHCIP or AHCIP, however, the plan for the elderly would be a federal program administered by the Social Security Administration.

The plan for the elderly, which would cover all persons currently eligible for Medicare (except for the nonelderly disabled) and federal, state, and local government employees, would be financed as at present by premiums and payroll tax revenues. The reduced cost sharing for lower-income elderly persons would be borne by general revenues and state contributions. Elderly persons not now covered by Medicare would be eligible for the assisted health care plan.

Cost-sharing requirements of the federal health care insurance plan

16. If there are economies of scale in the administration of insurance, coverage of AHCIP may reduce the unit cost of administering other non-AHCIP insurance plans, and hence increase the profitability of other business. Insurance companies would also have an incentive to allocate as many overhead costs to AHCIP business as possible.

17. Some states, however, may elect to provide these services for the poor, even without federal support.

Table 8-4. Cost Sharing under the Federal Health Care Insurance Plan, by Annual Individual Income

Individual income class (dollars)	Premium (dollars)	Amount deductible per person (dollars)		Coinsurance rate (percent)	Maximum liability (percent of income)
		Drug	Other		
Under 1,750	0	0	0	10	6
1,750–3,499	0	25	50	15	9
3,500–5,249	90	50	100	20	12
5,250 and over	90	50	100	20	$750[a]

Source: Same as Table 8-3.
a. The maximum liability is $750 at all incomes above $5,250.

(FHCIP) are based on individual income rather than family income. Cost sharing for each individual income group is shown in Table 8-4.

The premium, estimated to be about $90 in 1975 dollars, required of all elderly persons with individual income in excess of $3,500 is similar to the Medicare premium for physician services (estimated to be about $80 in fiscal 1975). The deductible of $100 would replace the current deductible of $84 for hospital care and $60 for physician services. The coinsurance rate of 20 percent, however, would apply to all medical services including hospital care, not just to physician services as is the case with Medicare. Unlike Medicare, FHCIP places a ceiling on patient payments for medical services ranging from 6 percent of income for the very poor to $750 for persons with incomes above $5,250.

The revised Medicare plan would eliminate many of the weaknesses in the current program. By reducing the cost-sharing requirements for all persons with lower incomes, disparities in use of services among the poor should be eliminated. Instead of channeling a greater proportion of benefits to higher-income elderly persons, as is the case under the physician portion of Medicare, lower-income persons would be encouraged through lower deductibles to make greater use of medical services. By making the benefit package more comprehensive (including drugs and no limits on hospitalization) and by placing a ceiling on patient payments, many elderly persons who now face severe financial hardship in meeting their share of large medical bills would be adequately protected.

However, some elderly persons would be worse off under the revised plan. Elderly persons now covered by both Medicare and Medicaid may face some cost increases. Medicaid pays all cost-sharing amounts for the covered elderly; under the new plan even very poor elderly people would be required to pay 10 percent of medical bills up to a ceiling of 6 percent of individual income. Higher-income elderly persons with moderate hospital stays would also be worse off under the new plan, since coinsurance would apply to the entire hospital stay rather than just to very long stays as under the current program. FHCIP would not cover the nonelderly disabled and persons with chronic kidney disease now covered by Medicare. Although such persons could obtain coverage under the assisted health care insurance plan, all except the poorest of these would undoubtedly be worse off.

Limiting Costs under the Administration Plan

The administration's proposal relies on a number of strategies to restrain increases in medical care costs. First, the benefit package under all three programs is comprehensive, encouraging the use of lower-cost alternatives where possible. Second, the programs generally require payments to patients to give them and their physicians an incentive to "police" the market and weigh the value of various forms of treatment against the resource cost of providing the services. Third, all persons, whether poor, elderly, or working, could elect to receive coverage under a health maintenance organization rather than from conventional providers of services. Such organizations are paid a fixed sum for each person covered rather than on the basis of services provided; hence, they have an incentive to use the lowest cost combination of resources to provide any given level of care. Thus care might be provided on an outpatient rather than on an inpatient basis, by family practice physicians rather than by specialists, and, where possible, by paramedical personnel rather than by physicians. Health maintenance organizations with a long-term, stable enrolled population can also be expected to provide those preventive services which will reduce the cost of medical care over time.[18]

Finally, the administration's plan attempts to hold down costs by its provisions for reimbursement of providers of medical services. The plan creates two types of providers: full participating providers and associate participating providers. Full participating providers would

18. See Charles L. Schultze and others, *Setting National Priorities: The 1973 Budget* (Brookings Institution, 1972), pp. 232–34, for a discussion of the pros and cons of health maintenance organizations.

have to agree to accept state-established reimbursement levels for all treatments and types of patients.[19] Associate participating providers extending care to poor and elderly patients under AHCIP and FHCIP would have to agree to accept state-established reimbursement levels as payment in full, but would be free to charge other patients higher fees provided patients were notified of this practice in advance.[20]

The effectiveness of this strategy in controlling costs depends in large part upon the states and upon the willingness of physicians to cooperate with the plan. Since state governments will be responsible for about 25 percent of the cost of the assisted plan for the poor, some states may try to limit their share of the cost by setting very restrictive reimbursement levels. Such an action may lead many physicians to refuse to treat the poor, or physicians may attempt to subvert the restricted fee schedule by increasing the number of services offered (by giving more laboratory tests, having patients for repeat visits, limiting the length of consultations). The result could well be a system that neither effectively controls cost nor guarantees high quality care to all persons.

There is little rationale for permitting associate participating physicians to earn larger incomes from the treatment of persons covered under the employee plan than from poorer patients covered under the assisted plan, and such a reimbursement policy may well reinforce a system of two-class medicine and limit the supply of high quality medical care available to the poor. Furthermore, permitting associate participating physicians to charge their patients fees in excess of amounts which will be reimbursed by insurance plans may pose financial hardships even on nonpoor patients, particularly in the case of very expensive services such as complex surgery. Thus the two-part reimbursement system may undermine the national health insurance objectives of ensuring access to medical care for all persons and preventing the financial hardship caused by high medical bills.

19. Hospitals, nursing homes, and home health agencies would be required to be full participating providers, but physicians and other providers could elect to participate as only associate providers. Services from full participating providers would be charged to a "health card" issued to all covered persons. Insurance carriers would then reimburse the providers directly according to state-established reimbursement levels. Patients would be billed for any cost-sharing amounts for which they are responsible and could pay over a period of time.

20. Associate participating providers would have to do their own billing and collection of fees. Providers are not prohibited from discriminating among patients on the basis of insurance status (or any other basis), and may well refuse to accept patients for whom compensation is lower.

Other Approaches to National Health Insurance

A number of other national health insurance proposals have also been advanced in the past few years. The American Medical Association, the American Hospital Association, and the Health Insurance Association of America have all backed bills that would rely heavily upon basic and catastrophic health insurance by private insurance companies, with government subsidies given either directly or through tax incentives.

Two alternatives to the administration's proposal which would reduce or eliminate the role of private insurance companies include the Long-Ribicoff and the Kennedy-Griffiths bills. The Long-Ribicoff bill would retain private insurance coverage of basic medical bills for all except the poor, but federal programs would cover catastrophic expenses for all persons under social security and provide basic medical services for the poor. The Kennedy-Griffiths bill would replace private insurance with a federal program covering virtually all medical bills for U.S. residents.

The Long-Ribicoff Bill

The Long-Ribicoff bill has three parts: a catastrophic expense provision that would assist all persons covered by social security; a plan to replace Medicaid that would pay virtually all basic medical expenses of low-income persons; and provisions to promote the sale of health insurance policies with a minimum standard of coverage to the nonpoor.

CATASTROPHIC EXPENSES

The catastrophic expense portion of the Long-Ribicoff bill is unchanged from the bill introduced by Senator Russell B. Long in 1973.[21] It would cover all medical services currently provided by Medicare (which excludes out-of-hospital drugs), but payments would be made only after sizable deductibles had been incurred.[22] Senators

21. See Edward R. Fried and others, *Setting National Priorities: The 1974 Budget* (Brookings Institution, 1973), p. 121, for a brief discussion of the 1973 bill.

22. Hospital benefits would not begin until after sixty days of hospitalization, and then the plan would pick up approximately 75 percent of costs. Coverage of physicians' bills and other medical services would begin only after a deductible of $2,000, and individuals would pay coinsurance of 20 percent on expenses above $2,000. Coinsurance payments for covered hospital and medical services would be limited to $1,000 in one year for an individual.

Long and Abraham Ribicoff estimate this provision would cost $3.6 billion annually.

LOW-INCOME PROVISIONS

The second part of the Long-Ribicoff bill would replace the Medicaid program. Eligibility would be open to all whose annual family income was below specified amounts which vary with family size ($4,800 for a family of four) without regard to age, family status, welfare eligibility, employment, or state of residence.

Patients covered by the low-income plan would make only minimal contributions toward the cost of care—$3 for each of the first ten visits to a physician. Persons above the income cutoff would be eligible for benefits only after income net of medical outlays fell below the income limit. Thus a family of four with income of $4,800 could receive comprehensive medical services with a maximum payment of $30, while a similar family with income of $6,000 and medical bills of $1,200 would be required to pay all of their own medical expenses.

Senators Long and Ribicoff estimate that this provision would cost $5.3 billion more than projected expenditures under Medicaid, with financing coming from state and federal general revenues. The state's share would be determined by current Medicaid payments and benefits under the new plan received by residents of the state.

CERTIFIED PRIVATE INSURANCE

The third part of the Long-Ribicoff plan would encourage the sale of certified private insurance to defray the deductible amounts under the catastrophic expense plan.[23] Insurance companies would be asked to develop a standard policy covering the first sixty days of hospital care and at least the first $2,000 of medical expenses per year. The maximum deductible allowable on the hospital part and the medical part would be $100 a year apiece. No further cost sharing would be permitted under the hospital plan, and total cost sharing under the

23. The U.S. Department of Health, Education, and Welfare (HEW) would check such policies to see if they meet minimum requirements concerning coverage, benefits, and premium charges. Premiums on group policies would have to meet some minimum standards established by HEW for the ratio to benefits paid out, and individual policy premiums would be based on the ratio established for the smallest groups. A plan certified by HEW could use the certification emblem in its advertising. Only insurance companies selling certified plans would eventually be eligible to serve as intermediaries or carriers under Medicare and the low-income program.

medical portion could not exceed 10 percent of total expenses (or $200 on a $2,000 policy).

The Long-Ribicoff bill would also exempt insurance companies from antitrust laws, ostensibly to permit insurers to enter into arrangements to establish insurance pools to offer certified health insurance plans. However, since the catastrophic expense plan would cover those rare claims running into tens of thousands of dollars, the need for such pooling would be greatly reduced and the antitrust exemption might have undesirable effects on competition.

THE LONG-RIBICOFF BILL has few provisions that would help to curb increases in costs. The low-income plan has virtually no cost sharing by patients. Reimbursement to providers under the low-income plan would be on the same basis as Medicare, namely, reasonable costs and charges, and providers would be prohibited from collecting charges from low-income persons above the amounts established as reasonable by the Social Security Administration. No restrictions would be placed on charges which could be assessed for benefits under "standard basic policies" sold by insurance companies.

The Kennedy-Griffiths Bill

The Kennedy-Griffiths approach to national health insurance is far more ambitious than either the administration or Long-Ribicoff approach. It would replace the existing system of private insurance coverage and public programs for the poor and elderly with a single comprehensive federal system. Under the Kennedy-Griffiths bill, the entire population would be covered for a broad range of health services with no payments whatsoever required of the patient. In addition, the proposal includes provisions designed to reorganize the delivery of health services, improve health planning, and increase the supply of health care manpower and facilities.

HEW originally estimated that the total federal cost of the program would be $90 billion in 1974. Since the Kennedy-Griffiths program would replace current federal outlays to finance medical care (including Medicare and Medicaid), and since additional federal revenues would be generated by the elimination of medical expense deductions in the current income tax law, the net cost of the program to the federal government would be about $60 billion. About $52 billion would represent replacement of privately financed expenditures; the other $8 billion would represent additional medical expenditures. Half of this cost would be financed by the imposition of an additional federal payroll tax and a tax on unearned income; the other half of the funds would come from general revenues.

The plan would meet the objectives of removing financial barriers to medical care for the poor and preventing financial hardships from high medical bills. By establishing one system for all persons with a uniform reimbursement policy, the plan would go a long way toward eliminating two-class medical care. Furthermore, by being the sole source of financing for medical care services, the federal government would have tremendous leverage to control medical care costs, encourage more efficient forms of organizing and delivering services, and influence the distribution and availability of medical manpower and facilities. However, the absence of any consumer payments might lead to rapid increases in health care costs, and the tax revenues required to finance existing privately borne costs as well as any increased costs would be substantial. Moreover, without some patient payments and automatic market incentives, all decisions regarding reimbursement, proper utilization of services, and appropriate allocation of resources must be made by regulatory bodies.

Basic Differences in Approaches

Nearly all of the proposed national health insurance plans share common objectives of ensuring access to adequate medical care for the poor, preventing severe financial hardships caused by large medical bills, and controlling costs. Both the Nixon and Kennedy-Griffiths plans provide a comprehensive benefit package available to all persons. Both plans would also create elaborate mechanisms for controlling the level of payments. However, they differ in three major respects: first, the extent of patient payments (and hence the remaining cost, which must be financed by premiums or taxes); second, the sources of financing (premiums, payroll tax, state and federal general revenues); and third, the role of private insurance companies and state governments.

Patient Payments for Medical Care

One of the major differences between various approaches to national health insurance is the extent to which the patient is required to share directly in the cost of medical care through deductible and coinsurance features. The issue is whether imposing direct patient payments is an equitable method of financing care and whether such payments lead to a more desirable distribution of medical care services, greater efficiency in the provision of services, and a more appropriate allocation of resources between medical care and other goods and services.

There are strong justifications for retaining substantial direct patient payments in a national health insurance plan. First, it reduces the cost of the plan which must be financed through taxes or other sources. The Kennedy-Griffiths plan, which contains no deductible and coinsurance provisions, requires massive increases in payroll and income taxes to finance expenditures that are currently made in the private sector. The plan would move into the federal budget private outlays for normal medical expenses that are now being made by middle- and upper-income groups with little financial strain. If the large tax increases necessary to finance the program were adopted, the nation might have to give up other high priority objectives. Experience with Medicare also suggests that even with adequate financing of medical care services, budgetary funds would still be required for specific health care delivery programs that will eliminate barriers to access to medical care for minority groups and rural residents. Attempting to finance the entire cost of medical care through the federal budget, therefore, may impede other social programs as well as restrict budgetary outlays for medical care.

Second, cost sharing reduces (but does not eliminate) the need for administrative control over the use of medical services. Deductible and coinsurance amounts give patients and their physicians an incentive to weigh alternative forms of care: inpatient hospital care versus care on a less costly outpatient basis, care from family physicians rather than specialists, greater use of physician extenders and nurse practitioners for those services not requiring a physician. In addition, it is important that the advantages of additional units of medical care services be weighed against the resources that must be devoted to providing them. While an extra day of hospital care, a follow-up visit to the physician, an extra battery of laboratory tests may make some contribution to improved health, the resources required to provide these incremental services may have greater social value if diverted to other uses. In the absence of financial incentives to consider the cost of medical services to society, regulatory bodies must be established to review the necessity of hospitalization, the appropriateness of the length of hospital stay, and the efficacy of laboratory tests and ancillary services. Controls on the numbers of specialists, family physicians, other health personnel, and health facilities must be created and enforced. Unfortunately, the expertise or accumulated knowledge to handle such an undertaking is not yet available, nor is the question of who should serve on such regulatory bodies resolved.

Not only can cost sharing have important automatic incentives for the appropriate utilization of medical services, it can help reduce the charges which physicians and hospitals request for their services. This is especially important if the national health insurance plan contains no effective mechanism for placing a lid on reimbursement levels. For example, a physician who charges $5 to a patient without insurance may charge $20 when the patient only pays 25 percent of the bill, and the charge may be even higher when the patient pays no share of the bill. Similarly, hospitals have been found to increase charges and revenues as insurance has grown, and hospital administrators have experienced no difficulty in finding ways to spend the increased revenues. Competition among health care providers, which admittedly works far from perfectly even in the absence of insurance, will not work at all without some direct patient payments since patients have no reason to go to a physician charging lower fees even if he or she provides exactly the same care with regard to convenience, quality, sensitivity, and all the other dimensions of this very personal service. Nor will either the patient or the physician have any incentive to select a lower-cost hospital even if other considerations are the same. Direct controls on costs are very difficult to enforce without some incentives for those who make the decisions.

Finally, if cost-sharing provisions are related to income, additional desirable consequences can be obtained. Experience with Medicare and Medicaid has illustrated that when lower-income persons are not required to pay deductible and coinsurance amounts while higher-income persons share in costs, a more equal utilization of medical care services among income classes results. Relating cost sharing to income in a systematic way should help eliminate major disparities in the use of services among income classes for persons of comparable health status.

Income-related cost-sharing provisions are also one mechanism for reducing adverse work incentives which might be created by an abrupt termination of benefits as income rises, as in the Long-Ribicoff plan.[24] Such an abrupt termination of benefits may discourage a second family worker from seeking a job, or discourage even a primary earner from moonlighting or undertaking overtime work.

While the arguments for substantial cost sharing are many, they cannot be implemented without some ill effects. A complex schedule of payments is frequently difficult to understand, and may result in many persons not taking advantage of the benefits available. This danger is minimized if the plan assumes responsibility for paying providers and billing patients for their share—such as in the administration's health card scheme. If cost sharing is related to income, some administrative mechanism must be devised for obtaining income information in a way that protects the individual from all the losses of privacy that are possible. Preferably, under a health card administrative device, the Internal Revenue Service would be charged with issuing cards coded with the appropriate income class. Imposition of cost-sharing amounts may also discourage some needed medical care, deter patients from seeking early treatment for a serious symptom, or cause patients to forgo beneficial preventive care. Preventive services of proven efficacy, however, can be exempted from deductible amounts.

The efficiency gains of cost-sharing provisions may be eroded in two ways: first, many people may purchase supplementary private insurance to pick up the deductible and coinsurance amounts, and, second, the importance of fixed cost-sharing amounts may be reduced over time by inflation in medical care costs. With national health insurance there is no rationale for subsidizing the purchase of supplementary insurance. Any employer contributions to supplementary insurance should be counted as taxable income to the employee, and not as a legitimate business expense of the firm. Deductions for health insurance and medical expenses under the personal income tax should also be eliminated.[25] The real value of cost-sharing amounts can be

24. For example, a family of four loses one dollar of medical benefits for every dollar of income above $4,800.

25. See *Setting National Priorities: The 1974 Budget*, pp. 109–20, 184–91, for a discussion of current tax subsidies for health care, as well as Bridger M. Mitchell and Ronald J. Vogel, "Health and Taxes: An Assessment of the Medical Deduction" (Rand Corporation, 1973; processed), and Martin S. Feldstein and Elizabeth Allison, "Tax Subsidies of Private Health Insurance: Distribution, Revenue Loss and Effects," Health Care Policy Discussion Paper 2 (Harvard University, Harvard Center for Community Health and Medical Care, 1972; processed).

retained by escalator clauses which automatically adjust deductible and maximum liability amounts to changes over time in average health expenditures per capita.

Unfortunately, the complete ramifications of cost sharing are not well known. Very little is known about how much private insurance supplementation would occur with various income-related cost-sharing schedules; even less is known about how such schedules would affect the mix of essential and marginal care. A national health insurance experiment was recently initiated by HEW to find answers to some of these questions, but even preliminary results will not be available for a couple of years.[26] In the meantime, experience with Medicare emphatically suggests that uniform cost-sharing provisions will lead to wide disparities in utilization among income classes but that reduced cost sharing for lower-income persons can move them into patterns of medical care utilization resembling middle- and upper-income persons with similar health problems. Given the unknown consequences of either including or omitting cost sharing, retention of cost sharing and flexibility to alter schedules over time as experience is gained seems to have many advantages.

Sources of Financing

A decision about the appropriate method or methods of financing national health insurance must weigh a number of objectives: (1) avoiding a regressive tax structure; (2) preventing adverse employment effects; and (3) minimizing any windfall gains to those currently financing medical care. The objectives are not absolute and may be altered by the mix of financing for other public goods and services.

Financing for most national health insurance plans is based upon premiums, payroll tax revenues, and federal and state general revenues. Financing by premiums paid directly by employers or private individuals to private insurance companies has the effect of limiting the federal budgetary cost of the plan. If the premium is mandatory, however, this lower budgetary cost is largely illusory because the compulsory premium contribution is in reality no different from a tax assessed on the employer for purposes of providing the benefits. In fact,

26. For a description of the experiment, see Joseph P. Newhouse, "A Design for a Health Insurance Experiment," *Inquiry*, Vol. 11 (March 1974), pp. 5–27.

if a firm responds to this premium by lowering cash wages or raising them less than it would otherwise, the premium is borne by the employee. In this case, it becomes a regressive tax, representing a much higher share of income for low-income groups.

The only case in which the employer cannot shift the cost of the premium back onto employees is when wages are already at the minimum wage level. For these low-wage employers, the premium is much the same as an increase in the minimum wage and raises the cost of workers to the firm. If the increase in cost is substantial (and a $450 annual employer premium as in the administration plan will represent 10 percent of the earnings of a minimum-wage worker employed for forty hours a week, fifty weeks out of the year), some employers of low-wage workers may either go out of business or substantially reduce their labor force.[27] Employers would also have a strong incentive to hire part-time workers, secondary family earners, or those who decline the insurance.

The use of premiums under the assisted plan in the administration's proposal—even though related to income—can also be criticized as punishing people who are poor health risks and those who do not belong to groups. A self-employed person with median income would be required to pay much more for equivalent coverage than some-

27. Although the administration proposal relies heavily upon compulsory premiums for financing coverage for working families, an excellent discussion of the adverse effects of premiums is contained in the internal HEW criticism of the earlier administration proposal:

Employer mandated health insurance coverage would have the following economic effects:

1. The income distribution consequences would be regressive with regard to both the financing and to a lesser extent, the benefit structure. NHISA [the former administration plan] would be financed by a fixed tax per employee that is unrelated to earnings. Thus, the proportion of earnings that would be devoted to NHISA premiums would be greatest among low-income workers. . . .

2. The economic effect on the labor market of mandated coverage is identical to that of an increase in the minimum wage of an amount equivalent to the employer's share of premiums. . . . The dislocation occurs for those marginal workers who are at the minimum wage. A strong equity argument can be made that, if the Federal government wishes to mandate coverage, it ought to help pay for it.

3. Since small employers as a group offer their employees less generous health insurance benefits than large employers, they would be most affected by the requirement to offer a minimum benefit package.

From *Casper W. Weinberger to be Secretary of Health, Education, and Welfare,* Hearings before the Senate Committee on Labor and Public Welfare, 93 Cong. 1 sess. (1973), Pt. 2, p. 21a.

one with the same income but employed in a two-person firm, even though the administrative cost difference be minuscule. Furthermore, people who are high health risks could face exorbitant premiums. For example, someone who suffers from severe kidney disease and is unable to work may be able to make ends meet on, say, a $10,000 income from disability insurance and past savings. However, although his medical bills are currently paid almost in full by Medicare, under the new plan he would be required to pay a $900 premium to purchase insurance coverage and his additional out-of-pocket payments are sure to come to $1,500.

The Kennedy-Griffiths plan would avoid these pitfalls by financing benefits through a combination of payroll taxes and federal general revenues. The payroll tax, while not a progressive source of financing such as the income tax, is markedly less regressive than a fixed premium per family. Furthermore, the Kennedy-Griffiths plan would attempt to reform the payroll tax by making the employer's share of the tax applicable to all earnings, and extending the earnings base to $15,000 for the employee's share. The large increase in the payroll tax which would be necessitated by the Kennedy-Griffiths plan, however, would undoubtedly intensify many of the burdens of the payroll tax placed on two-worker and low-income families, although this could be rectified by providing rebates or subsidies to low-income workers.

Unlike the Long-Ribicoff plan, the Kennedy-Griffiths plan would not attempt to recoup the $5 billion in benefits paid by state governments under Medicaid. Thus state governments would gain from the plan.

By patterning financing along current sources of funds for medical care, the administration approach has the advantage of not producing windfall gains either to state governments or to those employers who now pay for comprehensive private health insurance. However, the regressivity and adverse employment effects of compulsory premiums make it an undesirable method of financing the EHCIP component. Replacing these premiums under the administration plan with a payroll tax (split among employers and employees according to current shares of private insurance premiums) would represent a substantial improvement, particularly if the payroll tax were extended to cover all earnings. Another option would be to replace the fixed premium with an income tax or with an income-related premium. To avoid windfall gains to employers, they could be required to contribute toward the income-related premium at least as much as is currently paid under private health insurance plans.

Role of Insurance Companies and State Governments

Wide differences exist in proposed national health insurance plans in the roles of private health insurance companies and state governments. The Kennedy-Griffiths bill would eliminate any role for private insurance companies and would largely bypass state governments. The administration's proposal, on the other hand, would vastly increase the size of the private insurance industry, and would vest in state governments virtually all responsibility for the regulation of insurance companies and providers of medical services and the establishment of reimbursement levels.

Private insurance companies, including the nonprofit Blue Cross and Blue Shield organizations, are expected to sell over $31 billion of health insurance in 1975. In addition, insurance companies, acting as administrative agents for the Medicare program, will cover another $13 billion of medical care expenditures in fiscal year 1975. The administration plan would increase private health insurance business to about $36 billion in 1975 dollars (including supplementary plans that companies could be expected to sell). In addition, private insurance companies would act as administrative agents for plans covering the poor and the elderly which could involve up to another $40 billion of medical care expenditures. Thus, private health insurance could become a $75 billion industry—about the same size as the Social Security Administration.

Another source of concern under the administration proposal is the heightened possibility of price collusion on the part of insurance companies. Competition in the past has taken the form of tailoring policies to the unique needs of consumers. With all companies selling an identical policy, it is a relatively simple matter for firms to reach a mutually agreeable premium. Since Blue Cross and Blue Shield currently have 44 percent of the private insurance business, the concentration of market power necessary for effective collusive agreements is a genuine danger.

Proponents of a greater role for private health insurance companies note that the industry has accumulated a great deal of expertise and administrative skill which would be essential in the administration of any comprehensive national health insurance plan. They argue that regulation of insurance companies by state governments would be sufficient to curb potential abuses.

Nonetheless, some are reluctant to trust private insurance companies with an enhanced role because of their relatively poor performance in certain respects in the past and the heightened possibility of price collusion and noncompetitive behavior under the administration plan. Insurance companies have exhibited far more concern over limiting their risks than over providing consumers with adequate protection. Such practices as excluding high-risk persons from coverage, exempting preexisting conditions, and setting limits on amounts paid by the companies rather than by the patient form much of the basis of the need for national health insurance. Private health insurance companies have also had no noticeable success in restraining hospital costs or physician charges. Moreover, since insurance companies incur substantial marketing costs, over a billion dollars could be saved by federal administration.

Arguments about the appropriate role for state governments are no less divisive. Backers of the administration approach believe that the extensive regulatory and rate-setting powers required by the administration of comprehensive national health insurance cannot be adequately handled by a single federal agency and must be decentralized to the state level. Skeptics point to the wide variations among states in administrative skills, reimbursement patterns, and benefit generosity manifested in the federal-state Medicaid program, and note the absence of effective planning and regulation under existing decentralized health programs.

Perhaps what is more important is that perverse economic incentives could be created by disparities in reimbursement levels across states. Mobility of medical manpower could lead to greater concentrations of physicians and other health personnel in those states with generous reimbursement levels—which, if Medicaid is any indication, would also be the states with the least need for additional health manpower.

In the absence of a better track record for private insurance companies and state governments, a healthy skepticism toward enhancing their role seems justified. However, since the dislocation induced by the elimination of a $31 billion industry would not be negligible, one compromise would be to retain private insurance companies to act as administrative agents for a federal plan. There is little justification for permitting insurance companies to make a profit on policies sold to working families but prohibiting profits on coverage for the poor and the elderly. Instead, all insurance could be administered as under the Medicare program, with private insurance companies restricted to a fiscal intermediary role. Private companies, however, could still be permitted to sell supplementary insurance, although tax subsidies for the purchase of such insurance do not appear warranted with a comprehensive national health insurance plan.

A Compromise Solution—the Kennedy-Mills Plan

While each of the major national health insurance proposals has unique advantages, no plan is without serious flaws. Senator Edward M. Kennedy and Congressman Wilbur D. Mills have recently offered a compromise plan that combines many of the strengths of the administration, Long-Ribicoff, and Kennedy-Griffiths plans. It would create one system with uniform benefits. By requiring state contributions and consumer payments that vary with income, the plan would limit future tax increases. Budgetary resources would be focused on those with the greatest need for financial assistance—the poor and those with large medical bills. The plan would greatly reduce potential variations in benefits among states by establishing a single federal reimbursement policy, rather than permitting separate reimbursement policies for each state. An intermediate role for private insurance companies is proposed—one which would neither increase the profitability of the industry nor eliminate the industry entirely.

Benefits and Cost Sharing

The benefit package provided to all persons under the Kennedy-Mills (K-M) plan is identical to that of the administration, except that significant restrictions are placed on covered drugs. Cost sharing under the K-M plan, however, is more limited than under the administration plan. All services other than preventive care (family planning, prenatal and well-child care, and dental, eye, and ear care

Table 8-5. Maximum Liability under the Administration and the Kennedy-Mills National Health Insurance Plans, by Annual Family Income

	Maximum liability			
	Administration assisted plan		Kennedy-Mills plan[a]	
Family income (dollars)	Amount (dollars)	Percent of income	Amount (dollars)	Percent of income
2,000	120	6	0	0
4,000	360	9	0	0
5,000	600	12	50	1
6,000	720	12	300	5
8,000	1,200	15	800	10
10,000	1,500	15	1,000	10

Sources: H.R. 12684, 93 Cong. 2 sess., introduced February 6, 1974; H.R. 13870, 93 Cong. 2 sess., introduced April 2, 1974.

a. Based on a four-person family.

for children) would be subject to a deductible of $150 per person, not to exceed two deductibles per family, rather than three as in the administration plan. All services, except drugs, would also be subject to a 25 percent coinsurance payment. Drugs would be subject to a separate payment of $1 per prescription drug.

A maximum ceiling, however, is set on each family's contribution. For families of four with incomes above $8,800, the ceiling would be $1,000 rather than $1,500 as in the administration plan. No payments would be required of families with incomes below $4,800. For families of four with incomes between $4,800 and $8,800, the maximum ceiling is increased by $250 for each $1,000 of income over $4,800. As shown in Table 8-5, lower-income families would face substantially lower maximum payments under the K-M plan than under the administration's assisted plan.

While there are substantial differences between the maximum payments required under the two plans, few middle-income families would be required to make the maximum payments. Differences in average payments would be substantially less. Figure 8-1 shows the difference in the plans for a family of four with one member incurring $750 of medical expenses, a second family member $150, and the other two $50 each (with no drug or preventive care expenses). Family payments are substantially lower under the Kennedy-Mills plan for families with incomes below $6,000. Benefits decline much more rapidly with income in the Kennedy-Mills plan, however, as families

Figure 8-1. Comparison of Cost Sharing for Four-Person Family with $1,000 Annual Medical Expenses, Assisted Health Care (Administration) and Kennedy-Mills Plans

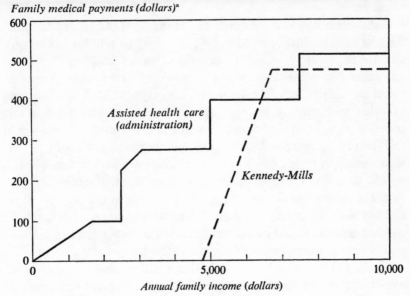

Family medical payments (dollars)[a]

Assisted health care (administration)

Kennedy-Mills

Annual family income (dollars)

Source: H.R. 12684, 93 Cong. 2 sess., introduced February 6, 1974; H.R. 13870, 93 Cong. 2 sess., introduced April 2, 1974.

a. Family medical payments do not include premiums for health insurance.

with incomes slightly above $4,800 find medical benefits reduced by 25 cents for each additional dollar of income.

Medicare would be retained for the elderly, but its benefit package would be expanded to include unlimited hospital care and prescription drugs. A ceiling of $1,000 would be placed on cost sharing for an elderly family. Presumably, lower ceilings would be placed on payments by the elderly poor, but exact requirements are unclear. A new long-term noninstitutional and custodial care benefit would be available to the elderly, with financing from premiums and federal and state general revenues.

Administration

Responsibility for administration of the K-M national health insurance plan would be vested in the Social Security Administration, which would be reestablished as an independent agency outside the Department of Health, Education, and Welfare. Private insurance companies would administer the plan for the Social Security Administration (SSA); however, employers with 1,000 or more employees could choose the insurer to administer the program on behalf of employees.

Elaborate provisions are contained in the K-M plan for controlling the cost of care. Institutional providers would be reimbursed by prospective payment systems with various incentive features. Physicians and other professionals would be reimbursed by fee schedules established by the professions themselves, but adjusted by SSA according to price and earning changes in the economy. Physicians could charge any patient more than the established fee schedule, but would then be responsible for collecting all patient payments. Just as in the administration plan, every insured individual would be issued a health benefit card for charging medical services from participating providers accepting the fee schedule. The program would pay providers and bill patients directly for deductible and coinsurance amounts. All covered services would be subject to review by professional standards review organizations within two years after the program begins.

The K-M plan would also establish a health resources board which would be charged with assuring availability of medical services in all parts of the country. Funds for this purpose would be $400 million in fiscal 1976, $600 million in fiscal 1977, and 2 percent of benefit payments in fiscal 1978, declining to 1 percent of benefit payments after fiscal 1979. The funds of this board could be used to sponsor health service programs in minority neighborhoods and rural areas to ensure a more equitable distribution of benefits.

Sources of Financing

The program would be financed by a combination of payroll taxes, taxes on unearned income, and general revenues. A 4 percent payroll tax on employment earnings up to $20,000 a year would be shared by employers and employees, with the employer responsible for at least 3 percent. Self-employed individuals would pay a single rate of 2.5 percent on their covered earnings up to $20,000. For those without annual earnings or self-employment income totaling at least $20,000, a tax of 2.5 percent of unearned income would be assessed. Thus, a family with interest, rent, and dividend income of $20,000, but no employment earnings, would be required to pay $500.[28] Reduced cost

28. Income from transfer payments would also be taxable as unearned income, except that benefits from the aid to families with dependent children (AFDC) and supplemental security income (SSI) programs would be taxed at the rate of 1 percent on the recipient and 3 percent on the state.

sharing for lower-income families would be met from general revenues and states are required to make a continuing contribution.

Senator Kennedy and Congressman Mills estimate that their plan
would have approximately the same net cost as the administration
plan, requiring about $8.5 billion of additional revenues in 1975.
They argue that any additional costs would be offset by the more
limited benefits for drugs and elimination of marketing costs of
insurance companies.

Possible Drawbacks

While the Kennedy-Mills plan is a promising step toward resolution of the basic issues that have impeded progress toward national
health insurance, it still contains some questionable provisions. Perhaps its most serious deficiency is its potential impact on costs. Since
physicians are permitted to charge all patients more than the federally
established reimbursement levels, they will undoubtedly take advantage of the increased insurance to charge higher fees and earn higher
incomes. It is somewhat ironic that the Kennedy-Mills bill provides
this escape clause for physicians while at the same time establishing
an elaborate mechanism for determining reimbursement under the
system. The Kennedy-Mills bill would also create complex review
procedures. All medical services would be subject to review for necessity and appropriateness by professional organizations. These regulatory provisions could prove quite cumbersome. Finally, the bill does
not eliminate tax subsidies that encourage purchase of supplementary
insurance, mitigating market forces that help to constrain costs.

Budgetary Implications of National Health Insurance

Predicting the budgetary consequences of any national health insurance plan is a precarious venture, as experience with Medicare and
Medicaid has amply demonstrated. Accurate estimates require pre-
dictions of the number of persons to be covered, the quantity of various medical services likely to be demanded and received, the level of
reimbursement of providers of medical services, and administrative
costs. Any miscalculations can lead to serious under- or overesti-
mates of costs.

Our limited knowledge and forecasting ability can impede informed
debate on alternative national health insurance proposals. Further
confusion is introduced into this sensitive area by apparent attempts

to minimize the budgetary implications of any specific plan. This takes two forms. The first is the tendency for most major advocates of national health insurance plans to quote the budgetary cost of the plan in incremental terms—over and above amounts that would be spent by existing Medicare and Medicaid programs, even if the latter plans are to be eliminated. Since Medicare and Medicaid are expected to cost $25 billion in fiscal 1975 (of which $5 billion would be paid by states), an incremental cost of $7 billion, for example, translates into total budgetary expenditures of $32 billion.

Another possible form of evasion is to use various devices to keep part of the cost of the program out of the budget. The administration plan would finance coverage of workers and their families by premiums of $32 billion paid directly to private insurance plans. In addition, employers and individuals would be required to contribute $6 billion for those covered by the assisted plan and the plan for the elderly. Since these contributions are compulsory, at least on the part of employers, it is equivalent to a tax, even if it does not appear in the budget. The Kennedy-Mills bill would also attempt to hide a large portion of the cost of the program by establishing a trust fund which would not be counted in the federal budget. Additional payroll taxes on employers, employees, and self-employed and on unearned income under that bill would amount to approximately $32 billion in 1975.

When all of the costs of both the administration and the Kennedy-Mills bills are counted, there is little major difference between them. This is not surprising, given the similarity in the benefit package available in both bills. However, as shown in Table 8-6, the sources of financing are quite different.

Rather than requiring only a modest increase in expenditures reflected in the estimates of $5 billion and $8.5 billion of additional budgetary resources, an accounting of the total cost of national health insurance indicates that quite substantial expenditures will be required. In part these will substitute for public expenditures which would have been made under the Medicare and Medicaid plans, in part they will substitute for expenditures which would have been made by employers and employees for private health insurance coverage. About $6.5 billion of the total cost represents new expenditures induced under either plan.[29]

29. These induced costs represent additional use of services, which patients demand (and receive) with better insurance coverage. This cost more closely reflects the addi-

Table 8-6. Estimated Cost of Alternative Health Insurance Plans, 1975

Billions of dollars

Cost item	Administration plan	Kennedy-Mills plan
Premiums paid to insurance companies	31.8[a]	...
Premiums paid to government[b]	6.3	1.7
Additional payroll tax and tax on unearned income	...	31.5
Public expenditures under current programs[c]	27.8	27.8
Federal	20.5	20.5
State	7.3	7.3
Incremental costs from general revenues	4.9	8.5
Federal	5.9	n.a.
State	−1.0	n.a.
Total cost[d]	**70.8**	**69.5**

Sources: Administration plan: U.S. Department of Health, Education, and Welfare, cost estimates prepared for HEW Secretary Casper W. Weinberger testimony before the House Ways and Means Committee of the U.S. Congress, April 24, 1974; Kennedy-Mills plan: payroll tax, tax on unearned income, and general revenues from Kennedy-Mills press conference, April 2, 1974; other data, from HEW estimates cited above. The cost of the Kennedy-Mills plan does not include long-term care.

a. Excludes premiums paid for the supplementary medical insurance.

b. Includes employer contributions and individual premiums paid for the assisted and federal health care programs under the administration plan and Medicare premiums under the Kennedy-Mills plan.

c. Includes Medicare and Medicaid as well as other federal and state medical care expenditures that would be covered by the plan. Excludes individual Medicare premiums.

d. Excludes out-of-pocket payments by patients and supplementary medical insurance (about $13.3 billion and $4.3 billion, respectively, in the administration plan).

n.a. Not available.

The net cost of various plans to the federal government is also sensitive to the treatment of payments to private health insurance companies under the federal income tax. In the absence of any major changes in private health insurance coverage, tax subsidies will result in $6 billion of forgone tax revenues in 1975. Since the Kennedy-Mills bill will greatly reduce the amount of private health insurance purchased, this subsidy would be far smaller. Under the administration proposal, however, forgone tax revenues from existing tax treatment of health insurance coverage could well increase by about $2 billion.

An informed choice about the best method of financing national health insurance can only be made if all of these costs and changes in current sources of financing are specified, the underlying assumptions explicitly presented, and the distributional consequences explored.

tional real resources that will be devoted to medical care with the implementation of national health insurance.

IN VIEW OF THE SUBSTANTIAL NEED for major changes in the way medical care is financed, the administration and the Kennedy-Mills proposals come at a welcome time. Even if neither approach is approved in its entirety, both will stimulate needed debate—the outcome of which may satisfy various objectives even better. The one disconcerting feature is that budget implications are covered up. Excluding large expenditures for health care from the budget will not encourage careful choices between alternative uses of budgetary resources; the true cost and budgetary implications of the proposals should be faced and openly discussed and justified.

9. Planning Future Federal Budgets

IN THE SHORT RUN the federal budget is difficult to change. Many expenditure programs have automatic increases built into them—social security benefits are altered to keep pace with the cost of living, interest on the federal debt changes automatically with the size of the debt and interest rates, federal payroll and retirement costs change with private wages and salaries. In fiscal 1975 these uncontrollable outlay increases accounted for two-thirds of the increase in total expenditures. Built-in expenditure increases of this magnitude seriously inhibit the government's ability to make significant policy changes that involve additional spending or tax reductions.

In the longer run, however, the budget becomes much more amenable to policy changes. The combination of rising incomes and the generally progressive federal tax system typically provides enough revenue to support the semiautomatic increases in spending under existing laws and to fund many new programs besides. During the past ten years, for example, the United States was able to fight a long and costly war, enact several Great Society spending programs, launch a general revenue sharing program for state and local governments, and make large cuts in personal and corporate tax rates. Such initiatives eventually have a very strong influence on the size and type of federal spending.

But greater long-run flexibility still does not make it easy for the President and Congress to alter budgetary priorities. As time goes on, many new claims on the federal budget develop: for defense spending,

247

national health insurance, income support programs, grants to state and local governments, reductions in taxes. It is costly to satisfy any one of these claims, let alone all of them together. Thus, even though rising incomes cause revenues to expand over time, budgetary choices continue to be constrained by limited fiscal resources.

This is why fiscal planning is important. Budget decisions should not be made in isolation—when some type of expenditure goes up, some other type must go down or taxes must rise if the budget is not to become more expansionary than intended. Budget decisions should also be forward-looking—current decisions should not build in so much future spending as to create uncomfortable dilemmas.

Recently both Congress and the administration have become more aware of these problems. Last year's attempt by the administration to make large expenditure cuts stimulated Congress to begin reforming its own procedures for making budgetary decisions, and it is now considering the Congressional Budget Act of 1974 (see Appendix B). In response to the need for more long-term budgetary planning, the Office of Management and Budget has recently begun presenting five-year projections of expenditures and revenues under current and proposed programs. While neither of these innovations will lead to explicit multiyear budget decisions, they hold out the hope that the budget will be developed in a more comprehensive and farsighted manner than in the past.

In this chapter we examine these issues in relation to the administration's 1975 budget. After reviewing the budgetary outlook for fiscal 1974 and 1975 and how it has changed in the past year, we examine the long-run implications of the budget—the way projections are affected by economic growth and inflation, and what plans the administration has to spend additional revenues in the next few years. We then discuss a few new plans to increase expenditures or reduce taxes that might be considered along with the administration's program—or treated as alternatives to it.

The Current Budgetary Outlook

The budgetary outlook for fiscal 1975 differs from the outlook one year ago in two important respects. The economy appears weaker than it was last year, requiring less drastic efforts to hold down government expenditures and maintain tax rates. Moreover, the budget itself has changed, with inflation causing revenues to grow at faster rates than anticipated, and also faster than expenditures. These two developments have led to a fairly sizable increase in the revenues that could soon be available for new programs. The budgetary picture is more optimistic than it was a year ago, when it looked as if there would be little unclaimed revenue until 1977 or 1978.

The outlook one year ago was for a full employment surplus of $0 and $2 billion respectively in 1974 and 1975. This is shown in Table 9-1 that compares the budgetary outlook presented in the budget documents submitted in January 1973 and February 1974.

Inflation in 1973 and the early part of 1974 was much more rapid than the administration had expected, and these estimates were soon outdated. Full employment revenues are now expected to be $9 billion and $17 billion higher, respectively, because of inflation. On the expenditure side, however, the short-run effects of inflation have been much weaker—actually lowering anticipated expenditures for 1974 and barely raising them for 1975. This was due to the sharp rise in food and fuel prices that led to a decline in farm price support payments and larger receipts for offshore oil properties (which are considered negative outlays). These decreases offset the inflationary growth in expenditures in other programs.

Revenue increases were made even larger by some new changes in tax laws recommended by the administration. The most important of these is the emergency windfall profits tax for petroleum producers (discussed in Chapter 6), that the administration believes will boost revenues by $1 billion in fiscal 1974 and $3 billion in fiscal 1975. The earnings ceiling for social security taxes has also gone up beyond what was expected one year ago (from $12,000 to $13,200), and the administration is proposing a few other minor tax changes.

At the same time, a combination of congressional actions and other factors have increased outlays beyond what was expected. Table 2-2 recorded those outlay increases not attributable to inflation at $8 billion for fiscal 1974. Further increases now planned by the administration should raise 1975 spending $14 billion beyond the 1974 forecast (see Table 9-1).[1]

---

1. Both here and in Table 2-2 our attempt to divide expenditure increases into components which do and do not result from unanticipated inflation should be interpreted with caution. Some of the increases we have attributed to congressional or administrative action may really be reactions to rising prices; similarly, some of the higher revenue from offshore oil leases can be attributable to increases in the number of properties leased.

Table 9-1. Comparison of the Budgetary Outlook in Fiscal Years 1974 and 1975
Billions of current dollars

Description	1974	1975
Full employment revenues, 1974 budget document	268	290
Change due to inflation	9	17
Other changes[a]	1	4
Full employment revenues, 1975 budget document	278	311
Full employment outlays, 1974 budget document	268	288
Change due to inflation[b]	−2	1
Other changes[c]	8	14
Full employment outlays, 1975 budget document	274	303
Full employment surplus, 1974 budget document	0	2
Change due to inflation	11	16
Other changes	−7	−10
Full employment surplus, 1975 budget document	4	8

Sources: *The Budget of the United States Government, Fiscal Year 1975* and *Fiscal Year 1974.*
  a. Includes increases in the social security taxable earnings base, effective January 1, 1974, and January 1, 1975; windfall profits tax for petroleum, reduction in telephone excise taxes, tax reform proposals, liberalized deduction for pension contributions, other minor items. See *Budget, Fiscal Year 1975*, p. 46.
  b. Includes net interest payments, farm income stabilization, receipts for government-owned petroleum reserves, cost of living adjustments for food stamps and civilian retirement payments (see Table 2-2).
  c. All other expenditure changes.

Thus while it appeared last year that the full employment budget surplus would be close to zero in both fiscal years, it now looks as if it will be higher. Inflation and the effect of some discretionary revenue increases have more than offset other expenditure increases.

The Long-Run Outlook

The amount of revenues available for new programs in the future can be estimated by projecting present tax and expenditure programs for the 1975–80 period. On the revenue side, the projections assume that current tax rates and other regulations remain the same until 1980. The values of the present exemption and tax bracket limits for income taxes are therefore fixed in dollar terms. The earnings ceiling for social security taxes is increased in line with wage rates, as is now established by law.

On the expenditure side, the projections allow only for those increases in spending necessary (a) to meet multiyear funding plans in such areas as general revenue sharing and transportation, (b) to meet projected expansion in numbers of beneficiaries in existing transfer

Table 9-2. Projections of Full Employment Revenues, Outlays, and Budget Surplus, Various Inflation Assumptions, Fiscal Years 1975–80[a]

Billions of current dollars

Assumption and budget items	1975	1976	1977	1978	1979	1980
Private GNP deflator remains constant						
Revenues	310	325	342	361	380	401
Outlays	303	317	326	336	345	356
Surplus	7	8	16	25	35	45
Surplus (1975 dollars)[b]	7	8	16	25	35	45
Private GNP deflator rises 3 percent a year						
Revenues	313	339	369	403	438	478
Outlays	303	324	343	363	384	406
Surplus	10	15	26	40	54	72
Surplus (1975 dollars)[b]	10	14	24	36	48	61
Private GNP deflator rises 5 percent a year						
Revenues	315	349	387	432	481	537
Outlays	303	329	354	382	412	444
Surplus	12	20	33	50	69	93
Surplus (1975 dollars)[b]	12	18	29	43	56	71

Source: Brookings projection model.

a. The projections are based on current tax rates and expenditure programs. See the text for specific assumptions.

The private GNP deflator is assumed to grow at 7.5 percent in calendar year 1974 in all three projections, and at the assumed rate thereafter. (The private GNP deflator is the same as the overall GNP deflator, except that it does not include wages and salaries of government workers. Since these wages, like private wages, normally rise more rapidly than prices, the overall GNP deflator would be growing about 0.3 percent per year more rapidly than the private deflator over the 1975–80 period.)

b. Deflated by the private GNP deflator (fiscal year 1975 = 100).

and grant programs, and (c) to maintain the real level of all programs when wages and prices increase.

The Impact of Economic Growth and Inflation

With the above assumptions, the effect of economic growth alone is to increase the full employment surplus from an estimated level of $7 billion in 1975 to $45 billion in 1980. This is indicated in the top part of Table 9-2, which projects budgetary totals under the assumption that the aggregate price level for all goods and services (the private GNP deflator) will rise by an amount anticipated by economic forecasters in calendar 1974, but after that remain absolutely stable.

Because revenues respond more sensitively to inflation than expenditures, the surplus rises even more when prices grow between 1975–80. If a 3 percent rate of inflation is assumed, the full employment surplus grows from $10 billion in 1975 to $72 billion in 1980, a striking increase even when corrected for the higher price levels in this

Table 9-3. Projections of Government Outlays Assuming a 3 Percent Inflation Rate, by Major Category, Fiscal Years 1975–80[a]

Billions of current dollars

Category[b]	1975	1976	1977	1978	1979	1980
Total Outlays	303	324	343	363	384	406
Defense, space, foreign affairs	96	100	105	109	114	120
Cash income maintenance	97	107	115	124	134	144
Helping people buy essentials	33	37	39	41	44	47
Aid for social programs	18	19	20	21	22	22
Investment in physical environment	17	18	19	20	20	21
Revenue sharing	7	7	7	8	8	8
Direct subsidies to producers	4	4	4	4	4	4
Net interest	22	22	23	23	23	23
Other programs	23	24	26	28	29	31
Financial adjustments	−14	−14	−14	−14	−14	−14

Source: Brookings projection model. Detail may not add to totals because of rounding.

a. The private GNP deflator is assumed to grow at a rate of 7.5 percent in calendar 1974 and 3 percent thereafter.

b. For definitions of categories, see page 5, note 1.

projection. If the assumed rate of inflation is as high as 5 percent, there is an even sharper increase.[2]

The Composition of Expenditures

These projections show a continuation of many of the trends described in Chapter 1. For example, with the 3 percent inflation projection, defense spending should grow by $24 billion between 1975 and 1980 (see Table 9-3) simply as a result of rising prices and wages.[3] There is likely to be continued growth in cash income maintenance expenditures, primarily because of the sharp growth in expected numbers of social security beneficiaries between now and the end of the decade. There will also be a rise in spending on programs to help

2. The full employment surpluses in Table 9-2 differ from those of the administration estimates in Table 9-1 because of the differing inflation assumptions and the different methods for projecting budgetary magnitudes. In general, for comparable rates of inflation, our method projects higher federal revenues because of a higher assumed sensitivity of the personal income tax to total income (see Joseph A. Pechman, "Responsiveness of the Federal Individual Income Tax to Changes in Income," *Brookings Papers on Economic Activity* [2:1973], pp. 385–413). This also means, in reference to our discussion in Chapter 3, that the federal budget appears to us to be even more restrictive in the upcoming fiscal year than is shown in the administration's estimate in Figure 3-1.

3. The $24 billion growth in spending in defense, space, and foreign affairs consists of $7 billion due to higher wage costs even with stable prices and $17 billion due to higher prices. We consider the remaining increases in defense spending, including the fact that outlays are likely to "catch up" with obligational authority, as program initiatives and discuss them as such below.

Table 9-4. Effect on Full Employment Surplus Assuming a 3 Percent Inflation Rate, Initiatives Proposed by the Administration, Fiscal Years 1975–80[a]

Billions of current dollars

Surplus items and initiatives	1975	1976	1977	1978	1979	1980
Full employment surplus (before initiatives)	10	15	26	40	54	72
Program initiatives	...	3	15	22	28	33
Defense	...	3	7	12	17	21
National health insurance	...	...	8	9	10	11
Unemployment insurance reform	...	...	...	1	1	1
Net full employment surplus	10	12	11	18	26	39

Source: Brookings projection model.

a. The private GNP deflator is assumed to grow at a rate of 7.5 percent in calendar 1974, 3 percent thereafter.

people buy essentials, even apart from the cost of the new health insurance plan which is not included in these projections for existing programs. Other categories are not slated to rise much above current levels; this means a continued downward trend in the relative importance of subsidies for producer groups and net interest, and the reversal of an upward trend for aid for social programs.

The Administration's Initiatives

Although the budget surpluses depicted in Table 9-2 are very large, they should be interpreted cautiously because there are many potential claims on this revenue. The administration has already proposed three programs that would absorb a large portion of the projected surplus—changes in the nation's defense posture (discussed in Chapter 4), national health insurance (Chapter 8), and a reform of the unemployment insurance system (Chapter 3)—none of which are included in the previous totals. When these initiatives are deducted, they lower the full employment surplus to $12 billion in fiscal 1976 and $39 billion by fiscal 1980, as indicated in Table 9-4.[4]

4. We estimate that to carry out the administration's defense policies with respect to force levels, weapon modernization, and support policies will raise spending a total of $45 billion by 1980, of which $21 billion can be considered a new initiative. The health insurance increase represents projected net government costs under the administration's program, for which most of the insurance premiums are not part of the federal budget. Other health insurance plans, such as the Kennedy-Mills proposal, involve much larger gross federal outlays because they are financed by a payroll tax, but similar net costs.

Additions and Alterations to the Administration's Program

The available revenues shown in Table 9-4 seem large enough for program initiatives to be made beyond those suggested by the administration. After first considering whether high full employment surpluses are necessary to prevent private investment needs from outrunning private savings, we then review alternative possibilities for increasing federal expenditures or reducing taxes.

Private Investment Needs

There have been many indications that private investment needs will be very heavy in the next few years. It will be necessary to build houses for large numbers of new families, to construct equipment to satisfy environmental requirements, and to develop new sources of energy. If private savers do not make sufficient funds available for these projects, heavy investment demands could drive interest rates to very high levels and slow some of these projects. In order to prevent this from happening, the federal government could "save" by allowing a budget surplus to develop and using the funds to retire outstanding government debt, thus providing more money for private investment. In this sense, the possible imbalance of private investment and savings becomes a relevant budgetary issue just like the others we have discussed.[5]

It is difficult at the present time to determine the importance of this problem, but in Appendix C we review one study of long-term investment and savings. It concludes that while private investment demands do not seem to be outrunning saving by a great amount, the federal budget surplus at full employment required in 1980 to balance investment and saving without higher interest rates is on the order of $10 billion—and possibly higher if the underlying predictions are not correct. Thus one important use for the projected full employment surplus would be to allow for such a contingency.

Increases in Expenditures

There are two obvious candidates for more federal spending. One is income support payments to low-income people. In Chapter 7 we

5. See Tilford Gaines, "Financial Implications of Material Shortages," *Economic Report* (Manufacturers Hanover Trust Company, November 1973); and Murray L. Weidenbaum, "The Governmental Competition for Investment Funds," Tax Foundation, *Tax Review*, Vol. 34 (November 1973).

noted that even though such programs have grown rapidly in recent years, many poor families still receive meager income support benefits, or none at all. Possible changes might involve improving present programs—at the cost of $4 billion a year in the late 1970s— to a universal negative income tax—entailing net federal costs of $12 billion to $17 billion by that time.

A second candidate is more aid for social programs. These expenditures—mainly grants to state and local governments to support such programs as compensatory education, community development, health service delivery, and manpower training—grew rapidly under the Great Society legislation of the 1960s, but have not been viewed so favorably by the Nixon administration. The 1975 budget does not permit these programs to keep pace with price inflation, let alone with the wages of state and local government employees, which typically rise even faster than prices. If aid for social programs were merely to to remain at its 1974 percentage of state and local government expenditures—thereby implying that federally supported grant programs were growing roughly as fast as all other state and local programs—this type of spending would total $2 billion more than the present estimate for fiscal 1975 and $7 billion more than that projected by 1980.[6]

Beyond these two candidates, emerging needs in almost any other area might justify increased federal spending in the years ahead. For example, even though defense spending is now slated to grow sharply through 1980, it could go up even more rapidly if U.S.-Soviet relations worsen. There could also be rapid increases in physical investment programs if the government begins to subsidize domestic energy production, to stockpile petroleum and food grains, or to invest more heavily in urban mass transit. A number of programs to help people buy essentials could be expanded: housing allowances, college tuition grants, and child care vouchers are three that have already been proposed. Or it might be decided to enlarge general revenue sharing assistance for state and local governments.

6. This is of course a very oversimplified way of looking at whether aid for social programs should or should not increase. The ultimate justification for such increases is in terms of underlying program needs, which vary according to the possibilities of improving the delivery of services through grants, the speed with which other federal programs are increasing, and the demographic trends facing state and local governments. We give these numbers only as illustrative orders of magnitude.

Reductions in Taxes

Another way to use this growing full employment surplus would be to reduce taxes. By 1980 the ratio of personal taxes to personal income will be 14 percent in the stable price projection and 15 percent in the 3 percent inflation projection. While progressive personal tax rates serve a useful purpose in redistributing income from rich to poor, it is questionable that they were intended to increase effective tax rates in this manner during inflationary periods. If such increases in the size of the public sector are not justified by underlying priorities, taxes should be cut to restore private purchasing power. Several countries—Brazil, Canada, Chile, Denmark, Iceland, and the Netherlands—now make such reductions more or less automatically, and Senator James L. Buckley has proposed doing the same in this country.

Four different ways in which the personal income or payroll taxes paid by households could be reduced have been discussed in Chapter 3. These measures were justified primarily in terms of their ability to limit the expected rise in unemployment in late 1974, but each measure also has merit as a possible permanent change in the tax structure. The original Kennedy plan, which simply raises the dollar value of the personal exemption to adjust for the recent inflation, would reduce revenues by $6 billion in 1975 and somewhat more later on. The Mondale plan, which provides an optional tax credit in lieu of the present exemption, would have approximately the same effect on revenues, but would result in larger cuts for low- and middle-income households. The Kennedy-Mondale compromise plan would have similar implications.

The other two plans, each of which reduces social security taxes paid by households instead of personal income taxes, might be even better suited to today's circumstances. Regressive social security tax rates are now 12 percent (including the employer portion)—high enough to virtually eliminate the progressivity of the entire federal revenue system. If either the administration's health insurance proposal, which requires that employers pay premium costs and would thereby impose a hidden payroll tax on employees' wages, or the Kennedy-Mills bill, which explicitly assesses a 4 percent health insurance payroll tax, are enacted, total payroll taxes will rise by another one-third in the next three years. In these circumstances it would make sense to use some of the growing federal revenues to reduce payroll taxes, financing the associated benefits (whether for health insurance or the regular social security benefits) out of general revenues. Two such plans, implying revenue losses on the order of $9 billion by 1980, were also discussed in Chapter 3.

Alterations in the Administration's Program

The foregoing discussion illustrates that even the sizable revenue totals in Table 9-4 do not go far when measured against the many possible claims. By fiscal 1980, roughly $10 billion could be needed to prevent high interest rates from choking off certain types of investment demands, $17 billion for an expanded income maintenance program, $7 billion for aid to social programs, and $9 billion if it is desired to cut payroll tax rates by one percentage point. These items alone more than absorb the available fiscal margin. A broader menu of new initiatives would require either cutting back on expenditures or reducing tax preferences to increase this margin still further.

One possible means of doing so is by reducing spending under existing programs. The administration and others have recommended that certain types of expenditures be cut back, because there were less costly ways of achieving program objectives or because the objectives themselves were questionable. For example, in the defense area it appeared feasible to reduce the ratio of support to combat forces, to cut reserves, to delay some modernization programs, and even to reduce the number of some types of combat units. Cutbacks in domestic spending included farm price supports, because the subsidies seemed larger than needed to achieve supply objectives, and impact aid to some school districts, because money was not distributed according to educational needs. Many of these measures are already incorporated in the 1975 budget. Defense efficiency measures have been initiated. Farm price supports have been drastically slashed by the combination of high food prices and the fact that most support payments are now only made if prices drop below target levels. The administration is also proposing a sharp reduction in impact aid to districts where families do not live on federal land, though such proposals have fared poorly in Congress in the past.

While these expenditure reductions are being planned, it should be possible to attempt others. In Chapters 4 and 5 we discussed some of the assumptions underlying the administration's decision that defense spending should increase. It was suggested that uncertainties inherent in assessing the future military balance and in judging the role of military forces in world affairs could lead to alternative interpretations of future defense needs and to more limited projected increases in defense spending. In the domestic area, cutbacks could be made in such areas as public works projects and maritime aid, and in eliminating the duplication of benefits in some income support programs.

Tax reforms could provide a second source of additional revenue. We mentioned that a very large amount of revenues—an estimated $78 billion—is lost through special preferences in the personal and corporate tax system. Many of these "tax expenditures" have desired incentive effects and should be preserved, but many do not. As one illustration, we have discussed how some of these special preferences for domestic and foreign oil and gas producers did not create the proper incentives for a nation trying to cope with an energy crisis.

There are many other possibilities for increasing tax revenues without risking adverse incentive effects. With national health insurance, there is little justification for continuing the deduction for health insurance premium costs—if this provision were changed, revenues would increase by $2 billion a year. Tightening the tax treatment of capital gains and dividends, including gains realized at death, could raise revenues as much as $10 billion a year; revising regulations governing foreign income of domestic firms, $1 billion a year; eliminating real estate tax shelters, $1 billion a year; repealing depreciation provisions enacted in 1971, $1.5 billion a year; removing the deductions for gasoline taxes, $1 billion; and permitting deductions only for the amount of charitable contributions in excess of 3 percent of income, $2.5 billion a year. A relatively modest tax reform package that removes some of these tax preferences and also strengthens the present minimum tax provisions was recently estimated to raise $16 billion by 1978; a more ambitious package could raise as much as $33 billion.[7] Were these reforms enacted, it would be possible to make cuts in general tax rates or to raise low income allowances and thus make the overall tax system more equitable.

7. The basic figures came from Tax Analysts and Advocates, "Fiscal 1975 Tax Expenditure Budget," *Tax Notes*, Vol. 2 (January 21, 1974), pp. 4–19; the reform packages from *Setting National Priorities: The 1974 Budget*, p. 55. The reform measures are discussed at greater length in *Tax Reform Studies and Proposals, U.S. Treasury Department*, Joint Publication of the House Committee on Ways and Means and the Senate Committee on Finance, 91 Cong. 1 sess. (1969), Pts. 1, 2, 3.

THESE ILLUSTRATIONS MAKE CLEAR that there are many possibilities for adding to or revising present budgetary plans. If present expenditures and tax rates are maintained and prices rise at the rate of 3 percent between 1975 and 1980, revenues would exceed expenditures by $72 billion in fiscal 1980. The administration now intends to devote $21 billion of that amount for defense spending increases and $12 billion for domestic purposes, mainly national health insurance. After deducting a cushion for possibly heavy investment demands, another $30 billion could be available for further initiatives such as income support, increases in social grants, or cuts in personal income or payroll taxes. This budget margin is large, more than has appeared to be available in the past. But it is not large enough to eliminate difficult budgetary choices. Measures to increase the funds available for new programs, whether through cutting back old programs or reforming the tax system, are just as desirable now as in the past. Moreover, there should be continued resistance to the temptation to rush into new large-scale programs without understanding their long-run budgetary implications.

A Note
on Impoundment

IN SOME POPULAR DISCUSSIONS of impoundment, writers have referred to any withholding of appropriations or failure of congressionally approved budget authority to result in outlays as an impoundment of funds. But this kind of loose definition fails to take full account of how the budget process works.

As explained in Chapter 1, outlays in federal programs come at the end of a long chain of activities. Once budget authority is voted by Congress, the executive branch agencies obligate the funds and eventually the obligations are liquidated by payments to the public (outlays).

For some items of expenditure, particularly the federal payroll (nearly one-fifth of total outlays), budget authority, obligations, and outlays almost always occur within one fiscal year. But in the remainder of the budget, outlays in any given year may stem from budget authority voted in previous years. In recent years, about 40 percent of the outlays, outside of the federal payroll, derives from budget authority of previous years. Therefore, large amounts of spending in any year are unaffected by congressional action in that year.

Moreover, an administration can speed up or slow down the rate at which it incurs obligations in any year, simply by directing a federal agency to make the appropriate changes in its behavior. Congress has, at least until now, accepted this prerogative of the executive branch. The justification is usually on the basis that good management practices require some flexibility on the part of operating agencies to assure that contracts they make give the government its money's worth. Thus for many government programs it is impossible to define the "normal" rate of speed at which budget authority voted by Congress is supposed to be transformed into an obligation of federal funds. In any event, whatever the normal speed for a particular program, it will vary enormously between programs—for example, large construction projects obviously require longer to obligate funds than does office equipment rental.

Hence, many of the delays in spending budget authority are a normal part of the government's way of doing business. Nonetheless, the Nixon administration has acknowledged that it has delayed beyond the normal rate, and the cause of slowdowns bear examination.

In some cases, the administration has withheld funds from particular programs on the grounds that to allow the commitment of funds would worsen inflation either by driving up prices in a particular sector (for example, pollution control) or in the economy as a whole. There is considerable legal dispute over whether such slowdowns in obligating funds is constitutional, but there is little doubt that this practice has existed for a very long time.[1]

Another justification for slowing down expenditures—that has been invoked much more by the present administration than previous ones—is simply that it disapproves of the program. While previous administrations have refused to build nuclear-powered warships or airplanes for which Congress had appropriated funds, the present administration has applied *its* priorities over a much broader range of programs. There is little question that this way of slowing up a program—namely, allowing unobligated balances of budget authority to pile up year after year because of a policy difference between Congress and the administration—is the source of much of the recent furor over impoundment and congressional activity to control impoundments.

Under reporting requirements that have existed for several decades, Congress has required the executive branch to report on funds "in reserve," a part of the unobligated balances of budget authority. These reporting requirements do not seem to have prevented controversy from arising over the propriety of the actions of various administrations. In budget reform legislation under consideration in 1974, sev-

1. See Joseph Cooper, "Executive Impoundment of Appropriations," in *Executive Impoundment of Appropriated Funds*, Hearings before the Subcommittee on Separation of Powers of the Senate Committee on the Judiciary, 92 Cong. 1 sess. (1971), pp. 181–89; and Louis Fisher, "The Politics of Impounded Funds," *Administrative Science Quarterly*, Vol. 15 (September 1970), pp. 361–77.

eral changes are proposed in these requirements. The proposals explicitly limit the justifications for placing funds in reserve. The only allowable justification would be to "provide for contingencies, to effect savings . . . made possible through changed requirements, and through greater efficiency of operations, or other developments subsequent to the date"[2] on which the funds were made available. Failure to obligate funds for fiscal policy reasons or to achieve less than the full objectives and scope of programs enacted and funded would be prohibited. The executive branch would have to notify Congress in advance when funds are to be reserved, and the Comptroller General (who is responsible directly to the Congress) could contest in court any impoundments made for reasons other than those specified in the law.

Even if such a law passes, it is doubtful that practices will change much. An administration intent on slowing down programs will cite legally authorized reasons for reserving funds ("to effect savings . . . made possible through changed requirements") whether or not these reasons are the prime motivating factors. Some slowdowns will be reversed, but not through the courts. Political pressures will be brought to bear on administrations—as they have in the past—and a compromise will be struck. In short, good faith and a willingness to compromise differences between the branches of government, which have averted constitutional confrontations over impoundments in the past, are the probable paths to future resolution of the impoundment issue.

2. "Explanation of S. 1541, The Congressional Budget Act of 1974: Establishment of Committee on the Budget," *Congressional Record*, daily ed., March 19, 1974, p. S 3861.

Congressional Budgetary Reform

THE BUDGET DECISION-MAKING PROCESS has two important weaknesses: it is fragmented and it is short-sighted. One possible benefit of the administration's spending cutbacks last year was to stimulate Congress to begin reforming its own procedures for making budgetary decisions. By April 1974, both the Senate and the House had passed budgetary reform acts, and the conference committee is now attempting to reconcile differences in these bills. The question is whether these current reform bills will improve the congressional budget process.

The first problem with present budgetary procedures is that they are fragmented. Each revenue and expenditure item is considered separately without regard to its impact on overall totals in the budget and therefore on the economy. Those voting on individual bills in the various appropriations and tax committees never get the chance to ask whether additional expenditures are of sufficiently high priority that other expenditures should be reduced, or taxes increased, to pay for them. Those voting in favor of tax reductions never have to face up to whether such reductions require increases in other taxes or reductions in expenditures.

The second problem is that Congress acts too late on budgetary decisions. At best, it votes on appropriations bills within a few months of the start of the fiscal year; at worst it votes when the fiscal year is so far advanced that federal agencies have to operate under continuing resolutions and state and local governments have already begun spending the money they "expected" to get from the federal government. This tardiness severely restricts the ability of Congress to make significant changes in the budget: congressional committees can refine and modify previous programs or administration proposals, but it is very difficult for them to initiate their own.[1]

The Congressional Budget Act deals extensively with the first of these problems and not so extensively with the second. It creates a standing budgetary committee in each house, staffed by a congressional budget office. The committees are to receive estimates of specific expenditures and taxes from appropriate functional committees, along with recommendations on overall expenditures and tax levels from the Joint Economic Committee. They then propose a first concurrent resolution in each house by May 1 of each year, action on which is to take no more than a month; this sets out aggregate revenue and expenditure targets and targets for specific functional categories. The committees on specific expenditures and taxes then take their own actions, submitting proposed changes in budgetary subtotals to their respective chambers for a vote. They must also provide five-year projections of program costs and tax expenditures under these actions. When these steps are completed in mid-August, the budget committees report a second concurrent resolution that could:

• revise the totals in the first concurrent resolution in line with the specific actions voted by the respective chambers or in response to changes in economic conditions;

• direct certain committees to alter their actions;

• require proportional reductions in all controllable expenditures;

• require tax increases or decreases.

The specific committees then report reconciliation bills for final passage by Congress (after conferences between the House and Senate) before the fiscal year begins on October 1—three months later than it presently begins. During this time the congressional budget office would be making projections of revenues, expenditures, and tax expenditures for the next five years, and providing other types of assistance to the various committees.

The procedures are complicated, but they should enable Congress to make sensible reconciliations of specific expenditures and tax totals and the overall economic goals of the budget. The first concurrent resolution provides general targets for the appropriations committee

1. See "Reforming the Congressional Budget Process," testimony of Alice M. Rivlin and Charles L. Schultze before the Senate Rules Committee (January 15, 1974; processed).

—targets which presumably have been adopted after debate and consideration of the relative priorities of spending in each area. The reconciliation process connected with the second resolution then enables these targets to be adjusted in line with new developments. Thus the machinery both establishes targets that are useful in making initial budgetary decisions and permits their subsequent revision if Congress wishes to respond to changing developments in a flexible manner.

However, the procedure does not facilitate long-run budgetary planning much more than the present process does. Postponing the start of the fiscal year to October may make it easier to have all appropriations actions completed by that time, but it does not get the money to state and local governments any earlier in their fiscal years. Nor does it provide for much increased congressional flexibility in reversing programs already under way, or in initiating their own. The long-term projections of the congressional budget office are a step in the right direction, but they do not force Congress to deal explicitly with such questions as what programs should be cut in 1978 if Congress votes now for a program entailing sizable expenditures in 1978. Real improvement here can only come from procedures that require Congress to vote on budgetary measures more in advance of the actual spending, when there is still time to reduce other appropriations to provide the requisite budgetary flexibility.

This possible shortcoming in the current budgetary reform bill may not be quite as apparent in the next few years if the current projections of somewhat higher available federal revenues are validated. It is always easier to increase expenditures or reduce taxes if more fiscal stimulation is needed than to reverse directions when restraint is required. But the federal government has looked toward large available revenues before, revenues that never quite materialized at least in part because the future implications of current budgetary decisions were not adequately foreseen when new programs were first voted upon. Now that Congress has taken the first steps toward budgetary reform, it would be a great mistake not to be alert to further improvements.

Should the Federal Government Be Saving More?

ONE ISSUE raised in the long-run projections of Chapter 9 is whether the spending demands of various sectors will require the federal government to achieve large budget surpluses in the next few years. It is alleged that the United States needs to rebuild much of its capital stock in conformity with energy and antipollution requirements, and that this will place tremendous demands on capital markets in the years ahead and force a tight fiscal policy.

This argument is difficult to assess. In addition to estimating the long-run implications of current budgetary policies, it is necessary to estimate the effects of these policies and other forces on private investment demands and the prospective savings of households, businesses, and state and local governments. Most of these relationships have been notoriously difficult to estimate in the past, and may be even more so in the future.

Barry Bosworth and James Duesenberry have tried to investigate this problem by using an econometric technique. They use behavioral relationships involving investment and saving to estimate the government saving required over the late 1970s to bring aggregate investment and saving into equilibrium at full employment, maintaining current levels of long-term real interest rates. The results, in terms of percentages of gross national product, are given in Table C-1. The 1973 numbers are historical values; the 1980 numbers assume that

Table C-1. Investment and Saving in the United States, by Type, Calendar Years 1973 and 1980

Percent of current dollar GNP

Type of investment or saving	1973 actual	1980 projected at full employment
Gross investment	**15.8**	**15.4**
Nonresidential fixed	10.6	11.3
Residential structures	4.5	3.5
Change in inventories	0.6	0.8
Foreign (net)	0.2	−0.1
Gross saving	**15.6**	**15.3**
Personal	4.3	3.7
Business[a]	10.5	10.8
State and local government surpluses[b]	0.8	0.4
Federal surplus[c]	0.1	0.4
Statistical discrepancy	**0.2**	**0.1**

Source: Barry Bosworth and James Duesenberry, "Resource Claims in the 1970s" (Brookings Institution, April 1974; processed). Detail may not add to totals because of rounding.

a. Adjusted for inventory valuation; includes capital consumption allowances.

b. Includes the surpluses of employee retirement programs and general government.

c. Actual federal budget surplus (on a national income accounts basis) in 1973; difference between investment and saving in 1980.

the economy is at full employment by that time to be consistent with our budget surplus projections.

These numbers show that, while the capital requirements to develop new energy sources, to convert manufacturing plants and equipment to types of machinery that use less energy, and to satisfy government antipollution restrictions will be heavy—raising the ratio of private investment to GNP from 10.6 percent in 1973 to an estimated 11.3 percent in 1980—they could be met without drastic alterations in current saving behavior. Even if the goal of the 1968 Housing and Urban Development Act of 25 million new and rehabilitated housing units between 1969–78 is met, the ratio of housing expenditures to GNP seems likely to fall from its extraordinarily high 1973 level. Personal saving as a percent of GNP should fall over the decade, primarily because of the effect of the progressivity of the federal personal income tax mentioned earlier. But the business saving ratio, which is strongly influenced by the state of the business cycle, could rise slightly if the economy returns to full employment. The ratio of the budgetary surplus of state and local governments to GNP is likely to decline from its very high 1973 level, but the extent of this decline is limited by steadily increasing surpluses of employee retirement funds and by the fact that most general governments are legally prohibited from running current account deficits. The net effect of these projections is that a federal full employment surplus of 0.4 percent of GNP, from $8 billion in the stable price projection to $10 billion for the 5 percent projection, should prove adequate to handle expected future investment demands without leading to significant increases in interest rates.

At the same time, the table suggests that there is a rather large degree of uncertainty in these estimates. If all the savings relationships are accurate but nonresidential fixed investment demands account for 11.7 percent of 1980 GNP, an estimate which is well within the realm of possibility, the full employment surplus required to balance savings and investment will be twice as high. Similar adjustments would have to be made if other relationships go awry.

TYPESETTING *Monotype Composition Company, Inc., Baltimore*
PRINTING & BINDING *R. R. Donnelley & Sons Company, Chicago*